IN DEFENSE OF SOLIDARITY AND PLEASURE

W0019595

IN DEFENSE OF SOLIDARITY AND PLEASURE

FEMINIST TECHNOPOLITICS FROM THE GLOBAL SOUTH

FIRUZEH SHOKOOH VALLE

STANFORD UNIVERSITY PRESS

Stanford, California

Stanford University Press
Stanford, California

Printed in the United States of America on acid-free, archival-quality paper

Library of Congress Cataloging-in-Publication Data
Names: Shokooh Valle, Firuzeh, author.
Title: In defense of solidarity and pleasure : feminist technopolitics from the Global South / Firuzeh Shokooh Valle.
Description: Stanford, California : Stanford University Press, 2023. | Includes bibliographical references and index.
Identifiers: LCCN 2022059362 (print) | LCCN 2022059363 (ebook) | ISBN 9781503631366 (cloth) | ISBN 9781503636149 (paperback) | ISBN 9781503636156 (ebook)
Subjects: LCSH: Technology and women—Developing countries. | Information technology—Social aspects—Developing countries. | Feminism—Developing countries. | Solidarity—Developing countries. | Women in development—Developing countries.
Classification: LCC HQ1870.9 .S565 2023 (print) | LCC HQ1870.9 (ebook) | DDC 305.4209172/4—dc23/eng/20230111
LC record available at https://lccn.loc.gov/2022059362
LC ebook record available at https://lccn.loc.gov/2022059363

Cover design: Lindy Kasler
Cover illustration: Shutterstock
Typeset by Sabon LT Pro in 10/14.5

para mi abuela Mamita, Guillermina,
por todo

CONTENTS

ACKNOWLEDGMENTS

So many people, places, and experiences have sustained me during the long, arduous, and beautiful process of researching and writing this book. Like everything we do, this book is the result of a collective effort. A collective labor of struggle and love.

I want to thank Franklin and Marshall College for giving me the necessary time, resources, and support to complete this book. The Department of Sociology has provided me with a much-needed kind and warm space to initiate my career as a teacher and academic. The support of my wonderful chair, Caroline Faulkner, has been indispensable. My colleagues in Sociology—Amy Singer, Ashley Rondini, Carol Auster, Emily Marshall, Jerome Hodos, and Katherine McClelland—have offered encouragement in ways that I truly treasure. Thank you to the coordinator of the Department of Sociology, Samantha Binkley, for making so many things easier. My deepest gratitude also to our former coordinator, Kelly Smith, for always receiving me with a huge smile and helping me with absolutely everything. The People of Color Alliance at Franklin and Marshall has been a vital space of comradery and critical conversations.

My colleagues at Franklin and Marshall Cristina Pérez, Mark Villegas, Rachel Feldman, and Seçil Yilmaz have embraced me with endless *cariño*. Thank you, my friends.

At Northeastern University, I want to deeply thank my advisor, Kathrin Zippel, and the rest of my committee: Jeffery Juris (RIP), Nina Sylvanus, Suzanna Walters, and my external reader, Jocelyn Viterna. Nina has been a mentor, a friend, and a fierce supporter of my work. Doreen Lee, at Northeastern University, has also provided vital feedback and supported this project since the very start. Nina, Jeff, and Doreen have been fundamental in my intellectual formation by always challenging me to go deeper and think bigger. Debra Kaufman was the first person to tell me that I should study sociology. Thank you, Debra, for seeing the sociologist in me when I was a graduate student in journalism at Northeastern University and for teaching me so much about being a feminist.

The fellowship I was awarded by the American Sociological Association (ASA) Minority Fellowship Program when I was a graduate student made possible my initial fieldwork trips to Latin America. Through the program, I have also met a wonderful group of scholars of color who continue to inspire me. The fantastic former director of ASA's Minority Affairs Program, Jean Shin, has opened many doors for me throughout the years. The Feminist Development subsection of ASA's Sociology of Development section made me feel at home in the field of sociology. I am forever grateful to Kristy Kelly and Susan Lee for their support.

I lived in Cambridge, Massachusetts, for ten years. My daughter Marina and I missed our homeland Puerto Rico every single day of our lives. We were mostly on our own in Cambridge. My dear friend Liz Williams was my rock there and my home away from home. Ethel Mickey illuminated my time in Cambridge with her brilliant light. Ethel has also given me invaluable and critical feedback on countless versions and drafts of this book. In Cambridge, Yara Liceaga and Ivys Fernández brought much needed Puerto Rican warmth to my life. Gracias, *chicas*.

So many people read drafts of chapters of this book. I am in endless gratitude to Sasha Costanza-Chock and Manisha Desai for their insightful critiques. My dear friends Ellery Biddle and Manuel Clavell Carrasquillo also pushed me to think about technology and feminism in much more complex ways. Mi *amiga linda* Laura Vidal has always supported me and this project. She also translated my articles into Spanish with so much care. I am so lucky to have this group of kind and brilliant people.

My editor at Stanford University Press, Marcela Cristina Maxfield, saw something in this project that I had not even imagined. She has been such a supportive and engaged editor. Gracias, Marcela. Thank you also to the entire editorial team and staff at Stanford University Press including Barbara Armentrout, Elliott Beard, Tiffany Mok, Sarah Rodríguez, Adam Schnitzer, Michele Wetherbee, and David Zielonka, as well as the anonymous peer reviewers of the manuscript. My gratitude also goes to freelance copyeditor Amy Smith Bell.

This book would not have been possible without the collaboration of the members of the Women's Rights Programme of the Association for Progressive Communications and of Sulá Batsú in Costa Rica. They have contributed in so many ways to this research, which is also theirs. They gave me hours of their precious time to speak about their lives, work, and dreams. I want to specially thank the Sulá Batsú collective and its coordinator, Kemly Camacho, for letting me be a part of their community, for challenging and stimulating my analysis on technology and feminism, and for teaching me huge lessons of solidarity. Gracias, *son las mejores.*

Puerto Rico, that immensely beautiful and courageous Caribbean archipelago, is a never-ending source of inspiration and strength in my life. I am so proud of being Puerto Rican. The resistance of the people and the land to centuries of colonialism has shaped my work and who I am. Resistance has taken many forms in my homeland, sometimes as solidarity, other times as pleasure and joy. Always as dignity.

I could not have done anything without the boundless and borderless love from my friends in Puerto Rico. José R. Madera, Gabriel López Albarrán, and Camile Roldán Soto have always had my back. They have been the best, most wondrous companions through many moments of happiness and despair. Thank you, Tania Morales Maisonet, for knowing me so well. I am not exaggerating when I say that I would not have been able to persist without the love of my best friend, Mariela Fullana Acosta. Mariela, *mi hermana de la vida,* my soulmate. You are also my home. Gracias, Marie, *por todo lo que eres y das.* There is also a big piece of my heart in Barcelona. I have learned so much about integrity and honesty from my friend Mónica Rodríguez. *Te quiero, Mónix.*

Mi familia, without them, *imposible.* Thank you to my marvelous aunts Norma and Wilma Valle Ferrer. My cousin, *mi hermana*, Alana Alvarez Valle's unwavering solidarity and love have been *imprescindible*. *Te adoro, Nana*. Her son, my nephew, Víctor Manuel, a brilliant, spunky burst of light. My loving gratitude also for those who may not be here but live in our hearts: my *abuelo* Víctor Valle Negrón and my uncle Ariel Ortiz Tellechea. My grandmother, *mi Mamita* Guillermina Ferrer Rodríguez, passed away when I was writing this book. This was one of the most devastating moments in my life. I dedicate this book to her revolutionary love—the kind of love that demolishes the bad and rebuilds with hope. Her love continues to flourish every day.

I owe my mother, Diana Valle Ferrer, everything I am and everything I have been able to do. Gracias, Mami, for the infinite love and kindness, the countless hours of conversation, the indefatigable support, the patience, the guidance. Thank you for your brilliance and rigorous feedback and critique of many drafts of this book. Thank you for teaching me what being a feminist truly is: *justicia, resistencia y humanidad*. Thank you for believing in me, always. Gracias *por salvarme tantas veces*, Mami.

The fierce and bountiful love of my partner, Antonio "Tony" Ayala Rivera, has nourished me in so many ways. My ride or die. The hours of laughter, conversation, and tears on our little balcony in West Philadelphia have been my refuge from the world. I could not have been able to write this book without his immense love and sustenance. *Te amo, Antonio*.

My daughter, Marina Isabel Pineda Shokooh, the love of my life, was eight years old when we moved to the United States. We left our family, friends, our beautiful *barrio* of Old San Juan, and our deep, immense, blue sea behind. We have only had each other during the most difficult, heartbreaking, and painful of times. We have also had each other during moments of immeasurable joy. It has always been us against the world, an unbeatable team. I have had the honor of witnessing how she has become a generous, wise, and strong young woman. She inspires me every day. Gracias, *mi amor, por tanto*.

LIST OF ACRONYMS

APC WRP	Association for Progressive Communications, Women's Rights Programme
CSW	Commission on the Status of Women
ECLAC	Economic Commission for Latin America and the Caribbean
ECOSOC	Economic and Social Council
ICT	information and communication technologies
ICT4D	information and communication technologies for development
ITU	International Telecommunication Union
SDGs	Sustainable Development Goals
UNCTAD	United Nations Conference on Trade and Development
UNDP	United Nations Development Programme
UNESCO	United Nations Educational, Scientific and Cultural Organization
UNFPA	United Nations Population Fund
UNGA	United Nations General Assembly
UNICEF	United Nations International Children's Emergency Fund
WSIS	World Summit for the Information Society

INTRODUCTION

Feminist Technopolitics and Development

Many of us have seen the image. Black, Brown, Indigenous women gathered around a laptop or a computer or using a mobile phone, mesmerized by the promise of the sleek, modern-looking machine. It implies a story about technology providing new opportunities, knowledge, capital.

But there is more to this image. Much more.

In the summer of 2015, I traveled to San José, Costa Rica, to study the technology-focused organization Sulá Batsú. I expected to find depoliticized frameworks based on women's "empowerment" and entrepreneurial talents, and visions and practices that centered technology as a magic wand that would cure all the world's injustices. Yet what I found was quite the opposite: Caring relationships built on solidarity and tied to dissension, elastic organizational structures that accommodated feelings, an emphasis on collaborative design and process, and practices that were at once bound to technology while decentering it. Technology was not the magic wand. Relationships were at the center. And rather than being seen as a luxury or an afterthought, the quest for joy was a fundamental value. "We work to the rhythm of happiness, not capital," one member told me during a rainy afternoon in San José.

As I looked at feminist digital activism in the global South, I was struck by how, in the face of online gender-based violence, the Associa-

1

tion for Progressive Communications Women's Rights Programme (APC WRP) centers the body and pleasure. Instead of calling on women of color, Indigenous, LGBTQI+, nonbinary, disabled, and so-called Third World individuals to be more restrained online, APC WRP calls for online disobedience, while acknowledging issues of harm, trauma, and safety. The emphasis on pleasure and play is a technopolitical feminist strategy between bodies, sexualities, and technologies. Amid increasing violence, APC WRP's activists are reimagining the internet as a feminist space that enables different ways of thinking and being.

These are the seeds of this book.

Digital technologies are a major part of the agenda of a development industry that is becoming increasingly corporatized.[1] Capitalist, white supremacist, and cis- and heteronormative interventions in technologies seem to have buried utopian dreams of a liberatory technological world. Data extraction for profit, state and corporate surveillance, algorithmic oppression, biometric data collection policies, online violence, proprietary knowledges, precarious labor, and electronic residues have progressively made our relationships with technologies fraught, to say the least.[2] Activists and many oppressed communities have certainly appropriated digital technologies for advancing social justice, communicating, and feeling joy. Yet it seems more and more challenging to envision care in relationships with technologies.[3]

Over the past twenty-five years, state and transnational institutions, the private sector, foundations, and nongovernmental organizations have been in a race to include women and other marginalized communities in the digital society. The importance of integrating women as users, consumers, designers, and developers of technologies has become a global mantra against inequality. But this exciting future being constructed, in which women are considered key figures full of potential, contains in its fold subtle and not so subtle forms of violence. In this book I ask the following questions: How does development discourse couple women and digital technologies as a frontier of expansion and inclusion? What forms of feminist technopolitics are flourishing in certain regions of the global South? What kinds of compromises and negotiations have been necessary? I examine these questions by studying two organizations that focus on gender and technology in the global South—the transnational network APC WRP and the cooperative Sulá Batsú in Costa Rica—as well as analyzing reports, documents, and other publications from private foundations and technology corporations, from the UN and ECLAC (UN Economic Commission for Latin America and the Caribbean), and from state entities, supplemented by organizational literature.

Drawing from online archival and ethnographic methods as well as interviews I conducted, this book makes two arguments. First, development discourse preys on care in producing an ideal Third World Technological Woman who combines technological dexterity and entrepreneurial instinct with caring qualities without addressing the histories that have erected the very barriers that these women are supposed to miraculously overcome. Second, feminist digital activists who are involved in development work mobilize a politics of care rooted in solidarity and pleasure in negotiating and defying technocapitalist paradigms of digital inclusion. Therefore, care is used in numerous ways, from making profit and furthering exploitation to building collaborative worlds. This book studies how care is mobilized in the inexorable path of digital inclusion: the ways in which it is both liberatory and urgent, as well as uncomfortable and entangled with violence. Thus the making and unmaking of a Third World Technological Woman lies at the crux of *In Defense of Solidarity and Pleasure: Feminist Technopolitics from the Global South*.

The implications of the ubiquity of digital technologies and of technosolutionist discourses and policies for solving the complex problems inflicted on historically oppressed communities are at a critical juncture. Women, queer and gender nonconforming/nonbinary communities, immigrants, poor people, people with disabilities, Black and Indigenous people, and people of color are increasingly considered both threats to and instruments of social, political, and economic stability and prosperity. We must continue to examine both the possibilities and the challenges embedded in inclusionary practices and policies. The stakes are high for feminist politics, especially in times of growing injustices and ecological devastation.

Sugiero que el camino de la historia será el de retejer y afirmar la comunidad y su arraigo vincular. (I suggest that the path of history will be one of reweaving and affirming the community and the roots of its bonds.)[4]

—RITA LAURA SEGATO

In grappling with what I call a feminist technopolitics of care, I found myself immersed in numerous understandings, practices, and theories. Care as both liberatory and repressive. Care to flourish; care to discipline. Care as a collective force; care deployed as an individualistic strategy. Care as romantic and bucolic; care as pragmatic and raw. Care as vulnerable. Care essentialized and exploited as "women's work"; labor that is essential for capitalism yet simultaneously decimated, unvalued, and unequally distributed along racial and class divides.[5] Care as a vital feminist commitment and principle.[6] Care as an indispensable force in building the worlds we want to inhabit.

Care flourished in my fieldwork as a political, ethical, and affective force—following feminist science and technology scholar María Puig de la Bellacasa—that moved activists.[7] These acts kept reminding me of the many conceptualizations of care from the margins of US academia by Latin American, Black, Indigenous, queer, and disabled scholars and activists. The ways in which I use *politics of care* are indebted to this lineage. To foreground care and emotions as sites of politics interrogates the modern/rationality paradigm, built on objectivity and reason, and legitimizes other forms of being and knowing.[8] For many communities, care—in the forms of love, protection, eroticism, rage, joy and pleasure, spirituality, solidarity, dissent, discomfort—has been embedded in their production of knowledge, an act of political resistance, of survival and protection, and of building coalitions across difference.[9] These registers offer "visceral, material, and emotional heft to acts of preservation that span a breadth of localities: selves, communities, and social worlds."[10] Sociologist Raquel Gutiérrez Aguilar says in her analysis of the recent feminist protests in Latin America: "We know that we need to reject, impede, inhibit, deactivate, confront, and blockade the multiple apparatuses of dispossession that attack our most intimate and decisive creations, everything that allows us to *care for* and regenerate life as a

4

whole, both human and nonhuman life."[11] Care is the ultimate sustainer of life, always, but particularly during catastrophic times.

Care is all this, yes, but we must also "unsettle care," following historian of science Michelle Murphy's work and warning in her critical examination of the entanglement of feminist practices, empire, and colonialism with caring politics.[12] Development has aimed to "care for" certain populations: mostly those marked as poor, marginalized, and forgotten. The state mobilizes the value of care so that it can be unburdened of the responsibility of caring for the most marginalized populations. Care has been embedded in discourses and practices of rescuing the "other," of white saviorism, of waging war and causing death.[13] Care is also too often associated with ideals of beauty and purity in a system that erases the ugly, painful, and exhausting work of care.[14] Care is about "getting your hands dirty" in both literal and metaphoric ways. Care is hard.

In this book I use *politics of care* to understand how care gives meaning and value to life *in relationship*, human and nonhuman. It is vital to understand that concepts of interdependence, communality, and relationality, for instance, are prevalent in bodies of thought and praxes of numerous Indigenous peoples across the world—within their own specificities—that have been both undermined and exploited by Western/colonial thought.[15] Hiʻilei Julia Kawehipuaakahaopulani Hobart and Tamara Kneese explain that care is "a relational set of discourses and practices between people, environments, and objects."[16] I use *care* to understand how feminist digital activists relate to each other, to the communities they serve, to the principles they stand for, the technologies they live and work with, and the worlds and futures they are building.

I also use *care* to understand how development builds on tropes aligned with femininity such as nurturing and self-sacrifice in a race to include women in the "digital revolution," as well as the complexities of feminist organizational caring politics. My use of *politics of care* is thus also attentive to power, governance, and control, as it borrows from the term *politics of life* attributed to Michel Foucault's theories on biopolitics.[17] It attends to the "vexation of care," as Murphy says, by looking at its limitations as well as its possibilities. Development discourse on technology skillfully uses care as a mechanism to counter the cold, impassive, market-oriented prescriptions for the place of women in the digital society. In feminist digital activism, care is both liberatory and brimming with conflict and negotiations. "Relationality is all there is, but this does not mean a world without conflict nor dissension," Puig de la Bellacasa argues.[18]

Solidarity and Pleasure as Politics of Care

We want to create new visions, imaginaries, and narratives that open up the possibility of conceiving technology from another perspective and design futures that ensure life in community.[19]

—PAOLA RICAURTE

Solidarity and pleasure do not inhabit separate silos. They are intertwined as parts of a politics of care, although my analysis might focus on one more than another in relation to activists' priorities and work. They are not only ideas. They are also fundamental dimensions of economic, political, and social practices. Psychoanalyst, cultural critic, and curator Suely Rolnik argues that "our challenge is in overcoming the nefarious dichotomy between micro- and macropolitics, seeking to articulate them in all of the relational fields of our daily life and our collective insurrectional movements."[20] There is power and a tremendous capacity for transformation in micropolitical spaces and tactics. If we aim to "defend life," to live life with dignity—human and nonhuman—amid the increasing precariousness of life, solidarity and pleasure anchored in our daily lives must also structure our politics.[21] We have seen iterations of both throughout numerous bodies of social theory, starting from centuries of Indigenous thought. Solidarity and pleasure have been deployed as instruments to advance capitalist accumulation as well as to sustain life in the face of devastation and violence.

In the contexts I study, politically located in the global South, solidarity and pleasure are not only means of survival for activists but also subversive tactics. They are woven into the fabric of how they take care of each other and the communities they work with. As such, these bonds are a target of colonial and capitalist schemes. My definition of solidarity stems from the field, and by it I mean horizontal forms of collaboration, kindness, and a profound sense of integrity and justice. I employ solidarity not as a blind form of unity and harmony, but as what feminist theorist Chandra Talpade Mohanty describes as an acknowledgment of shared interests that centralize the value of difference.[22] This is in line with political theorist Jodi Dean's "reflective solidarity" that both recognizes common oppressions and individual specificity arising "through critique and discussion."[23]

In this book pleasure is mostly concerned with sexual and erotic pleasure, but it is theorized expansively to include joy, desire, play, and experimentation expressed and enacted by historically oppressed and dissident communities.[24] Pleasure is thus a collective tactic of defiance in the face of violence. But pleasure, and moreover sexual pleasure, is not meant to convey an unblemished form of happiness; pleasure is entangled with power, violence, and risk (as amply theorized by Foucault).[25] In her deft analysis of *sexual optimism*, cultural theorist Maggie Nelson says that often the terms *pleasure* and *desire* exasperate her because they seem to presume a happiness that does not necessarily align with the realities of sexuality. And, yet, she argues: "No one wants the price of desire to be fatal disease or a life-shattering assault. Expanding the space for the practice of freedom means working to diminish the likelihood of such things for ourselves and for others."[26] "Expanding the space" for solidarity and pleasure is also a practice of justice.

Solidarity is akin to feminist anthropologist Rita Laura Segato's "politics of connections."[27] I use Segato's powerful framework of a "politics of connections" throughout this book to examine the politics of care of both feminist digital activist practices and global development discourse. Amid a world in which extreme violence—particularly against racially minoritized women and feminized bodies in all their diversities—and ecological destruction is rampant, Segato proposes a "politics in feminine key" that "reweaves community using the fragments that are left."[28] This politics in feminine key breaks away from the statist masculinist politics of a historically destructive public sphere, based on bureaucratization and the modern-rational paradigm, by extending the politics of domesticity and its "technologies of sociability and management."[29] Far from establishing binaries or essentializing women and women's work, a politics in feminine key is a subversive and radical politics of transformation. It does not center identities but relationships. This re-politicized politics of connections is not instrumental, but *a way of being*. Segato counterposes a politics of connections to a "politics of things" and the "thing-ification of everything" produced by capitalism as the ultimate sign of happiness and success.[30] The persistence of colonial practices exercised by modern states and corporate capital both targets and appropriates "connections" because these threaten their extractive and accumulative objectives, thus also "thing-ifying" these bonds.

The goal of a politics of connections is not to take over the state, but rather to be "amphibious" with inter- and extra-state projects created by the communities themselves. In other words, the objective is not to take over already established institutions but rather work with and beyond them. The objective is that communities with a shared vision for the future trace their own paths. The activists of Sulá Batsú and APC WRP take a similar approach with projects that target state and transnational institutions and others that center community building and autonomy.

Similar to solidarity, the disciplining and control of sexuality (and pleasure and joy)—of women's, men's, trans, and nonbinary individuals—have been central to colonial, modern, and developmental projects.[31] These sexualities have historically been constructed as nonnormative in relation to a universalized and unmarked white bourgeois sexuality that represents heterosexuality, cisnormativity, restraint, and modesty.[32] With practices and discourses on sexuality deployed to control and stigmatize marginalized communities across political geographies, the use of pleasure is particularly subversive. "The colonial-patriarchal-modern expression adequately describes the priority of patriarchy as the appropriator of the bodies of women, and the body as the first colony," Segato explains.[33] Pleasure thus disrupts colonial paradigms by centering subaltern bodies and sexualities deconstructing imaginaries of victimhood as well as of heroes and saviors.[34] It unravels these tropes because pleasure is *both* bountiful and messy. Feminist development scholars have insisted on calling for scholarship that explores the complexity of sexuality and pleasure in the global South.[35] Gender and development scholar Andrea Cornwall, for instance, argues that discomfort surrounding pleasure is precisely what is needed to disrupt development contexts: "Talk of 'pleasure' takes us beyond monochromatic representations of abjection, reminding us of the humanity of those whose lives development agencies would wish to improve. Pleasure-based approaches suggest more prospect of enhancing well-being and saving lives than current development models."[36]

Pleasure and joy are central to anticolonial justice. It is impossible to think about the gendered body as a site of colonialism and struggle without delving into what theorist and activist Lorena Cabnal has argued about the body being a "central part of the decolonial project." Cabnal calls for the "defense of the territory-body-earth" to enable emotional and spiritual healing as well as land restitution.[37] In Latin America and the Caribbean, for instance, Black and Indigenous women are making a resounding call in defense of pleasure and joy as sites of resistance and re-existence. Leading to the 2022 historic victory of the Left in Colombia, the vice presidential candidate Francia Márquez—a Black woman, former domestic worker, single mother, and climate justice activist— raised the slogan *Vivir sabroso* (Live deliciously), which she explains has been used in the Afro-Colombian community for years, meaning "living without fear, living with dignity, living with a guarantee of rights."[38] Cabnal says that the key is "to vindicate happiness without losing our indignation."[39] And the words of the Honduran Indigenous leader Berta Cáceres, murdered for her climate justice activism, reverberate: "There is no larger act of rebelliousness than preserving happiness" (as remembered by her daughter, Olivia Marcela Zuñiga Cáceres).[40] In a fascinating comparison, US Black feminists such as Audre Lorde have forged decades of scholarship and activism on the political significance of Black pleasure and joy.[41]

Sulá Batsú and APC WRP

In the cooperative Sulá Batsú, solidarity is part of its everyday practice in the ways the members organize, conceptualize their work, and relate to each other and the communities they serve. Care is an important part of their feminist technopolitical and economic praxes. Their workshops consist of training in basic internet skills, disassembling and reassembling computers, programming with open-source code; training women in online security and privacy; and fostering networks between rural women in STEM fields and creating local entrepreneurial endeavors.

The cooperative has conducted workshops with sex workers, domestic workers, environmental activists, and Indigenous women and led digital storytelling projects throughout Central America using photography, video, and graffiti. The co-op's administrative structure, its principles of sharing knowledge, participatory action research, and public art projects are all important pieces of its politics. In Sulá Batsú technology is anchored in relationships of solidarity among its members and with their communities and the planet. Their work is enabled by a commitment to solidarity, critique, and reflection.

Using a similar set of strategies as Sulá Batsú, rooted in care, APC WRP's activism against online violence and the increasing corporatization of the internet focuses on advocating for novel forms of sexual agency and pleasure online. Its feminist strategies against online gender-based violence embody a politics of care through the celebration of online pleasure. It works at the intersection of research, policy advocacy, movement building, and on-the-ground grassroots capacity building and training. Its projects—such as the annual campaign Take Back the Tech, the exploratory research EROTICS Project on the internet and sexuality, and its collective-based Feminist Principles of the Internet—all center sexuality, fun, and pleasure as fundamental dimensions of feminist relationships with digital technologies.

In both Sulá Batsú and APC WRP there have been complicated entanglements between visons and practices of care. Sulá Batsú, for instance, reproduces the entrepreneurial model, with a woman as an ideal technological figure. Its members are savvy activists who have been able to survive financial turmoil and precariousness and internal tensions and have learned to use institutional language to advance their projects. The micropolitics of these "uneasy alliances" (which I examine in chapter 4) reveals that while Sulá Batsú centers a particular technological woman, its practice of care also challenges corporate development agendas.[42] In the case of APC WRP, the tensions between pleasure, harm, violence, and the increasing criminalization of online violence sit uncomfortably together. There is global trend of passing laws against perpetrators of online violence amid important claims of how criminalization has been a neoliberal, racist, and classist project. In addition, APC WRP moves both within the transnational "UN orbit" and the local grassroots, making the multidirectional nature of feminist activism under globalization evident.[43] It has also had to negotiate its unapologetic feminist vision with global development agencies and funding agencies. Funding, including navigating the porous boundaries between co-optation and autonomy, is a significant part of feminist organizational politics and the complexities of enacting an ethics of care (examined in chapter 4).

Care, in its numerous manifestations—sometimes as solidarity, sometimes as pleasure—has also been subjugated, erased, co-opted, depoliticized, and commodified. But what is the alternative to enacting a politics of care? Forget care? Abandon solidarity? Continue to deny pleasure? Or has care become a hollow concept? A flowery rhetorical device that obscures labor and economic exploitation? I stand by the liberatory dimensions of the notion and the practice of care—life-sustaining, fairly valued, redistributed, non-extractive—and suggest that the key is in forging care while reckoning with how it has been deployed to advance violence, racism, colonialism, and capitalism. In this book, care is not frivolous, and it is not meant in any way to absolve institutions from their responsibilities. In their introduction to the new edition of Peter Kropotkin's *Mutual Aid: An Illuminated Factor of Evolution*, the late anthropologist David Graeber and coauthor Andrej Grubačić argue that contemporary social theory has "stubbornly dismissed pretty much anything suggestive of generosity, cooperation, or altruism as some kind of bourgeois illusion" because "conflict and egoistic calculation proved to be more interesting than 'union.'"[44] Practices of care and cooperation come from time immemorial. Their erasure has served abuses of power and led to unsurmountable violence. Care may be convoluted, but *se nos va la vida en ello* (our lives depend on it). Puig de la Bellacasa insists that care is too important to leave it to hegemonic appropriations.[45] Micronetworks of care—that stem from everyday life, the body, and relationships—defy increasing state and transnational forms of violence. I am committed to the critique of care as well as believing in its capacity for sustaining and transforming our relationships with ourselves, each other, our planet, and our technologies in significant ways.

Development has aimed to make the "Third World" legible (exploitable, marketable) to enforce a series of socioeconomic and political interventions, as anthropologist Arturo Escobar's groundbreaking scholarship has revealed.[46] But for many years international development agencies ignored women. Then, in the 1970s, greatly attributable to Ester Boserup's work, development started to incorporate "Third World women" in funding streams, policies, and discourses.[47] Development began to "see" women in terms of James Scott's analysis of how the modern state meant to control and discipline populations once considered "illegible."[48]

Women stand in a ripe space for interventions designed to make them legible, particularly the figure of the Third World woman—historically wrapped in imaginaries of poverty, Blackness and Brownness, sexuality, submission, and wilderness. Legibility is about *including*. What is legible can be included in systems of power and control. My critique of legibility may seem contradictory, even counterproductive. After so many years of struggling for visibility, I would be advocating for a return to invisibility. Nothing could be further from my objective. My work builds on a robust tradition of critical development feminist scholarship.[49] My goal is to excavate the hidden scripts behind "well-intentioned" development discourses that claim to advance women's liberation, in, as Gayatri Spivak says, "a persistent critique of what one cannot not want."[50] These texts have bright spots and moments of potent analyses, and development has provided a terrain for feminist appropriation and resistance. Yet I am examining troubling emerging *patterns* at the intersection of gender and digital technologies. Unveiling these discourses, a cornerstone of critical development studies, will, I hope, provide new imaginaries, concepts, and practices.[51]

The inclusion of women in development has gone through many iterations since the 1970s.[52] I focus on the race in the past twenty-five years to include women and other marginalized communities in the digital society. I look at the ways in which development discourse, mostly produced by the UN and some major technology corporations, has focused on the importance of integrating women into the digital society, and more recently into the so-called Fourth Industrial Revolution as a global

mantra against inequality.[53] Prominent strategies include capacity building and training in digital information and communication technologies
(ICTs), ICTs for entrepreneurship, education in science and technology
fields, and a diverse array of plans to promote the entrance and retention
of women in science and technology fields in education and the work-
force.[54]

I examine four ways in which development discourse produces the
Third World Technological Woman: (1) through images of care and
the "multiplier effect" (e.g., if women are doing well, this will extend
to their families and communities); (2) by focusing on the urgency of
the financial inclusion of women enabled by digital means; (3) by emphasizing the need for a skilled and tech-savvy entrepreneurial woman;
and (4) by underlining women as the ultimate designers and creators of
technology. Gendered qualities of care and selflessness are a transversal
axis that cuts through all the elements that constitute this Third World
Technological Woman—the organizing concept of this book. The trope
of the "nimble finger" and the "cheap, docile, dexterous" woman of the
export-processing-zone assembly plants produced by global capitalism
in the 1980s and 1990s is also now the caring woman with the technological entrepreneurial mind.

But what is particular about digital technologies? Although mostly
focused on access, use, policy, labor, and leisure, literature on gender,
technology, and development has identified various forms in which development has exercised neoliberal rationalities in its discourses and
policies on ICTs, such as through ideas of governance.[55] Particularly
important is the work of scholars Anita Gurumurthy, Payal Arora, and
Radhika Gajjala in revealing the neoliberal and "Western" rationalities that undergird policies and narratives on digital technologies in the
global South and the numerous ways in which communities interact
with technologies beyond the design and framing of international development.[56] I build on this work to explore how development discourse
employs an intervention that is intimate and gendered: digital technologies evoke ideas about *connection*—connections that dwell in the intimacy of our everyday lives. Critical technology scholars have amply
studied these connections as sites of extraction and commodification in
the era of platform capitalism.[57] But who are considered ideal *connec-*

13

tors? Women, particularly poor, Black, Brown, and Indigenous ones, through feminized ideas of care, reciprocity, and collaboration.

Connecting is also about caring. I have found that these are the connections that development discourse on digital technologies and women aim to render legible and profitable, stripping them from their politically subversive potential. Digital technologies project the possibility of connecting people and can also be connected to numerous areas of life and work, such as the household, the family, the community, agriculture, health, education, and the workplace, as well as to political and social rights. There is a particular temporality about digital technologies that is anchored in the present while leaning toward the future. This makes digital technologies suited for advancing various political and socioeconomic interventions—such as financial inclusion, digital entrepreneurship, data extraction, biometrics, and surveillance—that are gendered and always racialized. The struggle for economic justice and autonomy are intrinsic to the defense of living with dignity, and this is precisely why it is vital to examine what ideas of economic justice are being deployed.

This book is inserted in both postdevelopment and critical development literature in its political aim to search for *alternatives* to Euro- and US-centric development while embracing plurality.[58] It does not give up on the quest for liberatory forms of development, even when this concept and practice are burdened by violence and injustice. As J. K. Gibson-Graham argues, "The challenge of post-development is not to give up on development, but to imagine and practice development differently. Thus post-development thinking does not attempt to represent the world 'as it is,' but the world 'as it could be.'"[59] This book studies different practices and imaginaries of development anchored in feminist politics that are "radical departures from the prevailing paradigm [of development]" but that are also working and resisting within this paradigm.[60] Liberatory strategies can be both short- and long-term, fastened in the present while making the future and embedded in micropolitics while transforming structures. As Rolnik beautifully expresses, the work of micropolitics "announces," while the work of macropolitics "denounces."[61] This book both denounces the violence of technocapitalist developmental discourses and announces feminist technopolitics of world-making in the

14

face of violence. The politics of solidarity and pleasure announce the possibilities of different worlds.

The Caring/Economic Woman

Global development discourse mobilizes numerous forms of care as commodities in an ever-expanding market that *needs* women, while simultaneously centering the need to fairly value care, particularly since COVID-19. The commodification of a politics of care is gendered not only because women are the main targets but because of how it uses gendered tropes that "soothe" ruthless neoliberal policies. Development discourse and policy centers women as prime "untapped resources" that require immediate "investment" and skillfully makes use of tropes of the caring and nurturing woman.[62] The woman who emerges is a Third World heroine who will pull herself, her family, and perhaps even the entire community out of poverty because of her capacity as a savvy entrepreneur who "always pays back" and who is naturally sensitive, giving, and self-sacrificing. Development scholars have pointed to the ways in which these policies not only create "calculative agencies"—through financialization, loans, technical devices, infrastructure, and so forth—but also how they use gendered qualities such as care and nurturing in their discourses.[63] Critical literature on microfinance provides important parallels with the gender and technology discourse, particularly in the critique of how it aims to configure gendered neoliberal subjectivities.[64] Global urbanism scholar Ananya Roy argues, for example, that "microfinance's productivity" counts on women as "selfless altruists."[65]

How can care and nurturing lie together with "calculative agencies"? In his analysis of the German version of liberalism, Foucault argues that the "return to the enterprise," a "policy of the economization of the entire social field," is "at the same time a policy which presents itself or seeks to be a kind of *Vitalpolitik* with the function of compensating for what is cold, impassive, calculating, rational, and mechanical in the strictly economic game of competition."[66] This *Vitalpolitik*, or "politics of life," is an appeal to "warm" "moral" and "cultural" values that are antithetical to competition, diffused and multiplied to offer the "basic units" of the social body the "form of the enterprise."[67] These basic units, according to Foucault (citing Alexander Rüstow), are private property, the household, and neighborhood communities, among others. In the development agenda, this "politics of life" extends, for example, to realms of knowledge and technology, which are arguably basic units of the digital society. Knowledge and technology also become "enterprised."

But what is exposed if we apply a gender analysis to understand this *Vitalpolitik,* which Foucault argues is inherent to certain neoliberal rationalities? This politics of life acquires feminized qualities: care, nurturing, love, self-sacrifice, cooperation. All become intrinsic to the making of the disciplined and responsible subject, as well as to neoliberal policies of dispossession such as privatization, austerity, and debt. These feminized qualities—which are internal to neoliberal logics, not external—compensate for the "cold, impassive, calculating, rational, and mechanical" nature of the competitive market society. The woman that emerges is thus an ideal neoliberal subject, containing the perfect combination: the rational economic *and* caring woman. I argue that to be able to function, development actually *needs* women.

Development discourse and policy have skillfully appropriated elements of feminist ideas, principles, and concerns about the value of participation and representation; of care/social reproduction and cooperation, equality, and human rights; and even of economic justice and redistribution. These images often continue to essentialize and overburden women. I agree with development scholars Ananya Roy, Julia Elyachar, and Andrea Cornwall that radical and feminist politics, critical theory, and even "antidevelopment"—meaning initiatives that oppose mainstream development approaches—have been appropriated by development policies and frameworks.[68] This process of appropriation is discursive and also intimate.[69] Care, cooperation, and solidarity—traditionally associated with the "feminine" and with women—have become crucial in furthering specific socioeconomic agendas.[70]

In her study of the affective rhetoric of development discourse on projects of "immersion" in the developing world, cultural studies scholar Carolyn Pedwell notes: "International development is also a site where the transnational politics of the 'turn to affect' are played out. Indeed, the idea is taking hold that creating social justice is not simply a 'rational' exercise but rather one that involves, and perhaps depends on, the generation of affect. In particular, compassion and empathy have been figured as central to contemporary development practice."[71] Appropriation thus transcends co-opting ideas and concepts, expanding into intimate realms invoking people's emotions, desires, dreams, and hopes. And technology is the substance of dreams, of imagining and reimagining ourselves and the world.

In many of the development reports I examine, there is a conflation between technology and entrepreneurship; technology is about being human, and being human is about being productive and financially self-reliant. The developmental agenda, which has become increasingly corporatized, reproduces the politics of self-discipline and individual responsibility, while rendering profound social problems as technical malfunctions.[72] Reports focused on technology construct a technologically savvy and caring entrepreneurial woman that will have a multiplier effect on her family and community. This makes for an ideal neoliberal actor. Anthropologist Carla Freeman says that "today it is entrepreneurship at all levels that occupies the space of hope," and this hope rests on a woman entrepreneur, specifically a "Third World" woman.[73] The emerging Third World Technological Woman is a heroine, who will contribute to the economy and to social transformation once she has the skills to make a computer, a mobile phone, and the internet work for specific purposes. She is embedded within powerful affective language and imagery in many of the reports examined for this book. Similar to Randy Martin's concept of financialization of everyday life, "a proposal for how to get ahead, but also a medium for the expansive movements of body and soul," technical mastery and skill and digital financial inclusion aim to create specific forms of being in the world.[74]

In some ways comparable to the microfinance strategy, the technological developmental intervention, mostly through digital information and communication technologies, is increasingly relying on formal financial institutional patronage and becoming prominent in the corridors of financial power through "fintech," broadly defined as technology-enabled financial services such as mobile apps that can be used to open accounts, make payments, and obtain loans. The use of fintech has exploded in the start-up world, disrupting traditional banking, and besides digitizing basic financial transactions, it can also enable trading cryptocurrencies.

Attracting US$210 billion in global investment in 2021, this booming industry has acquired prominence in digital development targeting low-income communities and the "unbanked."[75] Women are considered indispensable actors for the growth and success of digital financial inclusion (which I discuss in chapter 1).

Another recent digital financial frontier directed at women that has exploded is "femtech," defined as software, diagnostic tools, wearables, and other services that use technology to attend women's health issues such as menstruation, menopause, and reproductive and sexual health. The "femtech revolution"—headed by women entrepreneurs—had in 2022 a market size between US$500 million and US$1 billion and funding that reached US$2.5 billion in late 2021.[76] Critical technology scholars and advocates are already examining significant problems regarding femtech such as privacy, data mining, surveillance, and the lack of an intersectional perspective, among others.[77] The pairing of femtech and digital development is incipient, yet I expect that it will be prominent soon because it perfectly combines women, profit, and feminized qualities through ideas of motherhood and self-care, for example.[78]

The technological intervention relies on training, workshops, and capacity building in line with what Victoria Bernal and Inderpal Grewal contend: the "goals of development have shifted to empowerment and capacity building, involving the production of new subjects."[79] It is funded by traditional developmental actors (governments and bilateral and multilateral agencies) and increasingly by so-called new actors (corporations, private foundations, philanthropic institutions, and individuals).[80] If we consider the increasing textual production (reports, resolutions, briefs, fact sheets, working papers) across the UN, the World Bank, tech corporations (e.g., GSMA, Meta, Intel, Google, Microsoft), and philanthropic foundations (e.g., the Clinton Global Initiative, Omyidar, the Bill and Melinda Gates Foundation) as a sign, it is noticeable in the global development agenda. Funding for technical training and capacity building has been steadily increasing.[81] And women/technology has become a central locus of development policy as part of the "gender equality as smart economics" mantra.

Since I began analyzing development discourse in 2015, the sense of urgency to include women in the digital society has increased dramatically. UNESCO has literally described it as a "race against time." Numerous factors are at play: the looming shift to a "Fourth Industrial Revolution" that will leave millions without a job, particularly blue-collar workers, the service sector—mostly composed of immigrants and people of color—and the global South; the socioeconomic desolation laid bare by the COVID-19 pandemic and its effects on women; and the fast-approaching 2030 UN Sustainable Development Goals (SDGs) deadline.[82] In 2020, according to the UN's *Sustainable Development Goals Report*, nearly half of the global population is still not online, ICT skills training fell behind (mostly affecting women), and a disproportionate number of women lost their jobs, many due to having to care for children and elders during the pandemic. The 2021 International Telecommunication Union (ITU) report *Measuring Digital Development* indicates that although mobile phone ownership is widespread, women own fewer mobile phones than men, and there is still a large global gender gap in internet usage.[83]

There has also been a shift from an emphasis on access to a focus on the design of technologies.[84] This shift has occurred in NGO, state, and global development circles. Recent global data on women in science, technology, engineering, and mathematics (STEM) education and careers—relevant to Sustainable Development Goals on education (4), gender equality (5), and industry and innovation (9)—varies greatly across regions and countries, stages of education, and fields. But according to UNESCO's 2021 science report, fewer than 30 percent of the world's scientific researchers are women, including in AI, considered a fundamental field for the Fourth Industrial Revolution.[85] This does not mean that advocacy in favor of access has ceased to be important but rather that making women designers of technology—through scientific and technological education and careers—has become central in development discourse as well as on the ground. The goal, of course, is precisely what many activists and feminist scholars of science and technology have been advocating for: from being solely targeted as consumers to becoming developers and designers.

In recent years there has been an explosion of campaigns aimed at increasing girls and women in STEM both in education and the workplace. The idea is that women could design technologies that would, it is hoped, center feminist needs and desires as well as integrate race, sexuality, disability, and ecological awareness into design. Nevertheless, many of these inclusionary approaches are fundamentally driven by a market-oriented impulse. Therefore, although it seems like "Third World" women are being considered as much more complex human beings—beyond subjects with basic needs—the bureaucratic, marketized objective remains intact. Women should become designers and producers to "supply" their labor and knowledge to growing national and corporate needs. Women's knowledges and labor become what political theorist Wendy Brown describes as "little capitals": a neoliberal rationality of rendering humans as sites for entrepreneurialism, increasing competition and value, and boosting rankings and ratings.[86] This woman must be skilled, educated, knowledgeable, and willing to care for others.

Making and Unmaking

In the making always lies the unmaking.[87] This is an inherent paradox. Marx theorized that capitalism contained the "seeds of its own destruction"—this is not a new idea. Capitalism has proved to be an unsustainable system that has created abysmal inequalities, spreading poverty, violence, oppression, and exploitation of peoples, nature, and animals. Feminist scholar-activist Silvia Federici has amply theorized how capitalism has also thrived on the degradation and plundering of women's bodies and knowledges.[88] And development has been a fundamentally capitalist and colonial project. The alliance between capitalism and technology—which is not new but has acquired distinct forms with globalization—is an ideal ally of development with its increasing corporatization. Platform capitalism—business models across economic sectors and geographic boundaries built on the extraction of data for profit—is intertwined with racism and white supremacy, classism, misogyny, LGBTQI+ phobia, and ecological devastation.[89]

It is not a surprise, then, that the capitalist-colonial ethos of corporatized technologies is also the terrain of the *unmaking* of the Third World Technological Woman. In recent years, development reports have progressively focused on the dangers of technology for women and marginalized communities, such as online gender-based violence, data privacy,

20

automation, and biases in AI. The contradiction of creating an ideal digital figure amid these persistent threats generates the following question: What are we leading women into? Development makes this neoliberal subject and then claims it back. But there are always *remakings* and *reinventions*. This book studies the micropolitics of these "spheres of insurrection."[90]

In the 2020 UN Secretary-General's *Roadmap for Digital Cooperation*, released amid the COVID-19 global pandemic and massive protests in the United States and other countries against anti-Black racist violence, Secretary-General António Guterres says:

> Digital technology is shaping history. But there is also the sense that it is running away with us. Where will it take us? Will our dignity and rights be enhanced or diminished? Will our societies become more equal or less equal? Will we become more, or less, secure and safe? The answers to these questions depend on our ability to work together across disciplines and actors, across nations and political divides. We have a collective responsibility to give direction to these technologies so that we maximize benefits and curtail unintended consequences and malicious use.[91]

Again, these are surely well-intentioned words, and Guterres has publicly and forcefully criticized patriarchy and violence against women.[92] And yet the institutions being called upon are precisely some of those that have contributed to creating the unsafe, precarious, and violent online and offline realms that are mostly affecting marginalized communities. Overwhelmingly, it is poor, Black, Indigenous, and LGTBQI+ people and women who at once must *take care of* the digital world and its economy as well as avoid its demise.

Data and Methods

In Defense of Solidarity and Pleasure is a comparative case study that employs multiple qualitative methods including ethnographic tools, semistructured interviews, and textual analysis. The two organizations I selected—the Women's Rights Programme of the Association for Progressive Communications (APC WRP) and Sulá Batsú—provide ideal sites to explore the contested arena of digital information technologies and feminist politics. These organizations offer "opportunities to learn" because they engage in multiple and different (sometimes overlapping) areas of work: developing women as skilled users of digital technologies, fostering entrepreneurship in the area of technology and participating in local, regional, and transnational advocacy efforts on gender and information technologies.[93]

I also chose these organizations because of variations between them. APC WRP identifies as a feminist organization and is a transnational network that develops global campaigns on feminism and technology, while also providing on-the-ground training across the global South from Asia to Africa and Latin America. Sulá Batsú—a member of APC—engages in local training and capacity building with marginalized communities that generally are either "disconnected" or barely entering the digital society in Costa Rica as well as engaging in technology advocacy nationally, regionally, and globally. Sulá Batsú is focused on entrepreneurship and women in STEM, although it is increasingly working on Indigenous digital rights and the intersection of technology and climate justice. APC WRP has also been centering activism on the relationship between technology, capitalism, and the climate crisis. Sulá Batsú is a grassroots cooperative, while APC WRP is a transnational network.

These organizations are embedded either through funding, advocacy work, or networks with development institutions. Both organizations—mostly APC WRP—maintain ties to development institutions through networking and advocacy at local, regional, and global UN events such as the annual session of the United Nations Commission on the Status of Women (CSW) and the biannual regional conferences on women of the Economic Commission for Latin America and the Caribbean (ECLAC). In addition, in recent years Sulá Batsú has received funding from large technological corporations such as Google for projects with youth and women and girls. I consulted more than one hundred reports, working papers, briefs, blog posts, presentations, guides, websites, and news articles from these organizations.

A third "site" of fieldwork was the online archives and repositories of development agencies and technology corporations and foundations. The textual analysis focuses on documents published between 1995 and 2021. In total, I analyzed 203 documents on gender and technology, including digital technology in general, from the UN, including ECLAC, from technology corporations, from international NGOs, and from philanthropic foundations. The relevance of UN agencies—among other global development institutions—as authorities of development discourse and policies has been increasingly questioned by scholars and activists alike.[94] Nevertheless, these organizations continue to be important arbiters of knowledge and practices of development. In Latin America, ECLAC has an undeniable importance in both policy and the production of knowledge in the region. In addition, the feminist digital activists I collaborated with engage with the UN and ECLAC in various ways in terms of knowledge exchange, advocacy, and funding.

In total, between 2014 and 2021, I conducted seventy-six in-depth interviews. Interviews were conducted in Colombia, Costa Rica, New York City, and online via a video conferencing application. I spent most of my fieldwork with Sulá Batsú during the summers of 2015, 2016, and 2019. I conducted most interviews with APC WRP activists through phone calls and video-conferencing applications. I interviewed people in a spectrum of positions in the organizations: board members, administrative staff, activists and trainers, graphic artists, communication and social media editors, web developers, project assistants, and founders and directors. Doing so was important for understanding different aspects of the organizations. I interviewed state actors, gender and technology scholars in Costa Rica, and development agency officials, as well as staff and consultants at multinational technology corporations and foundations. I interviewed three individuals working at the UN in different capacities, but meetings with institutional representatives at the UN and technology corporations were extremely difficult to schedule, and most of my attempts to (via email and the phone) were never answered. Finally, I interviewed key gender and technology experts and feminist digital activists from the region to acquire a broader understanding of the current state and historical trajectories of feminism and technology in Latin America.

Participants were from Argentina, Canada, Colombia, Costa Rica, Lebanon, Malaysia, Mexico, South Africa, Sweden, and the United States. The organization with most diversity in terms of nationality was the Association for Progressive Communications (APC), because of its nature as a transnational network not based in any particular country. Activists from both organizations mostly self-identified as middle-class, educated, heterosexual women, and in Latin America as *mestiza*, although some also identified as Black, working class/poor, and queer, and I interviewed four men (all from Sulá Batsú). I reflect more on my research in the methodological appendix.

Concepts and Names

Vocabularies are constantly evolving. In this book I use a series of concepts that are in permanent flux and that many times are conflated, such as *development, digital development, digital society, neoliberalism, financialization*, and *capitalist-colonial order*. All these concepts have their genealogies, analytical purchase, and specificities across disciplines, bodies of thought, and geopolitical borders. I primarily use *digital society* to refer to the ways in which information, communication, and digital technologies are increasingly structuring our societies politically, socially, culturally, and economically. Scholarly and activist circles increasingly use *data society* to describe contemporary socioeconomic and political intersections of data, technology, and politics, also covering issues related to AI, robotics, the internet of things, automation, and so forth. In chapter 1, I explore the implications of these technological advancements in development discourse, yet my focus is on digital information and communication technologies (i.e., hardware and software, mobile phones, smartphones, computers, the internet, social media, and applications) in both their materiality and sociality.

Neoliberalism is another contested term I use. It has become shorthand in the study of an arsenal of contemporary social, political, economic, and cultural processes and, as such, can lose analytical purchase, but "the spacious character of the concept is also an opportunity."[95] Neoliberalism is a highly malleable concept and thus ambiguous and mutable.[96] Its death has been proclaimed, boosted by COVID-19 with the entrenchment of the state and of authoritarianism and fascism in parts of the world. But neoliberalism is and always has been uneven and tied to specific historical trajectories. In development discourse, neoliberal features of corporatism and market-based financial inclusion—even when the state may figure prominently—are very much alive. Logics of self-discipline and personal responsibility are invoked under the guise of feminized caring politics. Digital development narratives are tied to neoliberal politics, which as sociologist Kamala Kempadoo argues (cited in *Paradoxes of Neoliberalism*), are a prolongation of colonial and racial capitalist policies of extraction and dispossession.[97] These rationalities specifically construct "Third World" women as ideal digital financial warriors. This book approaches neoliberalism as an intensification of capitalism, as well as an economic, political, social, and cultural project directed at self-management and discipline and the making of subjectivities that are more legible and governable, productive, and caring, in tune with market rationalities.[98] This does not mean that I discard macroeconomic approaches of neoliberalism. The making of these subjectivities is connected to larger economic and political processes such as financialization.[99]

Financialization, increasingly pervasive in everyday life through "fintech" (financial digital technologies) and built upon ideas of individual self-reliance and responsibility, is particularly gendered in the ways it targets the connective fabrics of gendered, racialized, and classed social relations (which I discuss in chapter 1).[100] I borrow the term *colonial-capitalist order* from Latin American thinkers such as Segato and Gutiérrez Aguilar to illuminate the consequences of capitalism, colonialism, and patriarchy on bodies and territories.[101] I add *techno-* to the equation to point to the ways in which digital technologies are interconnected with these systems of oppression.

I use terms such as *Third World*, *global North*, and *global South* with hesitation. All these terms are contested and problematic. Particularly, *Third World* is now considered pejorative in many circles. I decided to use *Third World* as a critique referring to the developmental neoliberal figure of the "technological woman" to show how geopolitical and epistemic asymmetries embedded in the term are still alive and well and hidden under other guises. *Global North* and *global South*, although imperfect, help map asymmetrical global power relations. As Nour Dados and Raewyn Connell argue, *global South* refers to "an entire history of colonialism, neo-imperialism, and differential economic and social change through which large inequalities in living standards, life expectancy, and access to resources are maintained."[102] The *South* is not a simple "geographical or geopolitical marker" but rather "a plural entity subsuming also the different, the underprivileged, the alternative, the resistant, the invisible, and the subversive."[103] There are many "souths" and "norths" across borders. I do not attempt to flatten the enormous diversity of the "global South" and the myriad of histories, politics, and feminist tactics that circulate, but rather, I attempt to understand emerging technopolitical strategies anchored in a southern perspective that could offer insights for activist and scholarly communities. This book reveals feminist technopolitical practices beyond developmental discourses of technology as "imported magic."[104]

I use *marginalized* to describe certain communities and individuals that have been historically and systematically exploited and dispossessed. I also use *oppressed*. And as I write this, I wonder, *marginal* according to whom? Against what standard? This is the same question I ask myself when scholars use *invisible* or *surprising*: invisible and surprising to whom? Scholars and activists have criticized the term *marginalized* as a bland euphemism to describe the historically exploited, dispossessed, and excluded. But the "margins" are also a place of defiance and struggle, as bell hooks famously said in reference to Black life: "Marginality [is] much more than a site of deprivation. In fact I was saying just the opposite: that it is also the site of radical possibility, a space of resistance."[105] I use *marginalized* (with an emphasis on the *-ized*) to indicate oppression, while always representing agency.

I also use the term *women*. The development reports analyzed employ almost exclusively hetero-, cis- conceptions built on the woman/man binary even when using *gender*. LGBTQI+, gender nonconforming, and nonbinary individuals are practically invisible in this discourse. Race is also nearly absent. But white supremacy and cis- and heteronormativity have structured development discourses and policies. The Third World Technological Woman is a racialized figure, even when presented mostly as deracialized.[106] The organizations I collaborate with, however, engage in activism at the intersection of digital technologies, race, sexuality, and LGBTQI+ issues.

As with any critical research, this book runs the risk of reifying *and* demonizing both corporate digital technologies and development. That is not my intention. There are opportunities and challenges in both. I examine the entanglements, contradictions, and sites of contestation enacted through feminist praxis.

I have chosen to maintain the identities of the organizations studied to amplify their mission, but I have protected the identity of most participants by using pseudonyms (most chosen by the participants themselves). I use the names only of the coordinator of Sulá Batsú, Kemly Camacho (precisely because we have talked about and negotiated the politics of using names in research) and of some of the state officials I interviewed. All the interviews with members of Sulá Batsú and some with APC WRP activists were conducted in Spanish. All translations to English of interview transcripts and texts (news articles, essays, books) in Spanish are mine (when an English translation was unavailable). I am not a professional translator, but I hope to have faithfully captured the thoughts of these activists and scholars.

Citational Practices

In Defense of Solidarity and Pleasure advances sociology of development, specifically gender and development studies, by examining digital technologies as a central locus of power and feminist politics. The work of such scholars as Ananya Roy, Kalpana Wilson, Andrea Cornwall, Smitha Radhakrishnan, and Wendy Harcourt have been fundamental in helping me theorize the gendered and racialized politics of development to expand debates in the literature on development and digital technologies (commonly referred to as ICT4D, or information and communication technologies for development). These scholars center power in their analyses, offering key insights that dismantle the overwhelmingly utilitarian and economic growth model of much of ICT4D research.[107]

In Defense of Solidarity and Pleasure also advances the subfield of critical digital sociology, which, as Jesse Daniels, Karen Gregory, and Tressie McMillan Cottom explain, is concerned first with social problems and inequality and *then* with technology.[108] In this book, I put gender and development and digital sociology in conversation using theoretical tools that have remained in distinct disciplinary silos—such as Feminist Science and Technology Studies—to understand how care is mobilized as a contemporary site of technocapitalist-colonial practices in the global South as well as a terrain of feminist defiance and negotiation.[109] These sites of discourse and action are not in reaction to the other; they are in interaction and mutually constitutive.

In Defense of Solidarity and Pleasure employs various theoretical strands, but it is anchored in the work of theorists at the margins of US-based sociology, mostly theorists from and working in the global South, particularly Latin America.[110] The work of Lorena Cabnal, Verónica Gago, Raquel Gutiérrez Aguilar, Suely Rolnik, and Rita Segato has been especially fundamental. I traveled to the "South" to collect data, yes, but it is also where I found the theoretical articulations to understand my findings. The activists I interviewed for this book are also centered as experts and theorists of their lives, experiences, and knowledges. As a Puerto Rican tenure-track sociologist in US academia, it has not been easy for me to challenge US-based sociology's history of theorizing the South with theories produced in the North. And yet there was no other way of understanding my case studies—which are either in the South or catering to the South—without engaging with theory *produced* in the South. Theory from the South helped me "find [my] way," as Sara Ahmed argues.[111]

I recognize there are "souths" in the North and "norths" in the South, which disturb neat categories, and often theories produced in these "souths" are much more in conversation with Euro-US theory than the other way around. I thus include scholars from multiple "souths," yet I do not exclude scholars primarily identified as from the "North" or the geographies of power that the "North" represents because they are also part of the conversation. This book follows the work of sociologist Raewyn Connell in an attempt to break with the persistent asymmetry of the geopolitics of knowledge in Euro-US academia, and instead embrace, as Pallavi Banerjee and Connell argue, a "world-centered, solidarity-based approach to knowledge."[112]

Overview of Chapters

Each chapter traces the making and unmaking of the Third World Technological Woman, cutting across issues of international development and governance, digital technologies, violence, feminist activism, entrepreneurship, and care. Chapter 1 focuses on the textual analysis of global development agencies'—particularly the UN's—policies and discourses at the intersection of gender and digital technologies in the global South from the mid-1990s to the present. I find that these entities construct an ideal Third World Technological Woman who combines technological dexterity and entrepreneurial instinct with care and self-lessness providing technical solutions to social problems. There is an increasing sense of urgency to include women in the digital society. Thus, digital technologies provide yet another field for tactics of discipline that are gendered, racialized, and explicitly target women. I also compare global development discourses to Latin American discourse produced by ECLAC, which provides important differences by employing broader historical, social, and political context while increasingly embracing women as ideal digital entrepreneurs.

Chapter 2 examines the work of the grassroots feminist cooperative Sulá Batsú, in Costa Rica. Sulá Batsú is a leader in the field of gender and technology in Latin America. I discuss how Sulá Batsú's solidarity-based organizational practices enable a Technological Woman that challenges colonizing and market-centered entrepreneurial strategies by forging collectivized ways of living and working and the ways that technology is localized, collectivized, and felt. The cooperative's administrative structure, its inclusivity and reflexivity, and its principles of sharing knowledge, participatory action research, and public art projects are all important pieces of its feminist technopolitics. At the same time, conflicts and contradictions have emerged from the coop's feminist praxes around its relationships, as well as its work on entrepreneurship and market-based solutions to inequality. I also analyze Costa Rica's state policies on gender and technology in this chapter.

Chapter 3 examines feminist technopolitics of care anchored in the global South, specifically through the case study of the Women's Rights Programme of the transnational network Association for Progressive Communications (APC WRP), a trailblazing organization in the area of internet rights. APC WRP problematizes online violence through two main strategies: (1) by anchoring online violence in a southern epistemology that makes explicit the connections between online violence and broader structural contexts and (2) by advocating for novel forms of online pleasure and joy. Feminist activists foster a pleasure-based technopolitics that reinvents tropes on Third World women's victimization and "natural" heroism. This includes desires of women, trans and non-binary, LGBTQI+, and disabled individuals. I also discuss the ways in which activism on pleasure is entangled with harm, trauma, and pain.[113] I examine how some of APC WRP's proposed solutions to online violence, such as policies that criminalize perpetrators, often contradict the organization's feminist principles of intersectional justice. Also examined in this chapter is the surge of development documents on the dangers of online violence against women and other marginalized communities.

Chapter 4 examines how feminist digital activists of Sulá Batsú and APC WRP negotiate their relationships with international development and corporate funders to be able to advance their projects. These "uneasy alliances" require compromises yet also provide a productive ground for subversion. It is vital to examine the subtleties of organizational everyday processes and forms of implementation to understand the complexities that lie at the intersection of feminist politics and funding. The chapter frames these negotiations within the broader context of the increasing corporatization of development and its implications for achieving a more just world.

I conclude that amid the inexorable path of inclusion in the digital society and expanding forms of capitalist-colonial practices within online and offline realms, feminist digital activists in the global South uplift a Technological Woman that is not uniquely an economic—or even a technological—actor but a fully human, complex individual. To explain the importance of their work, I understand feminist activists as building what Donna Haraway calls a "thick present" in which the "task is to make trouble, to stir up potent response to devastating events, as well as to settle troubled waters and rebuild quite places."[114] And yet I add that this present simultaneously makes a more caring future. I conclude by stressing the urgent task of transforming the present into a world in which digital technologies—and the possibility of their refusal—contribute to justice and truly liberatory politics.

ONE

The Politics of Discourse

Twenty-five years since the World Conference on Women in Beijing, the world has witnessed two things: a global digital revolution and not a single country having achieved gender equality.

—ACTION COALITION ON TECHNOLOGY AND
INNOVATION FOR GENDER EQUALITY[1]

There is a global digital revolution and women are being left behind. In this race, discourse produced by the United Nations and corporations on the "equalizing" potential of digital technologies provides yet another field for targeting women. "Care" as a site of economization through digital technologies is yet another iteration of capitalism's historical exploitation of the value of care/social reproduction.[2]

This chapter focuses on the making of this particular gendered and racialized subject and how she occupies center stage at this historical conjuncture of hopes for the future—especially since COVID-19, which brought the frantic need for internet connection and digital know-how and the "revelation" that care is indispensable for anything to work or survive, in addition to growing economic precariousness. Through textual analysis of more than two hundred documents, I examine (1) how this discourse preys on care to uplift women in the global South as ideal technological subjects; (2) the history of the coupling of digital technologies and women in international development; and (3) the particular

31

trajectory of ECLAC in Latin America.[3] Care as a central component of financial profit is contingent to economic geopolitical shifts such as the neoliberalization of development in the 1980s, the "benevolent" policies of the "post-Washington" consensus of the 1990s,[4] the 2008 global financial crisis, the expansion of digitalization and the fintech industry (which is largely unregulated), the increasing corporatization of development, and, of course, COVID-19. Since COVID-19 UN discourse has increasingly centered the importance of fairly valuing care while simultaneously exposing care as site of financial profit and extraction. The developmental approach to gender often seems benevolent, inclusive, and "feminist."

Again and again in these texts, *inclusion* in the digital society is often a code word for some form of extraction, either material or immaterial. Even with increasing references to the dangers and risks of inclusion— such as online gender-based violence, unethical data practices, AI bias, or the automation of labor and suggestions on how to "mitigate" these harms—the digital "revolution" remains unquestioned.[5] It is a given that we are advancing into this technological future, and the only option is to get on the bus or be left behind, as stated in the preamble to the resolution on the SDGs (Sustainable Development Goals) adopted by the UN General Assembly.[6] Critical scholars have been studying the ills of numerous forms of inclusion for decades, and recently development discourse on ICTs (information and communication technologies) has also started to recognize that it is not a magical solution. But inclusion in the digital revolution has become so urgent that warnings often seem like afterthoughts or problems to be solved through technical and bureaucratic interventions. One of the chapters of the 2021 *UNESCO Science Report* puts it succinctly: "To be smart, the digital revolution will need to be inclusive."[7]

Richard Heeks, who studies ICTs for development (ICT4D), has introduced the critical concept of "adverse digital incorporation" to explain how digital inclusion leads to inequality in times when internet access and mobile phones have dramatically increased in the global South.[8] In other words, people are "included," yet "inequality is increasingly associated with those included in digital systems in the global South" through patterns such as exploitation (i.e., of workers for the platform gig economy), commodification (of the bodies of women and children), legibility (surveillance, biometrics), and digital enclosure (expropriation of common knowledge into private digital systems). Not surprisingly, "adverse digital incorporation" disproportionately affects communities across gender, race, class/income, and ability. These issues traverse geopolitical borders. In her analysis of racial capitalism and digitalization in the United States, sociologist Tressie McMillan Cottom explains how the "platform-mediated era of capitalism" specializes in "predatory inclusion": "the logic, organization, and technique of including marginalized consumer-citizens into ostensibly democratizing mobility schemes on extractive terms."[9] And inclusion is increasingly urgent, reminiscent of the language of modernization. In effect, discourses on women and digital inclusion have assumed a rhetoric based on "urgency." The global COVID-19 pandemic has magnified the necessity of "leaving no one behind."

The Caring/Economic Third World Technological Woman

The Third World Technological Woman is *made* as the ultimate neoliberal actor, a combination of the "rational economic woman" with the caring woman.[10] In global development discourse, digital technologies are often framed as essential to caring for others. This is not a frame of arid economic empowerment; it is full of emotion. The image of the woman entrepreneur is that of a modern warrior, connected to digital technologies both as a consumer *and* a producer. This is the spectacular Third World woman of the future. The digital future is a gendered and racialized category, and the message is that women who have been at the margins can overcome barriers through digital technologies, framed as an intimate necessity.

The Care Collective states that "neoliberalism . . . has neither an effective practice of, nor a vocabulary for, care."[11] I agree that the capitalist-colonial order is inherently contrary to care and the defense of life, what feminist economist Amaia Pérez Orozco has called "the capital-life conflict."[12] And yet neoliberalism does have a vocabulary for care, or rather it has appropriated a vocabulary for care. This is the vocabulary that I have found. This vocabulary for care confers avenues for control and extraction of what Rita Laura Segato calls a "politics of con-nections": a vital site of political mobilization that has historically been the target of patriarchal-capitalist-colonial institutions. Global develop-ment's focus on digital technologies, women, and care is an intimate project that makes these connections legible and profitable. I turn to Michel Foucault's "politics of life" to understand how certain gendered and feminized qualities serve to counter the cold and market-oriented objectives of these discourses that manifest through four main modes that are interconnected.[13] These modes are (1) imageries of care and the "multiplier effect," or the essentialized talent of women to help every-one around them; (2) women's financial inclusion facilitated by digital means; (3) the need for a skilled and tech-savvy entrepreneurial woman; and (4) women as the ultimate digital designers.

In this way, numerous areas of life and work can be made into sites of potential profit connected to finance and market-based approaches to in-equality, or what Julia Elyachar calls the "financialization of indigenous social practices."[14] These discourses often obscure the political and so-cioeconomic structures that have produced the inequalities this techno-logical subject is supposed to overcome by providing technical fixes. The Third World Technological Woman is supposed to miraculously thrive amid numerous forms of violence and precariousness.

Caring and the Multiplier Effect

Helping women and girls develop digital skills translates into stronger women, stronger families, stronger communities, stronger economies and better technology.

—MARK WEST, REBECCA KRAUT, AND
HAN EI CHEW, *I'D BLUSH IF I COULD*[15]

Care and the care economy, both paid and unpaid, have increasingly appeared in UN reports and documents since the 1995 Beijing Platform for Action. It is a Sustainable Development Goal target under the gender equality goal and has become even more central during the COVID-19 pandemic.[16] Discourses about the care economy in the documents under study are polyvalent and often contradictory. Certain documents offer intersectional and redistributive analyses of care work, address structural issues and power relations as the root of gender inequality, and call on states to provide the necessary infrastructures and social protections for caregivers. In other documents, care is seen as something to be taken care of so women can have more time to be productive (ostensibly in the formal workplace) and for "leisure" and "self-care."[17] Technologies are fundamental for this freedom. The UN Women's 2018 *SDG Monitoring Report* assures that "mobile phones can contribute to important aspects of women's empowerment: They enable women to keep in touch with family and friends, facilitate financial transactions and save time coordinating and managing everyday activities."[18]

The recognition, valorization, and redistribution of care work has been a central claim of feminist movements, albeit approached from divergent political perspectives and struggles. Development scholars Susan Bergeron and Stephen Healy argue that although many feminist scholars have been critical of the incorporation of care and cooperation in development as new targets of marketization, not recognizing the importance of this inclusion "forecloses ways of imagining how they might be starting points for a different conversation around the economy" while reifying global capitalism.[19] But the authors admit that the ethics of care in mainstream development discourse "becomes a means, an instrument of economic growth."[20] I agree with Bergeron and Healy's contention that there is space for reimagining feminist politics, yet at the same time critical research has been essential in revealing challenges of what Gayatri Spivak calls "what one cannot not want."[21] Women in many parts of the world are the primary caretakers of their families and communities as well as the majority of workers—mostly poor, Black and Brown, and immigrant women—in the care economy. This is not new or disputed. But in these reports, technology is mostly framed as assisting women in their caretaking responsibilities, as a DAW (now UN Women) and UNESCO report states: "Women spend a large amount of time performing labour-intensive tasks. Technology can support them in their multiple roles in production, community management, domestic and care responsibilities, such as the provision of care to children, the sick and the elderly."[22] Actually, technology and its many benefits, including information, will support women in their "triple roles" of production, reproduction, and community organizing.[23] Women are consistently framed

35

as caring about their families and committed to their communities; thus, digital technologies will aid them in their purpose in life while ostensibly increasing their financial opportunities. This is the making of the caring/economic technological woman in all her magnificence.

The multiplier effect is prominent in this discourse on women and technology. There is a typology of sorts: women will have access to technology—as users, consumers, developers, producers, scientists—and will save themselves, their families, communities, and countries. "Saving" is also aligned with caring. In a May 8, 2015, email interview, two women who worked at Intel on relevant projects expressed: "With greater use of technology, women conquer the power to transform their life, their family, their community and the environment around them. Girls and women are called masters of the multiplier effect. When they are mothers, their children are more likely to complete their studies and have a better quality of life and health, as they will be incentive and inspire knowledge and good daily practices."

Intel has played an important role in the gender and technology conversation, with a series of reports including the 2013 "Women and the Web: Bridging the Internet Gap and Creating New Global Opportunities in Low and Middle-income Countries" cited across numerous UN reports.[24] The Intel executives—who answered my questions via email as a team, not individually—mentioned a couple of stories of women's experiences with technology through their program Intel Learn, which was aimed at digital skills training for children and youth in the "developing" world. They told me about Peruvian entrepreneur Dany, who "before the program, did not know how to turn on a PC" and "now uses the Internet to look for better options for her business." They shared the story of Ana, a Colombian who worked ten years at "the center of waste collection in Cali and could not appropriately manage the money received from the sale of recycled materials." When the center closed, they explained, Ana had no income. She learned how to write, read, add, and subtract after taking a computer course that applied the Intel Learn methodology. Ana learned Excel so she could systematize the reports of an organization that she now directs. "By using technology," they wrote, "she has achieved greater economic stability and has changed not only her life but also [that of] her family and many women who worked and

36

work with her." It seems as if humanity itself relies on the merging of life and technology through this caring, loving, selfless, gendered subject.

Technology, Skilled Women, and Financial Inclusion

Globally, digital data in the form of transaction records are used to determine creditworthiness, and women without a digital footprint may find themselves unable to secure a loan, rent an apartment or even connect utilities without a significant deposit. Digital skills also increasingly facilitate important life decisions such as selecting a partner, as dating moves more and more to online platforms.

—MARK WEST, REBECCA KRAUT, AND HAN
EI CHEW, *I'D BLUSH IF I COULD*[25]

This quotation connects some of the interrelated dimensions of the Third World Technological Woman: digital skills → financial inclusion → the capacity to live a full life. If women are incapable of learning digital skills, they will not be able to secure a livelihood, not even a partner. A UN Women working paper presented to the UN Secretary-General's Task Force on Digital Financing of the Sustainable Development Goals (which chose women as one of the main themes) states that the obstacles women face are huge, "but so is the opportunity if we manage to unlock the potential of digital finance to create a more equitable and sustainable world."[26] If digital finance does not unlock their potential—while managing and mitigating harms and barriers—equality is unlikely. Digitalization has become a feature of financial inclusion (incorporating individuals into the formal financial system), framing women as vital participants.[27]

The 2017–21 Financial Inclusion Global Initiative (FIGI)—partnering the World Bank Group, the Committee on Payments and Market Infrastructure (CPMI), and the ITU, funded by the Bill and Melinda Gates Foundation—assesses that as a "critical enabler for poverty reduction and inclusive growth," financial inclusion through digital technologies promises to incorporate the 1.4 billion people who remained "unbanked" or "underbanked" as of 2021 (1.1 billion got access to bank accounts between 2014 and 2021).[28] Financial inclusion can "improve resistance to economic shocks, boost productivity of businesses, facilitate female empowerment and help eradicate extreme poverty and increase shared prosperity."[29] This is how the internet and digitalization in general become "a symbol of economic progress—the promised land you'll reach with the right equipment and the right training," as information scholar Daniel Greene argues in his research on techno-solutionism and poverty in the United States.[30] In the texts under study, it is mostly women from the global South who will take you to that "promised land." The burden of economic progress lies on the backs of gendered, racialized, and classed subjects.

The World Bank's *Global Findex Database* reports—launched in 2011 with funding from the Bill and Melinda Gates Foundation—measure how "adults save, borrow, make payments, and manage risk," including through digital means or the use of fintech (broadly defined as the use of digital technologies for financial services).[31] The 2021 report shows that financial inclusion has risen globally—dramatically boosted by the COVID-19 pandemic—with 71 percent of adults in "developing economies" with a formal financial account, up from 63 percent since the last survey in 2017. Adults making or receiving digital payments grew from 35 percent in 2014 to 57 percent in 2021, outperforming advances in account ownership. For the first time the gender gap narrowed, from 9 percent to 6 percent in low- and middle-income countries since 2017.[32] But Bill Gates still assures us that "the world can do better. Leaders should focus even more directly on expanding account ownership and use among women."[33] Not surprisingly, in the 2021 report women figure as indispensable financial actors, with examples of women in Chile, India, Nepal, and the Philippines being able to take control of their lives—and their households—after gaining access to digital financial services. In Kenya, women who had access to savings through mobile phones could even reduce their "reliance on high-risk financial sources of income (such as transactional sex)."[34]

Even when the UN's 2020 *World Development Report* problematizes some of the failures of technological progress, it emphasizes the digital divide, the increasing value of being a "high-skilled" worker versus "medium-" or "low-skilled," and the importance of digital financial inclusion (i.e., account ownership) for "less advantaged people" to be able to enjoy the bounties of the so-called digital revolution. The report highlights Aadhaar as a success. Aadhaar, the system the Indian government launched in 2009, uses demographic and biometric data (collected through fingerprints, iris scans, and so forth) to create unique ID numbers. One of the uses of the ID number is to open financial accounts, and "by 2017, 80 percent of adult Indians had at least one bank account."[35] But critical technology scholars have examined some of the problematic issues with Aadhaar related to surveillance, data mining, and privacy, among others.[36]

In their analysis of how international development agencies used digital technologies, particularly the mobile phone, for advancing financial inclusion since the 2008 crisis, Daniela Gabor and Sally Brooks argue that "a defining feature of financial[ized] inclusion as enabled by new information technologies, particularly mobile technology, is what we refer to as the 'commodification' of a new class of financial consumer, or more accurately, of his or her personal data. Central to this vision is the potential of digital technologies to capture the data of the newly 'included' in ways that enable lenders to map, know and govern 'risky populations.'"[37] The authors contend that beyond the World Bank, there is a global "fintech-philanthropy-development complex" that profits on "digital legibility" of "irrational customers" with the objective of making profit through data extraction, behavior modification, and surveillance, disciplining the poor into financialized subjects.

Yet Gabor and Brooks do not engage in a gendered analysis, even though they mention that strategies of financial inclusion target "households," which are undeniably gendered sites of care. I suggest that beyond the goal of making profit through data extraction and surveillance, this fintech-philanthropy-development complex aims to profit from particular, intimate relationships of care in which women figure prominently. Luci Cavallero, Verónica Gago, and Celeste Perosino extend this research on fintech by looking at the ways in which Argentina implemented policies of financial inclusion during the COVID-19 pandemic amid growing precariousness.[38] The "unbanked" had to use a series of digital technologies, such as certain apps, to access state emergency funds. The authors offer a critical perspective on "inclusion" as a process embedded in gendered discourse and policy.

It is impossible to examine development's focus on digital financial inclusion without analyzing its gendered and racialized dimensions. The UN's Addis Ababa Action Agenda, the outcome document of the Third

Conference on Finance for Development in 2015 on the heels of the Sustainable Development Goals, centers both women as entrepreneurial actors and digital technologies in particular as vital to the financing of development, while promoting private sector financial cooperation.[39] Despite calling for "social protection and essential public services for all," the document has been criticized as a step backward from the previous Monterrey (2002) and Doha (2008) declarations. The Declaration from the Addis Ababa Civil Society Forum condemns the Action Agenda for emphasizing private sector financing, instrumentalizing women as economic actors, uncritically adopting digital technologies for development, and not calling for debt cancellation, among other issues, while ignoring systemic, historical, and political factors. As if foreshadowing the 2020 global pandemic crisis, the Doha Civil Society Declaration states: "If another crisis were to strike today, the world would be just as unprepared as it was in 2008 to reduce its costs and ensure that these costs are borne by those that with their reckless and greedy behavior caused it."[40]

Increasing violence against women, abysmal poverty levels, and massive health disparities and access to adequate health care for poor, old, rural, LGBTQI+, Black, Brown, and Indigenous communities during the COVID-19 pandemic indicate that strategies of inclusion have not avoided precariousness amid social, economic, climate change, and ecological collapse.[41] In moments of crisis, which will be more frequent and destructive, these are two vital questions: What truly gives people and communities the power to live with dignity and joy? What supports their ability to thrive (materially, socially)? Data on the relation between poverty reduction and fintech in the global South is mixed at best. One of the most cited examples of the success of fintech is the mobile-based money transfer platform M-Pesa in Kenya.[42] An influential article by Tavneet Suri and William Jack—focused on women's uses of the app—found that M-Pesa had raised 194,000 households (2% of Kenyan households) out of poverty. In their response, Milford Bateman, Maren Duvendack, and Nicholas Loubere examine how that article fails to consider debt, exit rates, corporate profit, and data mining, among other problems.[43] Speaking to the value of emotion in corporate development, Radhika Gajjala and Dinah Tetteh found that M-Pesa's marketing materials deployed leisure as an equivalent of economic empowerment and upward mobility. Emotion serves as both a site of extraction of labor under the guise of leisure and as a unique way to attract poor users to digital technology.[44] In addition, as Judy Wajcman theorized long ago about the mutual constitution of technologies, and Payal Arora has found among poor users in the global South, people use these technologies in ways that subvert the neoliberal financial goals imprinted upon them.[45] And yet, the UN's 2022 "Financing for Sustainable Development" report continues to pair women with digital financial inclusion, while incorporating warnings of the risks of algorithmic bias and lack of data protection.[46]

The Magical Tech Entrepreneur: The Dexterous, Skilled, and Tech Savvy Woman

Protect and promote global values.
Foster inclusion and transparency.
Work in partnership.
Build on existing capabilities and mandate.
Be humble and learn.

So read the priorities from the UN's Strategy on New Technologies, created by the office of Secretary-General António Guterres in 2018.[47] The nineteen-page document aims to support the use of these technologies in achieving the 2030 Sustainable Development Goals in alignment with the values of the UN Charter and the Universal Declaration of Human Rights. Unsurprisingly, the only time *women* appears in the document is to reaffirm women's role as exceptional digital entrepreneurs; Guterres says that he will "explore, with the UN senior leadership, how to further increase UN support to women entrepreneurs in technology fields, and how to increase their participation in UN forums where new technology-related issues are being addressed."[48]

The document—which focuses on digital technologies and emerging technologies such as robotics, AI, and biotechnology—gravitates between addressing the tremendous opportunities and the dangers of these technologies regarding privacy, ethics, and equity. Yet the examples in the document about UN support for design and development of new technologies are "the world's largest drone test corridor for humanitarian applications covering over 13,000 square kilometers" in Malawi and a "Virtual Farmers Markets where an app-based e-commerce platform connects farmer's surplus and buyers' demand for crops."[49] Repeatedly, a gendered and racialized form of "entrepreneurial citizenship" is called upon as a "promise of inclusion through the generation of economic and social possibility," as communication scholar Lilly Irani argues in her ethnography of the innovation and technological entrepreneurial ethos in India.[50]

Feminist scholars have demonstrated the ways in which development mobilizes women and girls as ideal economic neoliberal actors.[51] While this entrepreneurial woman has been touted as the cure of the developing world's problems, researchers have pointed out the dilemmas of emphasizing market-based approaches, such as microfinance, as solutions to inequality. The onus is on the caring, self-sacrificing, hard-working woman, while sociopolitical contexts are ignored, methods of shaming are deployed, and women's debt increases under the guise of "liberation." Gender and development scholar Kalpana Wilson notes that the focus on women as an agent of change and infinite possibilities neatly dovetailed with the neoliberalization of international development with its ideals of personal responsibility and self-reliance embodied in the microfinanced female entrepreneur.[52]

This empowered, altruistic, poor woman has become what Ananya Roy calls a "timeless image of aspiration."[53] The burden of progress rests on her shoulders. But, as Cavallero and Gago brilliantly argue in their feminist analysis of debt, victimhood and entrepreneurship are two sides of the same coin: "The 'farse' of inclusion through finance attempts to impose the idea that becoming an entrepreneur is the ideal to which we all aspire and that banks support. The entrepreneur is the complementary figure of the victim. Both are spaces of subjectivation proposed by a neoliberalism that wants to wash itself in pink. The feminist proposal is: *we are neither victims nor entrepreneurs*."[54] The focus on women's alleged ideal capacities as entrepreneurs is another iteration of including women in a broken global economic apparatus.

The making of this "worthy neoliberal subject"—a market actor and both an agent and a rescued subject of development—has fueled debates in the field of gender and development regarding the co-optation of feminist politics for state, transnational, and corporate interventions that are antithetical to feminist principles.[55] Feminists spent years advocating for women to be included in development, but their inclusion has not transformed the institutions that produce the very inequalities that feminists struggle against. Market-based approaches to economic development—such as entrepreneurship—financialize subjects while obscuring the conditions that have contributed to economic precariousness and the need for profound structural transformation. These same issues remain as discourse progressively embraces women as designers, creators, and developers.

The intertwining of technologies and entrepreneurship was evident in an interview I conducted on the phone with an International Telecommunication Union (ITU) official who mentioned that women need to be "fed" into the "pipeline," adding that "because ICTs are shaping our societies, we want to make sure that women and girls become creators of ICTs and not simply consumers. We want women and girls to have access to ICTs. We want them to be digitally literate, but we also want them to be creators, developing the technologies that are so profoundly impacting all of our lives." As our conversation continued, the emphasis on financial growth was evident:

> FSV: This is another broad question, but it's a question I like to ask, because it sometimes gives people the possibility to really think about the work they're doing: What kind of future do you think ICTs will bring for women in the developing world?
>
> ITU official: Well, I'd like to think it will bring many job opportunities for women in the developing world.

This new brave world of the digital society revolution *needs* women. Badly. But what do women (and which women?) need? This question remains unanswered.

Today it is hardly a secret that technology is shaping the future and is a lever of power. Women cannot continue to be absent or nearly absent from the labs, companies and offices where technology takes shape. This risks the perpetuation or even an acceleration of gender inequality.

—MARK WEST, REBECCA KRAUT, AND
HAN EI CHEW, *I'D BLUSH IF I COULD*[56]

There has been a shift from an emphasis on access to production and design of technologies. Under the "Education" section, the Beijing Platform for Action had already mentioned that it is "essential" for women to both benefit from technology and participate at all levels of its design. But the Platform does not define exactly what the benefits are for women in becoming designers and producers of technology. How will this shape gender power relations? How will this lead to a liberatory feminist future? Daniel Greene explains that the "access doctrine," based on techno-solutions to social problems, has proved to be mutable and malleable: from internet access (subsequently divided by gender, race, and class "gaps"), the doctrine shifted to the importance of mastering digital skills and currently, according to my findings, to the value of developing and designing technologies.[57] This shift in priorities has occurred from the grassroots level to global development circles. This does not mean that access or skills have ceased to be central, but rather that making women creators of technology—often through inclusion in STEM education and careers—has acquired prominence in global development discourse. In fact, according to the UN's data, the gender gap in access to the internet, computers, and mobile phones continues (it has narrowed in developed countries yet remains wide in the least developed countries), and the gap between men and women in ICT skills (particularly those considered high-level or advanced skills) is widening.[58]

The design narrative is an intensification of the skills narrative—that is, to be able to become developers, women must now acquire "high-level" digital skills. Inclusion in STEM could indeed yield valuable opportunities for historically marginalized communities. "Adding and stirring" can have important implications unimagined by policies that purport to advance diversity, equity, and inclusion (DEI)—a now almost notorious acronym in the US context. Sulá Batsú activists frequently use the term *appropriation* to describe how communities can subvert the parade of inclusion—and the hegemonic design of technologies—for their benefit.[59] In effect, I argue that feminist digital activists work within, against, and beyond many of these institutions—that is, global development agencies, big tech corporations, universities, and state agencies—in ways that center feminist principles. Thus there are no one-way avenues.

At the same time, scholars and activists have debated whether inclusion in capitalist, racist, and patriarchal institutions leads to transformative change or ends up advancing the problematic objectives of these institutions while contributing to an illusion of DEI. In addition, inclusion in these institutions often puts minoritized individuals in harm's way within these violent spaces. "Inclusion" showcases women, particularly Black and Brown women, while exploiting their labor, silencing and neutralizing critique, and erasing the global circuits of extraction (human and environmental) that these institutions often practice. Internet studies scholar Safiya Umoja Noble argues that including Black women and youth in Silicon Valley does not address structural racism and misogyny, while feeding into the neoliberal logics of an artificial inclusion in a structure/institution that "systematically excludes them": "Filling the pipeline and holding 'future' Black women programmers responsible for solving the problem of racist exclusion and misrepresentation in Silicon Valley or in biased product development is not the answer."[60] Diversity commitments from big tech corporations such as Google, Meta, and Twitter have reignited conversations on what "inclusion" really means for Black women.[61] Sulá Batsú, for instance, is also reflecting on the implications of its work supporting young women to enter the tech industry in Costa Rica (discussed in chapter 2).

In general, the emphasis on supporting women in technological and scientific careers often centers on eradicating stereotypes and "self-perceptions" of women and girls in science and technology, on making education "gender sensitive" or "gender responsive," integrating more women as role models and mentors, adopting measures to retain women and avoid the "leaky pipeline" (now increasingly called "pathways)" from K–12 education to higher education and employment, and integrating women in decision-making positions across public and private spheres.[62] Take, for example, the goals of the UN Women's Global Innovation Coalition for Change (GICC)—launched in 2017 with private sector, academic, and nonprofit organizations: "Build market awareness of the potential for innovations developed by women that meet the needs of women and girls; identify the key barriers to women's and girl's advancement in innovation, technology and entrepreneurship; and work collaboratively to identify and take actions to address these barriers and needs at an industry-wide level."[63]

Yet an analysis of how both educational and workplace institutions often advance capitalist logics of exploitation, extraction, and profit is absent even if it is urgent to avoid "leaving women behind." These inclusionary approaches are driven by a capitalist impulse that simulates an image of diversity. The assumption is that inequality will be eradicated when women become designers and producers. Therefore, although it seems that Third World women are being considered as much more complex human beings—beyond subjects with basic needs—the marketized objective remains intact. This time what is different is the approach. These women may lead simple lives, yes, but they are also needed as refined economic neoliberal actors, as the UNCTAD states: "Solutions are developed from women's knowledge, experience and understanding of the locality, soil and planting conditions, environmental and climate patterns, and animal behaviour. When refined and replicated, they can resolve a range of problems sustainably and affordably, while also serving as a means of increasing income generation."[64] Raw forms of knowledge and design can be refined to serve individually driven solutions to inequality. The incorporation of these once illegible knowledges outside "Western" scientific paradigms has also had the effect of commodifying them, as Vandana Shiva's scholarship and activism has showed.[65] Women are, in essence, the "potential linchpin" in the digital global economy.[66]

The EQUALS Global Partnership shows the connections between access, skills, and design in how women are centered as (hopefully highly skilled) digital financial warriors. The partnership was launched in 2016 by the ITU, together with founding partners Group Speciale Mobile Association (GSMA), the International Trade Centre, the United Nations University, and UN Women, with the objective of contributing to the UN

Sustainable Development Agenda "through actions and evidence-based research aimed at closing the global gender digital divide."[67] In their reports—five since 2019—I encountered an emergent frame of threat and emergency, further punctuated by the global COVID-19 pandemic. Women must get on the bus of techno-financial modernization toward the Fourth Industrial Revolution, which according to the UN, is defined by emerging digital technologies such as AI, robotics, the internet of things, big data, blockchain, and biometrics. The world is changing, and fast, automation is advancing—which in itself is not questioned—and women must master information and communication technology skills to become legible financial subjects, although some "alternative pathways" are mentioned, such as hackerspaces.

The EQUALS inaugural report, *Taking Stock: Data and Evidence on Gender Equality in Digital Access, Skills and Leadership*—which surveys global data on women's access, skills, and leadership—explains that a gender perspective in digital access, for instance, "puts structural issues and core concerns that women and girls face online at the center of our understanding of the problem."[68] Yet "meaningful access" is focused here on "meaningful use" of ICTs for financial transactions. A priority is the "use of ICT tools for financial transactions, and the potential to include the unbanked and underbanked in the formal financial system."[69] What seems "meaningful" is the capacity to create digital financialized subjects. Beyond these categories, there is a growing "third digital divide," meaning that even with access and skills, some people still do not enjoy the same "material outcomes."[70]

In other words, access and information and communication technology skills have proved to be insufficient. To be able to thrive, women (and men) need intermediate skills and mostly high-level digital skills to participate in the digital future. The case study on GSMA's Connected Women's Initiative, which committed mobile operators to reach "new women" with mobile money and internet services, claims that "mobile can help empower women, providing access to information, services, and life-enhancing opportunities."[71] Besides women being able to send and receive digital payments, access financial accounts, and purchase online, it is unclear what these "life-enhancing opportunities" are. Part 2 of the EQUALS report, independently authored by members of the EQUALS research group, presents more critical perspectives with analyses on the relationships between ICTs and the LGBTQI+ community, children and youth, women with disabilities, and women farmers; gender perspectives on digital security and privacy; and the potentials of AI for gender equality.

As feminists we must continue to question the interventions enabled by this transformation in discourse (and potentially in policy). Women will become producers of technology for what purposes? The idea is that women will not only consume to move economies but also produce to move markets. The best of both worlds. This is yet another instance of vacating feminist struggles from their political transformative principles.

But what are the origins and trajectories of these discourses? In what historical contexts have they been shaped? I examine this history in the next section.

A History of the Coupling of Women and Digital Technology

The triad of gender, digital technology, and global development in the 1990s was marked by the emergence of the internet during the violent neoliberal structural adjustment policies that harmed women's rights in the global South. Critical technology scholar Anita Gurumurthy explains that at the same time, the information and communication technologies in development discourse and policies also emerged against a background in which feminists participating in UN conferences and events were foregrounding the inseparability of socioeconomic and civil-political and cultural rights.[72] This crucial claim was a "starting point for feminist activism in the internet arena."[73] These divergences and negotiations are in tension throughout the body of discourse regarding women and digital development.

The women/technology/development triad, as well as women/science/development, had a breakthrough during the UN's Fourth World Conference on Women in 1995 in Beijing, China. The inclusion of women in media, science, and technology was incorporated in the Beijing Declaration and Platform for Action, considered a watershed moment. The now famous Section J "Women and the Media" in the 1995 Platform for Action centers the issue of women and representation in the media and access, a pivotal claim of global women's activism leading to Beijing (and remains a node around which activists mobilize, as I witnessed at the 59th Commission on the Status of Women in New York in 2015).[74] In the early 1990s, feminist activists were concerned with women's representation in the media—both as producers, writers, and directors as well as content sources and experts.[75] But, as Gurumurthy warns, "the Declaration did not go far enough in acknowledging the injustice of the global economic system."[76] Micky Lee concurs with this crucial point in her discursive analysis of the Beijing Platform for Action: it neglects to emphasize that communication technologies are not neutral tools or a part of an unequal global economy.[77] In effect, in my textual analysis of reports post-Beijing, the feminist claim of the "right to communicate" fades. Technology starts being mostly connected to economic development and digital inclusion—entrepreneurship is central—as well as issues of access and use, content creation, and sometimes political voice and participation.

The Platform for Action is considered a major achievement of feminist transnational activism, and it positioned women and technology on the global map. One of the problems is that making women visible had unexpected outcomes that have dovetailed with rationalities of women as "good investments." As gender and development scholars Sylvia Chant and Caroline Sweetman put it: "From Beijing onwards, gender equality and the empowerment of women became increasingly adopted as a goal which made simple economic sense."[78] While feminist activists were advocating for approaches to ICT more in line with the "right to communicate," the UN was increasing its partnerships with the technology corporate private sector and advancing information and communication technologies as the cornerstone of successful business. The 2000 UNDP Digital Opportunities Initiative (DOI), elaborated in partnership with the private consulting firm Accenture, framed ICTs as an economic motor of development normalizing "a depoliticized vision of women's empowerment, folding in a mix of women's entrepreneurship, enskilling and voice into a win-win, corporate-friendly approach."[79]

The UN ICT Task Force, formed in 2001, was integrated by numerous tech corporations, such as the Markle Foundation, Cisco Systems, Hewlett-Packard, and the Cisneros Group from Venezuela. Muhammed

Yunus, the founder of the Grameen Bank and considered the "father of microfinance," was also a member. The Grameen Bank has been at the forefront of linking mobile technology to the financial empowerment of poor women.[80] The alliances between global development institutions and the corporate sector have increased exponentially in recent years (examined in chapter 4), as evidence that digital technologies make economic sense.[81] And if it is a caring, selfless women using these technologies, better yet.

Post-Beijing

Since Beijing, the importance of women, technology, and science has been both central to specific women's agencies and bodies (UNIFEM [now UN Women] and the Commission on the Status of Women [CSW]) and mainstreamed across numerous UN agencies (UNDP, UNESCO, FAO, ITU, and UNCTAD, among others) in task forces, units, caucuses, commissions, and expert groups. There are hundreds of reports, working papers, briefings, resolutions, fact sheets, and repositories of information. Various scholars and experts in development, gender, and technology, such as Sophia Huyer and Nancy Hafkin—prominent in scholarship, advocacy, and policy—had argued since the early 2000s that information and communication technologies should be considered tools for economic empowerment for women, not merely for communication and networking.[82] It is in the Beijing + 5 Declaration (2000) that ICTs start making a stronger appearance in the context of economic progress, business and entrepreneurship, and poverty reduction.[83] Follow-up meetings Beijing + 10 and Beijing + 20 restated the importance of digital technologies as tools of market-based economic advancement as well as the inclusion of women in STEM.

The World Summit on the Information Society (WSIS), organized in two phases in Geneva (2003) and in Tunisia (2005), represented potential opportunities for transformative feminist digital politics.[84] But activists were critical of the scarce participation of women from the global South as well as how women were instrumentalized as actors in a digital society without an analysis of how that society had to change.[85] The 2003 Geneva Declaration and Plan of Action is peppered with terms such as *cooperation* and *solidarity*, uses *information* instead of *com-*

munication, and offers mostly "techno-libertarian" and technological determinist approaches in showing how ICTs will allegedly solve the world's problems.[86] In 2003, feeling that the Geneva Principles had not adequately represented their voices, civil society organizations launched an alternative declaration titled "Shaping Information Societies for Human Needs" that prioritizes the "right to communicate" and decenters techno-solutionism: "Redressing all forms of discrimination, exclusion and isolation that different marginalised and vulnerable groups and communities experience will require more than the deployment of technology alone. Their full participation in information and communication societies requires us to reject at a fundamental level, the solely profit-motivated and market-propelled promotion of ICTs for development."[87] For the Tunisia Summit, market-based solutions were in full sway, with millions of dollars invested in communications in the South through public-private-partnerships (PPPs). The Tunis Commitment boosts the instrumental view of ICTs as tools for economic growth and enterprise, relegating "gender" to Principle 23, emphasizing the "digital divide."[88] Thus "the future of the internet was crystallized in neoliberal terms, and normative explorations for its governance as a bulwark of global peace, equitable development and justice silenced."[89] This framing laid the groundwork for a persistent neoliberal and depoliticized understanding of digital technologies.

The Internet Governance Forum

The multistakeholder Internet Governance Forum (IGF) established in 2006 is one of the key outcomes of the World Summit on the Information Society. The forum has become an important place to discuss global internet policy and governance issues and is constituted by governments, civil society, the private sector, academics, the internet technical community, and individual experts. IGF's Best Practice Forums, launched in 2014, are "bottom-up," collective, and participatory intersessional events (between each yearly Internet Governance Forum) in which stakeholders exchange experiences on internet-related policy issues to engage in conversations, identify best practices, and inform policy decisions, but not develop new policies.[90]

An overview of the Best Practice Forums yearly outcome reports since 2014 offers an interesting perspective—gender is one of the topics, together with cybersecurity, local content, the internet of things, big data and artificial intelligence, and cybersecurity, among others. There are gender reports on online gender-based violence, issues of access and digital participation of trans, gender-nonconforming, and nonbinary individuals, and in the 2020 report there is even a call to emphasize issues of online pleasure over harm.[91] But Gurumurthy—who has been active at the Internet Governance Forum—warns that "multistakeholderism" conceals unbridgeable power differentials when organizations and individuals have to reconcile completely incompatible principles and objectives: "Engaging business and governments has meant adherence to a politics of process rather than a critical politics of resistance."[92] One of the feminist political issues most marginalized has been economic justice and redistribution.

The connection between women and digital technologies is in the UN's 2015–2030 Sustainable Development Goals (SDG)—which superseded the 2000–2015 Millennium Development Goals (MDG)—considered the UN's institutional agenda and international development plan of action. The sustainable development goals do not include a specific goal for information and communication technologies (different kinds of technologies are mentioned throughout the document), but ICTs are prominent in Goal 4 on "quality education," Goal 9 on "industry, innovation and infrastructure," Goal 17 on "global partnerships," and of course, Goal 5 on "gender equality": "Enhance the use of enabling technology, in particular information and communications technology, to promote the empowerment of women."[93] Digital technologies are a backbone of the Sustainable Development Goals in helping to "accelerate progress" toward every goal of the agenda, which launched the Technology Facilitation Mechanism to integrate multistakeholder collaboration on science, technology, and innovation.[94] Both the SDG's "aspirational, imaginary nature" and its financial and public-private partnerships foci combine with the inexorable race to include women in the digital "revolution."[95] The coupling of digital technologies with the private sector, as well as with women, is evident.

Feminist digital activists have made great strides, particularly on issues of internet governance (the IGF has been important), and in a series of thematic "special procedures" of the United Nations Human Rights Council (HRC), such as the Special Rapporteur on the Right to Freedom of Opinion and Expression, the Special Rapporteur on the Right to Privacy, and the Special Rapporteur on Violence Against Women.[96] Since 2011, a number of UN resolutions have incorporated language on digital technologies on issues related to online gender-based violence, freedom of expression, data privacy, mass surveillance, cybersecurity, artificial intelligence, and disinformation.[97] Much of the groundwork for the inclusion of online gender-based violence in international development, for instance, has been provided by the Women's Rights Programme of the Association for Progressive Communication since 2005. The 2011 report of Special Rapporteur on Freedom of Expression and Opinion Frank La Rue to the Human Rights Council has been exceptionally important. The report describes the internet as "a catalyst for individuals to exercise their right to freedom of opinion and expression" and "facilitating the realisation of a range of other human rights."[98]

The 2018 thematic report on online gender-based violence of the Special Rapporteur on Violence against Women is another pivotal document. This report contains language such as "systemic structural discrimination," connecting online gender-based violence to broader contexts of gender violence. It calls on states and internet intermediaries to provide data protection, legal frameworks, and clear protocols against online gender-based violence, among other recommendations.[99] In 2021, for the first time in the twenty-seven years of the mandate of the Special Rapporteur on the Promotion and Protection of the Right to Freedom of Opinion and Expression, Irene Khan dedicated her report to gender and freedom of opinion and expression, adopting a "feminist analytical framework" and an "intersectional approach" to examine the challenges that women face both online and offline.[100]

The particular incorporation of online gender-based violence in development discourse is discussed chapter 3, but it is important to understand that it is increasingly difficult to separate feminist social justice principles from development parlance.[101] The inclusion of feminist issues merges with the general shift of global development discourse to a warmer and highly gendered and feminized language that discursively disengages from neoliberal policies, while continuing to adopt many of its precepts. I argue that this language needs women and the use of feminized tropes to be able to convey its benevolence. Simultaneously there is an increasing emphasis on public-private partnerships and "philanthro-capitalism," market-based strategies to eradicate poverty and inequality, and decreased funding for feminist organizations in the global South, particularly impacting Indigenous, LGBTQI+, youth, and Black women's organizations.[102]

The Largest UN Women's Event since Beijing

Catalyze collective action
Spark global and local conversations among generations
Drive increased public & private investment
Deliver concrete, game-changing results for girls and women
—GOALS OF THE GENERATION EQUALITY
FORUM ACTION COALITIONS

The 2021 Generation Equality Forum—the largest UN women's meeting since Beijing 1995, convened by UN Women and cochaired by the governments of France and Mexico with civil society and youth-led organizations—provides an ideal recent scenario to understand the phenomenon of the corporatization of gender equality. On one hand, there is an explicit investment in attracting the private sector to sponsor the objectives of the forum—with fast solutions that are measurable—and, on the other hand, the language of feminist principles of structural transformation and a focus on process is evident throughout the documents.

The 2021 forum, celebrated in March 2021 in Mexico City and in June 2021 in Paris, officially launched the Global Acceleration Plan for Gender Equality—expected to provide "concrete" steps toward gender equality by 2026—structured around thematic blueprints of six Action Coalitions: gender-based violence, economic justice and rights, bodily autonomy and sexual and reproductive health and rights, feminist action for climate justice, technology and innovation for gender equality, and feminist movements and leadership.[103] Each Action Coalition is sponsored by Action Leaders (who make a five-year commitment) and Commitment Makers (minimum one-year commitment)—from member states, UN agencies and international organizations, civil society organizations, private companies, philanthropic foundations, and other institutions. The term Commitment Makers was adopted precisely "to promote non-hierarchical and inclusive language."[104] As of June 2021, for example, PayPal and the Bill and Melinda Gates Foundation were among the leaders of the Economic Justice and Rights Coalition, and Koç, Microsoft, the Rockefeller Foundation, and Salesforce were among the leaders of the Technology and Innovation for Gender Equality Coalition.[105] As of 2022, US$24 billion had been pledged (US$17.3 billion secured) to all Action Coalitions.[106]

The objectives for the Makers are financial, advocacy, policy, and programmatic commitments, and these should be "game-changing," "scalable," "measurable," and "preferably undertaken in concert with other stakeholders."[107] These criteria are clearly aligned with a neoliberal quantification of social justice, and yet throughout the documents there are references to the importance of the collective nature of the commitments and of feminist co-creation and joint accountability. Moreover, the Makers' commitments must reflect the Action Coalitions principles, which are "intersectional" (used to describe "intersecting forms of discrimination") and reflect "feminist leadership" (across axes of gender, class, sexuality, race, and ability, among others) and "transformation" (changing structural and systemic unequal power relations).[108]

A sense of urgency permeates the Generation Equality Forum's documents and posts—note the use of the word *acceleration*—due both to the gender injustices laid bare by COVID-19 and to the proximity of the SDGs' 2030 deadline for major changes that have not been met. The Action Coalition on Technology and Innovation for Gender Equality proposes, for example, reducing the gender digital divide in access and skills by half, increasing investments in feminist technology and innovation by 50 percent, doubling the number of women working in technology and innovation, and demanding that states and tech corporations take steps against online gender-based violence—all by 2026. The brochure of the technology Action Coalition states that "by 2026, women and girls in all their diversity [should] have equal opportunities to safely and meaningfully access, use, lead, and design technology and innovation with freedom of expression, joy, and boundless potential."[109] The race against time swallows everything in its path, even the feminist claim of "joy" that is meant to trouble neoliberal and corporate scripts and policies.

The View from Latin America

The UN Conference on Women in Beijing in 1995 is considered a watershed event for women, gender, and technology in Latin America and the Caribbean. That said, Latin America has a long and robust history of collective, alternative, local, independent, and community-based media—radio, guerrilla TV, print—produced by Black, working-class, and Indigenous peoples.[110] The Zapatista rebellion in 1994 is widely considered a groundbreaking event that inspired and ignited the use of digital technologies for social justice.[111] The Beijing Platform for Action—and the intense women's online networking before the conference in Beijing—does represent an important moment for awareness, advocacy, and mobilization around women and information and communication technologies.[112] But the region's historical, political, and socioeconomic specificities are imprinted on discourse around women and technology.

The Economic Commission for Latin America and the Caribbean (ECLAC)—one of five regional commissions of the UN—was founded in 1948 to contribute to the economic development of Latin America. In 1949 the Argentinian economist Raúl Prebisch became the executive secretary of the commission headquartered in Santiago, Chile, developing a strong political and socioeconomic legacy in the region. It is fundamental to acknowledge the ways in which Prebisch situated the ECLAC as an epicenter of knowledge and policy for the region, rooted in a historical structural analysis of economic development focused on global power and inequality leading to the elaboration of dependence theory.[113] This structuralist perspective, anchored in the specificities of the region, continues to influence the ECLAC to this day. This theoretical and political foundation also runs through ECLAC's discourses on women, gender, technology, and science in ways that contrast with general UN discourse, although increasingly there are similarities. Differences center on the ECLAC's critical approach by emphasizing state regulation of the market and economic redistribution, rejecting techno-solutionism and technological neutrality, incorporating intersectional and institutional analyses of identity and power, and including—from early on—attention to links between gender, technology, and violence. Increasing areas of overlap are on ICT-based entrepreneurship as a strategy for women's economic empowerment, the inclusion of fintech as a major player in the digital society, and issues around emerging technologies such as big data, the internet of things, AI, blockchain, automation, and robotics.[114]

Every three years since 1977, ECLAC's Division of Gender Affairs organizes regional conferences on women in Latin America and the Caribbean that includes representation from states and civil society organizations, producing regional agreements in the form of "consensus" documents that often use intersectional language that includes young, rural, Indigenous, and Afro-descendent women, women with disabilities, displaced and migrant women, and LGBTQI+ individuals. The most interesting publications from the ECLAC on women, science, and technology are niched under the working area of "gender," often as part of the multiyear processes associated with the regional conferences on women.[115] In 2013 the Twelfth Regional Conference in Santo Domingo, Dominican Republic, focused on gender, equality, and information and communication technologies. The Santo Domingo Consensus is an interesting document in how it approaches women and ICTs by (1) employing an intersectional perspective throughout the text; (2) condemning racism and ethnocentrism; (3) emphasizing the responsibility of the state in regulating tech industries and infrastructure; and (4) stressing the importance of feminist movements and organizations as agents in the digital society.[116] Although centered on potentializing women's place in the digital economy, the report prepared for this conference questions the neoliberal state-market relationship and offers a structural approach to transformation beyond techno-fixes.

The ECLAC has produced hundreds of documents and reports on women, technology, and science in Latin America and the Caribbean since at least 1990, through their Division of Gender Affairs (formerly the Women and Development Unit).[117] As a foundational 1990 report, *Women and New Technologies* is powerful in the way it interrogates the social dimensions of new technologies—mostly robotics and biotechnologies—and how they can shape the gendered division of labor.[118] The report—elaborated amid the devastating consequences of the World Bank- and IMF-imposed structural adjustment programs in the region—focuses on issues of power and inequality between women and men and between nations and regions, and it foreshadows and critiques the intervention of corporations as further disenfranchising states' ability to provide for marginalized populations. It asks a fundamental question that is still very relevant: "What should be the prevailing interests in the adoption, creation, and adaptation of new technologies? And how will national interests and those who have the least power in the social structure be protected—women from the popular sectors, for example—for whom improving the conditions of life is indispensable?"[119] This report is already questioning techno-fixes to social problems as well as the neutrality of technologies, including a powerful analysis of women and social reproduction that, instead of preying on care as a site of economization, unveils how reproduction and care are sites of power.

In the early 2000s, feminist scholar Gloria Bonder, coordinator of the UNESCO Regional Chair on Women, Science and Technology in Latin America in Buenos Aires, often collaborated on ECLAC reports on women and technology. In various reports she makes the usual recommendations on increasing access and training for women, collecting more data, promoting women to decision-making positions, and including gender in state digital policies. But Bonder also formulated a critical perspective incorporating analyses of technocapitalism, neoliberal development, and the value of celebrating and fostering pleasure, play, and imagination beyond productivity.[120] These were rare political statements at the time: "Even in adverse situations like in Latin America, it is possible and desirable to re-create the creative and playful capacity of women in their relationship with the internet. We need to create other narratives and metaphors, think about that bond outside the logic of productivity or citizenship, or at least not only in those terms. This is about giving women the opportunity to articulate their own imaginary and play to invent and reinvent themselves."[121]

Bonder consistently contextualizes the rise of the "digital revolution"

in Latin America with the devastation caused by neoliberal development policies in the region to explain how these forces combined, making a similar analyses to Gurumurthy's:

> The scandalous growth of poverty and of the levels of social inequity, together with the weakness of the national states and the lack of public investment in strategic sectors for human development, such as education or health; together with other alarming signs such as the lack of transparency of the state administration of budgets for social programs and purchase of technological infrastructure, the concentration of multimedia in the hands of transnational corporations, and the absence of regulations regarding the rates of telecommunication services, do not allow us to be very optimistic, at least in the short term.[122]

These topics resurfaced in my phone interview with Bonder in 2015, in which she stressed that women in STEM should not reproduce the status quo but aim to transform power relations: "It's not that I disagree that women should be in decision-making positions. What I wonder is what are they there for? To adapt to the world or to change it?" She added: "We live in a capitalist world. Capitalism is a stage of enormous expansion and of enormous brutality. By the way, technology is part of that economic order and therefore reproduces a particular order. Then we have to analyze technologies—why these and not others? Make a critical analysis, a deconstruction, understand the values, the messages that they emit . . . the power relations embedded in technologies."

This critical perspective can still be seen throughout ECLAC's corpus of knowledge on women and technology.[123] But, at the same time, ECLAC texts on women and digital technologies increasingly emphasize the "urgency" of inclusion in digitalization, particularly since COVID-19. There are concerns with gaps in access, skills, and design and development of technology, automation, the care economy, and digital entrepreneurship, as well as the dangers of online gender-based violence.[124] Explicit critiques, such as Bonder's, of capitalism and corporatization are increasingly scarce.

One of the most recent multistakeholder initiatives is the Regional Alliance for the Digitalization of Women in Latin America and the Caribbean, led by the Ministry of Women and Gender Equity of Chile to-gether with UN Women, Microsoft, Mastercard, and Eidos Global (a software and technology company), with ECLAC's technical support. The Alliance was launched in 2021 during the meeting of the presiding officers of ECLAC's Regional Conference on Women of Latin America and the Caribbean and presented at the Generation Equality Forum. In addition to supporting national programs to facilitate women's access to digital technologies, the Alliance has created an online platform called Todas Conectadas (Every Woman Connected) aimed at training 3.8 mil-lion women in digital financial competencies through free online courses, providing spaces for networking and a "marketplace" for women's digi-tal entrepreneurial businesses.[125] One of the "commitments" of Master-card, the multinational financial company headquartered in the United States, is to enable participants' incursion into fintech.[126] At the same time, ECLAC's then executive secretary, Alicia Bárcena, said in advance of the 2022 regional conference on women dedicated to the "care soci-ety" that the recovery from COVID-19 "will be feminist, or it will not be at all." She emphasized that the region needs a radical transformation of the development model to one that puts the "sustainability of human life and the planet at the center." Bárcena added: "We see the care society as a civilizational leap forward, as the most promising horizon for a trans-formative and sustainable recovery with gender equality."[127] It remains to be seen how a new development model that centers "care" along market-oriented and techno-solutionist strategies will unfold.

Conclusion

In global development discourse on women and digital technologies, care has become a precious commodity. The politics of connections nec-essary for individuals, communities, and countries to survive and thrive have become sites of economization ripe for socioeconomic, political, and technological interventions. It is often through care and caring rela-tionships of many sorts that people survive precarity and social and eco-logical catastrophes. These relationships maintain communities when all else fails. And these connections are gendered and racialized not only in their materiality and embodiment but also as sociopolitical constructs.

Neoliberal policies prey on care and thus on these women. Digital technologies are particularly suited for amassing these relationships both due to their capacity to connect as well as to inhabit the intimate spaces of our everyday lives. The expansion of digital technologies becomes a highly gendered, racialized, and intimate socioeconomic project. It is about much more than tools or spaces; it is about life itself. These discourses obscure the political and socioeconomic structures that have produced the inequalities this Third World Technological Woman is supposed to overcome as well as the need for deep sociocultural transformation. They portray an inexorable path that will lead nowhere for millions of people unless technologies are *reformed* and dangers are *mitigated*.

The rolling back of state social protections, deregulation, trade liberalization, militarization and criminalization, land grabbing, climate change and ecological devastation, and the corporatization of development, among others, are already obstacles to the digital justice that these reports claim to be striving for. But these discourses also make women and many gender issues visible, an important gain for feminist activists and policy makers that provides opportunities for appropriation and resistance. The increasing difficulty of parsing development language with feminist claims should continue to provoke deep reflection.

The Latin American discourse provides some noteworthy differences. In ECLAC publications and policies, the coupling of women and digital technologies is often examined within a critical perspective that centers power over techno-solutionism and corporate interests, although COVID-19 has increased the sense of urgency of including women and other historically oppressed communities in the "digital revolution." Under the incipient "threat" of women being left out the picture, digital financial proposals such as entrepreneurship and financial inclusion have acquired prominence.

The march forward is full-fledged. In a speech in 2020, the UN Secretary-General said that "looking to the future, two seismic shifts will shape the 21st century: the climate crisis, and digital transformation."[128] The Secretary-General's 2021 report *Our Common Agenda* proposes the creation of a multistakeholder Global Digital Compact with "shared principles for an open, free and secure digital future for all."[129] In 2022, UN Women's executive director Sima Bahous launched the Year of Action on Gender and Technological Change to "make digitalization a tool to achieve gender equality, social justice and poverty eradication."[130] In this context, how are feminist digital activists negotiating and reimagining the digital society? What are some of the points of consensus and contention? What spaces are feminist organizations carving amid technocapitalist development discourses and policies?

TWO

Solidarity

"We want to create a technology of feelings."

This is what an Indigenous woman from the Cabécar community of the Caribbean Alto Pacuare region of Costa Rica told Kemly Camacho, the coordinator of the local development cooperative Sulá Batsú, during one of their conversations. This goal blew Kemly's mind away. After having worked on technology-related issues her whole life and having founded the internationally recognized cooperative Sulá Batsú more than fifteen years ago, Kemly simply could not wrap her head around the implications of collaborating on the creation of "una tecnología del sentir." This "technology of feelings" drastically differed from the profit-oriented neoliberal technologies and ideas of technology that Kemly had worked with her entire life. But, after reflecting on it for many months after my visit to Costa Rica in 2019, I perceived this moment as a culmination of Sulá Batsú's work and organizational practices rooted in a politics of care and solidarity.

For the Indigenous Cabécar and Bribri women, whose communities are under the imminent arrival of internet connection, the meaning of codesigning a "technology of feelings" was grounded in practical results, such as creating a virtual application that could submerge users in their communities and cosmology or an application connected to sensors that

63

could detect when deforestation trucks enter their lands. But their request surpassed the practical. A technology of feelings is also about celebrating their knowledges and ways of being. It is about collaboration, joy, and respect. It is about being seen, heard, felt, and seeing, hearing, and feeling. It is about following rhythms not determined by linearity, assessments, outcomes, and results. It is about connecting with what is difficult to articulate in our languages, about "connecting technology to the divine, a technology that is more intuitive" as co-op member Andrea told me. "And to be able to create a technology that feels, we also had to feel them," Kemly told me. The Indigenous women told the co-op members that to be able to work together, they had to visit their communities, sleep in their houses, travel their lands, and participate in their ceremonies. And so they did. They crossed rivers and hiked mountains, under incessant rain, through flooding, and in paths of mud, to feel the communities they were going to start a project with. Kemly and Juan, a founding member of the co-op, took Bribri language classes to understand the community's worldviews and knowledges.

Founded in 2005, local development cooperative Sulá Batsú, which means "creative spirit" in the Indigenous Costa Rican language Bribri, follows a cooperative model where income is shared among the staff and workers "control and own the means of production as owners and workers of the business."[1] Sulá Batsú, housed in Casa Batsú, the beautiful community space *la coope* (the co-op) manages in the Barrio Escalante in San José, is funded through two main sources: their grassroots projects, which are funded through proposals and grants from state agencies and corporations, development institutions, and international nongovernmental organizations, and the *venta de servicios* (selling of services) that generates income through consultancies, workshops, evaluations, and trainings in the public and private sectors. The income generated from these sources is collectivized—that is, the person who acquires the contract receives a higher percentage of the cut, but the remaining salary is distributed among all the staff. Staff members are also included in different phases of the projects, even when their individual skills might be stronger in another area.

The co-op has approximately twenty associates and a core daily working staff of approximately ten people. The core staff is mostly women, but there are currently some men. The core staff of *la coope* in 2021 included Kemly, Lila, Daniela, Marina, Andrea, Pabru, Samuel, Gabriel, and Juan.[2] Some of them are founding members of the co-op. Most of the seventeen activists I interviewed self-identified as middle-class, educated, mestiza (racially mixed), heterosexual women, although some identified as working class/poor and queer, and I interviewed four men. Costa Rica is considered to be socioeconomically privileged in the context of Central America.[3] Some core staff live in the capital, San José, and some commute up to two hours to la coope from rural areas. Among the activists are anthropologists, sociologists, software engineers, graphic designers, artists, accountants, social workers, journalists, and car mechanics. Sulá Batsú has received funding for its grassroots projects from institutes of higher education, international development agencies, and technology corporations, including UN Women, UNESCO, Hivos, the Canadian International Development Research Center (IDRC), the University of Toronto, the University of Washington, and Google.

One of Sulá Batsú's main initiatives is to bring women and girls closer to digital technologies through associative technology-based entrepreneurship and supporting women in science and technology fields through trainings, workshops, and advocacy at the local, national, and transnational levels. Sulá Batsú has offered digital workshops to thousands of girls, young women, and their mothers, partnering with numerous municipal governments in Costa Rica and other countries in Central America. These workshops consist of training in basic internet skills and use, computer disassembly and reassembly, open-source code programming, application (app) design, and online security, as well as talks by leaders in science and technology fields on how to overcome stereotypes and gendered cultural norms.

Society and technology is only one of four of their main areas of work, the others being the free and open exchange of knowledge; art and culture; and creating a solidarity-based economy. Gender, the environment, intergenerational bonding, and fostering the commons are transversal axes of the co-op's projects. The activists of Sulá Batsú— whose slogan is "a society of shared knowledges"—mostly work in marginalized communities—rural, low-income, Indigenous—but also with universities, chambers of commerce, technology corporations, and local and national government agencies. They also participate in numerous international conferences on technology. La coope's advocacy is thus multiscalar, from the transnational and the state to the municipal level. But I argue that Sulá Batsú's most radical project is its micropolitical work that weaves a "politics of connections" based on solidarity and the defense of life both human and more-than-human. In Sulá Batsú, technologies are about and for life against violence. The Technological Woman is not uniquely a victim or an entrepreneur. She holds multitudes. I have come to know her—them—well since I started to conduct fieldwork with the co-op in 2015. This chapter traces the co-op's origins, trajectories, visions, and futures.

Technologies of Care

"Everyone, absolutely everyone, can design technologies," Kemly told me in one of our many conversations during a rainy afternoon in San José, Costa Rica. The coordinator of the cooperative Sulá Batsú made this seemingly innocuous comment in the midst of co-organizing a high-profile Latin American conference for women in the fields of STEM characterized as being corporate and business-oriented. A fifty-something woman with an overwhelming energy, Kemly is the heart of la coope. Her high-pitched voice can crack a mirror, and that, combined with her presence, makes it difficult not to notice her. Kemly was intent upon inviting Indigenous women from Costa Rica to open the conference with a discussion about Indigenous science and technologies. After weeks of difficult negotiations with the main organizers, the co-op made this possible. Kemly's message was clear: technologies must be understood within racialized, gendered, and colonial trajectories. The technological allure was thus decentered, and Indigenous women were centered as experts, makers, and knowers. The tactic—decided upon collectively by the activists of la coope and the Indigenous leaders—held both tremendous intellectual force and emotional intensity. It was a radical act of solidarity and a feminist vision of technology—and most important, of what has not been considered "technological."

Sulá Batsú is reimagining technology and the digital society in ways that enable different forms of thinking and being, built upon radical interconnectedness and solidarity. Arturo Escobar posits that there is currently a "political activation of relationality" in the context of increasing social and ecological devastation, and a need of repositioning design as "an ethical praxis of world making."[4] For the Cabécar women, relationality has been central to their ways of being and thinking for centuries. The Indigenous women's knowledges centered at the conference focused on STEM embody a rupture and a vision of designing a world in which technologies are intimately tied to a politics of life. It symbolizes a moment in which we can appreciate Indigenous science and technology beyond being labeled as "traditional"—a situated act of technopolitical agency that is far from deterministic models. When care is centered, technology is also decentered. How is it possible to do work on technology and simultaneously decenter the technological? In her magnificent book *Dark Matters*, sociologist Simone Browne does precisely this.[5] Browne's work—which has been influential in the co-op's evolution—excavates the history and the persistence of the surveillance of Blackness from transatlantic slavery to its afterlife. In other words, Browne decenters digital technologies, locating them as another iteration of the historical persistence of racism.

To be clear, this is not a debate about "newness," if these technologies bring new problems or not. It is about reevaluating the preeminence of digital technologies. Kemly mentioned, for example, how she was reflecting on the increasing emphasis of technology activists and funders on "digital security." "Focusing on digital security continues to represent a techno-fix to profound social problems," she said. There has always been something about the insistence on digital security that has bothered Kemly. She understands that empowering individuals to protect their data and privacy and demanding ethical approaches from tech corporations are important. But these are liberal patches to problems that will not be alleviated with more digital security. Thus Sulá Batsú's objective combines multiple knowledges, the technical and what is considered "nontechnical" to approach both social and individual forms of oppression. This point is crucial. The co-op has slowly undergone a transformation, distancing itself more and more from mere "inclusion" in the digital society. "This is the base of our project and of the transformation of the co-op," Kemly explains. As an example of this shift that is critical of inclusion, Sulá Batsú has recently started to collaborate in a project—guided, designed, and directed by the Cabécar women—to create an internet community network in their lands with the goal of achieving "digital sovereignty," a term that has become more and more common among digital activists in Latin America.[6] The community network defies state and corporate agendas of digital inclusion and offers a terrain—both literal and metaphorical—of Indigenous assertion and contestation.

Sulá Batsú conducted a two-year project (2014–16) on digital security training for women who work at pineapple cultivations on the Caribbean coast of Costa Rica that provides insights into the dilemma of focusing on digital inclusion as a solution to social problems. Similar to Browne's decentering, the *defensoras* against the pineapple corporations in Costa Rica both center and decenter the technological in their body-territory activism. This project—funded by the University of Toronto's Citizen Lab—focused on research on the digital vulnerabilities of women environmental leaders at the *piñeras* (pineapple-producing corporations). A highly destructive monoculture in Costa Rica, pineapple cultivation has exhausted the land, undermining the possibilities of other forms of agriculture, allowed multinational corporations to privatize lands, contaminated surrounding bodies of water, and exploited the workers.[7]

Elena, one of the co-op activists who led the initiative, explained that although funding from the University of Toronto focused on digital security training, the co-op immediately realized through their conversations with these *defensoras* that their priorities were the defense of their lands and their bodies. Elena recalls how these women who led the environmental struggle against the pineapple multinationals had a political awakening that connected the land to their bodies and intimate lives: "We saw patterns in the stories of these women that showed that an internal struggle ensued when they began participating in the defense of their territories. They started to struggle within their families, defending their bodies. They would tell us, 'Yes, when I started community organizing, I also started to go to school,' or 'That is when I left my husband.' So we identified that pattern: the connection between the defense of the territory and the defense of their bodies."

During our interview in 2019, Elena explained that the co-op had started the project with the sole idea of offering digital security training to these rural leaders. These women mostly use WhatsApp and Facebook[8] on their cell phones to communicate with each other, which puts them at a greater risk of surveillance and harassment by their employers. But as community organizers and environmental leaders, their struggles transcended digital security:

> When we started to discuss violence against activists in digital spaces, they were always bringing up the physical threats they receive in their territories. And then we went deeper and realized that there were three fronts of struggle: personal, territorial, and digital. In the manual we made together, we included the issue of digital security but also issues of safety in their communities. For instance, we pointed to the safest paths they could take to walk home, because basically their enemies [the employers] live one kilometer from them, and people started to find out that they were protesting, and this has also caused their neighbors (coworkers) to accuse them of trying to get them fired.

The body-territory assembly—theorized by various Indigenous feminist communitarian thinkers from Latin America such as Lorena Cabnal and Julieta Paredes—reveals three important and interrelated issues that defy the promise of digital inclusion: the digital is embodied, spatialized, and detached from the guise of abstraction; it demonstrates the ways in which violence is interconnected, crossing numerous realms from the intimate to the territorial; and technologies can be simultaneously centered and decentered (an issue I will return to soon).[9]

Elena recalled that part of the process was identifying the violence these women confronted because of being women. The community organizers had not realized that being women made them vulnerable in specific ways, such as threats against their children (mostly their daughters), sexual harassment, and feeling unsafe in their own communities and territories. Women became the target of sexist jokes in the workplace and communities, such as people telling their husbands to "control their women." "Men would not be threatened in these ways," Elena said. Sulá Batsú did conduct digital training sessions on privacy and data protection and codesigned a manual on digital security. But it was clear through their participatory methodologies with the community that these women's struggles were part of a much broader landscape of violence.

TIC-as

One of the co-op's most important projects is TIC-as, a three-year proposal initially funded by UN Women (2013–16), renewed for another two years by Google in 2017, and supported by the Inter-American Development Bank and UNESCO, to train, guide, and support young rural women and girls in the fields of science and technology. *TIC-as* is a play on words with *ticas*, the popular term for women from Costa Rica, and TICS, the acronym for Information and Communication Technologies in Spanish. The TIC-as project consists of eighteen initiatives including research on data, equity in STEM fields, online gender-based violence, technology cafés, Indigenous technologies, technology-based entrepreneurship, ecofeminism and technology, and biannual hackathons. In Costa Rica alone, by 2019, TIC-as had worked with twenty-five hundred participants. The TIC-as project offers workshops on computing, coding, and leadership for girls throughout their school years as well as support for young rural women, some of whom are studying in STEM fields.

Workshops for girls (ages 10–17) mostly consist of trainings in basic internet skills and use and computer disassembly and reassembly. Girls learn how to dismantle old computers that have been donated, reassemble them, and sometimes even make jewelry out of old parts. The idea is for them to understand that computers are not mysterious black boxes but legible and usable everyday objects.[10] This is a deeply emotional experience for both Sulá Batsú activists and for workshop participants. Activists explained that girls "fall in love" with technology through many of these experiences. Although girls are usually not afraid of technology—Kemly argues that fear appears at a later age—the process of demystification, including the tinkering, meddling, and opening of that black box, makes the computers a part of their lives. Sulá Batsú staff invite girls to participate in public art projects in their communities, such as murals and graffiti, that contain messages and images that encourage girls to explore and engage with technology and science.

Workshops for young women (ages 18–30) are mostly on open-source code programming, application (app) design, and online security. Other offerings include talks by leaders in science and technology fields on how to overcome stereotypes and gendered cultural norms. TIC-as has already collaborated with thirteen hundred girls and young women in San Carlos, the northern rural city in Costa Rica on the border with Nicaragua that Kemly identifies as having the potential of becoming a "technological pole"—a center for technological production and development—because of the industries and technical universities headquartered there. The workshops with young women are more focused on busting myths about women and technology, designing collaborative strategies to overcome gender barriers in higher education and the workplace, and supporting the creation of local and regional networks of women in science and technology. They also offer young women more advanced training in programming, design, and technological entrepreneurship, train them to become mentors for girls, and invite them to international technology conferences.

In March 2017, Google donated $400,000 to Sulá Batsú to expand the project to eighteen hundred rural girls and six hundred of their mothers in Costa Rica, Guatemala, El Salvador, Nicaragua, Honduras, and Panama. Initially funded by Google, the project became La voz de las chicas del Centro de América (The Voice of the Girls/Women from the Center of America). The project expanded from digital trainings on internet skills, data protection, app design, and coding to including workshops on audiovisual design and editing, musical composition, social media, and digital storytelling. In 2021 a group of young women from Nicaragua who had participated in the program created an impressive series of engravings depicting the ways in which technology harms the planet (see figure 1).

TIC-as, which has won numerous national and international awards, such as the 2019 UNESCO Prize for Girl's and Women's Education, has taken on a life of its own, becoming a network of young women throughout Costa Rica and Central America. It is now the heart of Sulá Batsú, because it has fostered relationships of care among participants, alumnae, and the co-op's activists. Many of the young women who have participated in TIC-as have become leaders in subsequent workshops and have even become associates of la coope. TIC-as encapsulates one

FIGURE 1. "Wired Forest" by Nathy Guevara (a pseudonym) is an engraving (artist's proof) made in one of the workshops of Sulá Batsú's TIC-as project, "La voz de las chicas del Centro de América." Reprinted with permission.

of the co-op's main goals: to encourage women to appropriate technology to improve their lives and communities, beyond merely consuming corporative technology. In Costa Rica the technology sector is dominated by multinational corporations in urban areas, such as Amazon, Microsoft, Hewlett Packard, Intel, and IBM (both in manufacturing and research and development). Rita Laura Segato argues that "there is no major obstacle for the historic project of capital in its expansionist path other than local and community connections."[11] Fostering the possibility of remaining in your community is central to Sulá Batsú's technopolitics of care. Home and community can be sites of violence, precarity, and binding traditions, and leaving could be necessary and urgent. Sulá Batsú activists are well aware of this. This is why I stress that activists collaborate with women so they have the *possibility* of remaining in and transforming their communities instead of having to migrate to capital cities, or Europe and the United States, searching for futures that they could not have at home. Sulá Batsú nurtures a "politics of connections" that surpasses the supremacy of technology, while simultaneously integrating it.

In the summer of 2015, I attended a Café Tecnológico (technology coffee hour), one of the monthly meetings Sulá Batsú holds with the TIC-as participants at the local technical college in rural San Carlos. In a huge conference room, about thirty college-age women were visibly eager for the *tertulia* (conversation) to begin. Two tech experts invited by Sulá Batsú discussed their experiences in the private sector, and a visiting professor from Spain and I were also invited to offer talks. The experts' talks were focused on how to survive and thrive in the entrepreneurial and private sector worlds in ways that reproduced heteronormative notions of gender, such as advice on how to be both a good mother and a successful businesswoman.

But what captured my attention were the visible affective bonds between the young women and the Sulá Batsú activists. In my subsequent encounters and interviews with some of the young women—all of whom are studying scientific fields in college or are interested in one way or another in science and technology—many of them remarked that the relationships they had created with Sulá Batsú activists had been fundamental in helping them survive the male-dominated world of science and technology. One of the participants said, "I feel that TIC-as gives us security. They make us feel that as a woman you're really doing valuable work. . . . I really like their attitude, how they motivate women. This has provoked a change in all of us. I have seen how we have grown." Another remarked: "TIC-as gives you the courage to keep on going. I don't know how to explain it. It gives you that thing, that *espinita* [gut feeling, inspiration] of growing, of being truly powerful, like they say."

Beyond the affective bonds between them, the TIC-as participants also frequently commented on how the project had made them feel "powerful," helping them gain respect in their families and communities. I interviewed a group of TIC-as participants during a stormy afternoon in rural San Carlos. We met at a local café, with couches and lounge seats, amid magnificent mountains lush with infinite shades of green. They were between eighteen and twenty-two years of age, studying software engineering at the local technical university, and from San Carlos (except one who was from the Caribbean coast of the country). They were eager to talk. We spent a whole afternoon together drinking coffee. One of the TIC-as participants told me: "You really feel powerful because with technology you create things, new things, and you feel 'Wow, I did something different; I achieved something no one has done.'" Another young woman said: "Technology gives you both the power to believe in yourself and help others. It's like a viral network, where one can share knowledge and do great things."

And another participant observed: "To be in this field makes others take you more seriously, because people do not expect you to study careers in technology. They expect you to be a teacher or something. And when you say you are studying to become a software engineer, they say 'What?!' You start to be taken seriously." When I asked them, "Why technology? Why become an entrepreneur?" one participant exclaimed: "I want to have superpowers! I want to be superpowerful. I want to think about doing something and be able to do it. I want to have the ability to say, 'I will develop software that many men will use, and they will have to recognize that a woman made it.' Because machismo often does not let men acknowledge that a woman actually made something."

This sentiment dovetails with mainstream ideas of "empowerment" and of becoming part of the exclusive STEM "boys club." Technology, as expressed by these young women, is a magic bullet that endows them with power just because they are women in a male-dominated space. Their aspirations are geared toward inclusion, not necessarily transformation. These ideas about technology are pervasive. Yet Sulá Batsú provides a rhizomatic and collaborative model that inspires practices that contest these individualistic forms of empowerment. These superpowers include a commitment to their communities, to their *compañeras* (friends, colleagues), and to the activists of Sulá Batsú with whom they have continued to collaborate by becoming mentors to younger TIC-as cohorts even after becoming professionals. Affective bonds have shaped their relationships and visions of technology.

When I asked these young women if they would identify as feminists during our interviews in 2015, they emphatically said no. Coming from Catholic rural families and dealing with their own emancipation while simultaneously abiding by cultural gendered norms, being a "feminist" was far too radical. For them, *feminism* still meant hating men and not wanting to get married or have kids, among other stereotypes. This had changed by the time of my trip in 2019. Actually, I noticed a political awakening among Sulá Batsú activists. "How could I not be a feminist during these times," said Samuel, the co-op's social media and communications manager and a talented artist. I had created a reputation in la coope of asking all of them if they were feminists. Lila told me that Samuel had been waiting for me to arrive so that he could amend his previous stance on feminism. In our interview in 2019, Samuel alluded to the extreme violence against women in Central America and affirmed the urgency of being a feminist in these times. One of the TIC-as participants I had interviewed in 2015—who in 2019 was working as a software engineer in her hometown San Carlos and had become a co-op associate—asked me: "Did I really tell you then that I was not a feminist?"

Firuzeh: Yes, you did! What has changed since then? Tell me.
TIC-as participant: Well, let me see, what has changed? I think that my process with TIC-as has led me to feel empowered because of the opportunities it has given me. Also, to be able to guide other

75

girls and young women. I have seen the impact, let's see, of that chain of knowledges, the impact of understanding that we are sisters, be with them when something has happened . . . I am surprised, Firuzeh.

Firuzeh: Really? Yes, yes, you told me that! I follow you on social media, and throughout the years I have seen a transformation. And I told myself, I have to talk to her . . .

TIC-as participant: Yes, yes, I think you are right, I remember a tweet I wrote in which I said that we should not get confused with this elitist feminism that we are sold. That kind of feminism we see in the tech world. For instance, companies put a woman as the director, and it's like "women have it easy—all women have it easy." And it is not like that at all. It seems like the path to get up there is not that hard. Obviously, I appreciate all those testimonies from women, but I do not share that philosophy that those journeys are perfect. Because when you tell college women that those journeys are perfect, then when they arrive, they get frustrated and feel lied to. We have to tell them how things really are.

TIC-as continues to be one of the souls of la coope. And yet, it is also undergoing a profound transformation. When I started my research on Sulá Batsú in 2015, TIC-as was overwhelmingly geared toward supporting young women who wanted to study and work in STEM fields as well as fostering technologically based entrepreneurship. The entrepreneurship dimension has remained strong and thrived, but the STEM part has changed considerably. Through a painful realization, as well as a feminist political awakening of sorts, Sulá Batsú activists have discovered that incorporating women in STEM companies ultimately furthers corporate gains. Tech corporations co-opt many of these young women after hiring them because TIC-as has become such a renowned project. Companies parade the recruitment of these young women to signal progress, openness, inclusion, and equity.[12]

Speaking about the emphasis on inclusion—specifically of Black programmers—as a solution to inequality in the tech industry, sociologist Ruha Benjamin argues that by "focusing mainly on individuals' identity and overlooking the norms and structures of the tech industry, many diversity initiatives offer little more than cosmetic change, demographic percentages on a company's pie chart, concealing rather than undoing the racist status quo."[13] This does not mean there are no spaces for agency. For decades, feminist research has studied the ways in which women negotiate, navigate, and resist STEM-related and other corporate spaces. Kemly described the process of young rural TIC-as participants' integration and co-optation in STEM corporations: "I have realized that after TIC-as, when these young women enter the business world, they are immediately co-opted. They have tremendous organizational skills as well as training in collective action. Then these corporations hire them, co-opt them, and use these capacities to fulfill their own interests. Once these women are embedded in the business world, it is very difficult to take them out of there."

The co-op has realized that, at the end of the day, corporations are driven by maximizing profits and "innovation" under the guise of gender equity, inclusion, and diversity. Of course, this is not news, but after years of advocating for women's inclusion in corporate STEM, the results have made Sulá Batsú members interrogate their original objectives. Kemly says: "When we started to work on this topic, more women in technology, and we realized that we were piled together with big tech corporations and states, then I started to ask myself, But do we want the same things? Why is there so much interest in this? Why are they so interested in women? And I would tell myself, 'But no one cares about women!' . . . Then we realized that we were advocating in defense of the corporate and state agendas, and we said, 'But what is this?'"

The co-op is increasingly critical of other well-known strategies of inclusion, such as inviting women who have "made it" to serve as role models for young women. Sulá Batsú has realized that centering "role models" is a fundamentally cruel strategy, because most of the young women they work with—crossed by differences of class, race, and nationality—do not have access to the same opportunities many of these women had. The role model system is built upon ideas of meritocracy and self-reliance, on individual stories of success that completely disregard structural barriers. These stories obscure the hardships and pain these role models had to go through to become prominent figures in STEM. Thus the co-op is slowly moving toward a more rhizomatic model in which young women can organize as grassroots STEM collectives where women can support each other, foster intellectual and affective bonds, teach and collaborate with each other, and establish local tech enterprises. This is the future the co-op envisions.

Hackathons

The biannual "feminine hackathons" are part of the TIC-as umbrella project. The co-op has organized five hackathons since 2014 in Costa Rica, and one included young women from Central America, Mexico, and the Caribbean. The hackathons have been held in the rural northern region, in the southern part of the country, in Limón on the Caribbean coast, and in the capital, San José, representing rural, Indigenous, Black, and coastal geographic social locations. Since 2014, 360 young women (sixteen to thirty years old) have participated. Under the slogan "This is not a competition, this is a community gathering," the hackathons are thirty-six-hour nonstop events where groups of girls and young women design technological "prototypes"—apps, virtual maps, wearable technology, and so forth—with a social objective in mind.

Participants belong to a spectrum of technological dexterity; the co-op mixes young women who might be in STEM or are studying a STEM field with women who might not have access to a computer or the internet, for example. The intermingling of multiple knowledges is fundamental for the project. There are no winners, but rather projects are highlighted. Each hackathon—held after a three-month process of selection and participatory research in the communities and regions where the events will be held—has organized under a specific theme, such as green technologies, feminist coding, urban sustainability, or satellite technologies. Participants have designed apps to help teenage mothers find resources, an Amazon-style app for shopping in local stores, an app that identifies nearby public transportation options, and a glossary of words chosen and defined by girls so that the adults in their lives understand what they mean by concepts such as "stereotypes," "conflict resolution," and "communication." The hackathons are designed according to seven principles:

1. Everyone should know how to design technology because it is a way to have a voice in the digital society.

2. No one should be excluded from this process by a technological elite.

3. No one should be excluded from this process because of their economic, cultural, gender, or geographical contexts, conditions, or status.

4. The communities for whom technologies are developed are the only ones that can judge if these technologies are useful.

5. Technological proposals belong to the groups that produce them.

6. There should be exclusive spaces for women to develop technologies.

7. Plural and diverse conditions must be created to foster technological proposals.

Sulá Batsú's hackathons are different from other mainstream, more competitive events. Although the main event is thirty-six-hours nonstop, the processes before and after are the most important parts of the hackathon for the co-op. Before each hackathon and during at least two to three months in meetings both online and in-person, the co-op offers workshops in leadership, capacity building, and technological skills. The formation consists of understanding the needs of the geographic region where the hackathon will be held. Kemly explained that for the hackathon in the Caribbean city of Limón, which has a major Black population, we "informed the young women in the history of the Black people of the region, and the problems they confront."

The participants define what they are looking for in technology based on the problems and the needs of the people of the region. One of the most important elements of the hackathons is that juries are composed of both experts in STEM—from academia and the private and public sectors—and members of community-based organizations. In the hackathon in Limón, surrounded by various Indigenous communities, Indigenous and Black organizations formed part of the jury. "This encounter between the tech community and the community is one of the most important aspects of the hackathons," Kemly said. The hackathon might officially "end" after the thirty-six-hour event, but the process extends throughout the network of women who continue to work in their communities, with each other, and with the co-op and offer continuity by participating as "godmothers" in future hackathons.

In the 2018 hackathon, held in the Caribbean town of Limón, two prototypes were highlighted: the digital application Okama Süei (translated as "White man's technology" in the Indigenous language Cabécar) and Cybertrash, a satellite technology that would survey the sea-devouring microplastics, one of the main contaminants of the ocean. It was in this hackathon that Sulá Batsú started working with Indigenous Cabécar and Bribri women from the Alto Pacuare semiautonomous region in the Caribbean coast. The app the women designed aims to counteract the potential extractivism and erasure of Indigenous knowledges in the face of imminent internet connection in their region. Through Okama Süei, Indigenous women intend for non-Indigenous people to "feel" their language, traditions, ceremonies, knowledges, and ways of being and thinking. They appropriate the way in which their knowledges travel through and beyond the internet in another iteration of the ways in which relationships both lie within and surpass technologies. One of the goals of the virtual map—which integrates videos, audios, images, and maps in the Cabécar language and Spanish—is to create awareness of the lives and richness of the Cabécar and Bribri communities in developing advocacy campaigns and a "course of action" generating policies and procedures to protect Indigenous knowledges in Costa Rica.

The relationship between Sulá Batsú and these Indigenous leaders has extended beyond the hackathon, and Okama Süei—which has been funded by the Embassy of Canada in Costa Rica, UNESCO, the Frida Program, and the College of Information and Computation Professionals of Costa Rica (CPIC in Spanish)—has now become a central project for Sulá Batsú and has transformed its visions for technology. In the launch of the Okama Süei application in July 2021, which I attended via Zoom, the women from Alto Pacuare presented their project and talked about codesigning the icons with one of Sulá Batsú's activists. The platform has twelve icons that represent themes that are important for their community, such as agriculture, food, the home, art, the economy, knowledges, medicine, women, and sound. One of the members of the Association of Women of Alto Pacuare said: "Sound is very important because everything comes in the form of oral transmission." The codesigner from Sulá Batsú mentioned that during the process of design, she had learned a lot and her perspectives "as a Western woman" had been constantly challenged, for instance, when the Indigenous women told her that the icon for the "economy" had to be represented by women holding hands. "It is very, very important to state that these women's knowledges can never, never be contained in a technological device. Their knowledges are built in everyday life," Kemly said during the event, emphasizing the limits of technologies and the ways in which life overflows the technological. This is the direction that Sulá Batsú is taking after sixteen years of work centered on digital technologies.

Finally, my conversation with Kemly veered toward the polemic issue of "entrepreneurship." An important objective of the hackathons, as well as of the co-op in general, is to foster women-led and collective enterprises that design technologies that attend to local needs. Kemly and the co-op have been emphatic on the importance of women being able to "make money" and thrive in their communities. She insists that *entrepreneurship* should not be a "bad word" within feminist or progressive politics and that women have the right to live with dignity by generating their own capital. The co-op's activists believe that by designing technologies "with a purpose" and participating in the construction of the data society, women can transform the political and socioeconomic conditions of their communities. They are not interested in filling multinational technology companies with women—although this has certainly been a consequence of their work with young women—but rather they hope to encourage women to manage their resources and design technologies through localized entrepreneurship.

Technology has a very particular place in this puzzle. The activists believe that through community-designed collaborative and ecologically friendly technologies, justice is possible. The key is not the technology per se but the relationships that are created: relationships with oneself, each other, the community, and the planet. Technology opens the possibilities of collaboration. Sulá Batsú's vision of entrepreneurship both complies and is in tension with national and transnational plans for the

Third World Technological Woman. In Costa Rica state policies employ an individualistic and entrepreneurial perspective that is important to understand because the co-op is constantly negotiating with state policies and discourses.

Costa Rica: Women and Technology

Costa Rica is categorized as an "upper-middle-income economy," according to the World Bank, and within the context of Central America it is considered to be socioeconomically privileged.[14] This classification limits the country's access to development aid, although numerous forms of inequality persist and have worsened due to the COVID-19 pandemic.[15] The IMF and World Bank structural adjustment programs (SAPs) in the 1980s that demanded governments slash social spending and adopt austerity measures, deregulation, export promotion, and privatization as means of economic development impacted the country. Although poverty and inequality increased after the implementation of SAPs, Costa Rica continued to be the most stable and prosperous country in Central America (the military had been abolished in 1948 after a civil war).[16] Costa Rica has been labeled a "mixed economy" with a combination of market and state-led economic approaches.[17] It has important social welfare provisions in universal health care, education, and telecommunications, and a mix of national, foreign, and corporate investment in eco-tourism, agriculture, and technology. Costa Rica also has a long and vigorous history of cooperatives, especially in the agricultural sector.[18]

Fostering entrepreneurship through micro-, small-, and medium-sized enterprises is a priority, with the Ministerio de Economía, Industria y Comercio (MEIC) at the helm of establishing public policy in this area since 1977. In 2017, 98 percent of the country's national enterprises (a 7 percent increase since 2012) were micro-, small-, and medium-sized enterprises with fewer than one hundred employees, 64 percent in the service sector, contributing to 35 percent of jobs and 36 percent of the GDP.[19] In the ICT sector, micro-, small-, and medium-sized enterprises depended mostly on national capital, while large enterprises (more than one hundred employees) depended mostly on foreign capital.[20] The ICT sector has thrived, both nationally and globally, mostly in software development.[21] One of the driving principles of the 2030 National Enterprise Policy, established by the MEIC in 2020, is gender inclusivity.[22] This national plan states that one of the main challenges in the creation of micro-, small-, and medium-sized enterprises in the country is the gap in adopting new technologies.[23] Starting in the 1990s, foreign big-tech companies such as Intel (which closed its manufacturing facility in 2014), Microsoft, IBM, Google, Amazon, Akamai, and Hewlett-Packard opened operations in Costa Rica, making electronics and software development prime industries (medical equipment is also an important sector of the broader technology industry).

Costa Rica boasts comprehensive digital policy frameworks. The country has one of the highest mobile broadband penetration rates in Latin America, with one of the most affordable costs of broadband access in the region, although gender and urban/rural divides persist.[24] As of 2019, statistics show that the internet penetration in Costa Rica is 85.9 percent (the highest in Central America).[25] The Ministerio de Ciencia, Innovación, Tecnología y Telecomunicaciones (MICITT) is the state agency charged with designing and implementing ICT policy. The MICITT has created important national ICT policies, such as the National Science, Technology, and Innovation Plan 2015–2021, the 2017 National Policy for a Society and Economy Based on Knowledge, and the National Telecommunications Development Plan (PNDT). The PNDT, first ratified in 2009, with a second phase comprising 2015–2021, and a third phase covering 2022–2027, is aimed at amplifying national competitiveness through digital inclusion, transparent electronic government, and the digital economy, closing the digital divide, developing universal access, building infrastructure, and improving broadband services. It includes the development of a Digital Solidarity Agenda focused on access for "vulnerable" communities, such as people with disabilities, Indigenous populations, the elderly, children and youth, women head of households, and "micro-entrepreneurial women."[26] The MICITT has also designed strategies to support national policies, such as the 2018 Strategy for Digital Transformation Towards the Bicentenary of Costa Rica 4.0, focused on inserting the country into the "Fourth Industrial Revolution."[27]

The need to include women in STEM fields is a definite priority for the country, where women occupy the 30 percent to 40 percent of jobs in these fields.[28] In 2017 the MCITT launched the National Policy for Equality between Women and Men in Training, Employment and the Enjoyment of the Products of Science, Technology, Telecommunications and Innovation 2018–2027 (Política Nacional para la Igualdad entre Mujeres y Hombres en la Formación, el Empleo y el Disfrute de los Productos de la Ciencia, la Tecnología, las Telecomunicaciones y la Innovación, PICTTI) —a multisectorial effort with numerous state agencies, the private sector, and civil society organizations, including Sulá Batsú. With support from the National Institute of Women (Instituto Nacional de las Mujeres, INAMU), the PICTTI's objective is to include more women in STEM education and jobs and "equalize the number of women and men attracted to training, skill development, quality employment, permanency, and research in the different fields of science, technology and innovation."[29] The five "strategic pillars" of the policy are (1) attracting women into science, technology, and innovation; (2) training and retention of women in careers in science, technology, and innovation; (3) promotion of women's research and employment in science, technology, and innovation; (4) social ownership of science with a gender perspective; and (5) sustainability and follow-up. The policy mandated the creation of a high-level commission and an interagency commission in charge of overview and implementation.

These policies often combine women, ICTs/STEM, entrepreneurship, and the importance of formal economic inclusion; thus the Third World Technological Woman is also made through state policy and discourse. In 2021 the MICITT added *Innovation* to its official name and created the Costa Rican Promoter of Innovation and Investigation (previously the Consejo Nacional para Investigaciones Científicas y Tecnológicas, CONICIT) in charge of implementing policies and providing funding for innovation, capacitation, and investigation in the technology sector.[30] The incorporation of the word *innovation* signals a fundamental shift toward entrepreneurialism. The CONICIT launched the first national-level project in 2021, CONSTELAR, which will be steered by the business incubator Impact Hub San José, part of a global network centered on the "construction of entrepreneurial communities to create high impact," according to its website.[31]

Developed by the Costa Rica United States Foundation for Cooperation (CRUSA) and the CONICIT and supported by the Spyre Group, an entrepreneurial organization from Israel, CONSTELAR is focused on training and supporting women's entrepreneurship in STEM. The project includes an incubation program (which in its first phase in 2021 selected twelve women for twelve weeks); clubs for students, researchers, and professors in STEM in universities across the country; mentoring in areas of education and financing; a national STEM event (the first one was celebrated in September 2021); and a platform to interact and exchange ideas. The goal of CONSTELAR is to "formalize ventures to be able to opt for venture capital funds so that women can take the first step in creating companies, and that at some point they can sell or produce large profits, find partners who help them expand, and provide jobs."[32]

One of the focus areas of the National Institute of Women (Instituto Nacional de las Mujeres, INAMU)—which had a vital part in the elaboration of the PICTTI—is science, technology, and gender, in addition to other issues concerning gender-based violence, economic autonomy, civic participation, and health and education. Although entrepreneurship is an area of focus of this state agency, the priority is to provide women with the educational and financial opportunities to thrive in STEM academic fields and the workplace. There is a pervasive sense that the digital society is running away and women are being left behind, more so due to COVID-19. INAMU offers grants and training for women's entrepreneurial projects, although not necessarily centered on entrepreneurship in ICTs but rather on ICTs as tools to develop ventures such as the Fund to Foster Productive Activities and of Organization for Women (Fondo de Fomento para Actividades Productivas y de Organización de las Mujeres—FOMUJERES) and Proyecto Emprende. INAMU also focuses on cooperatives, employment, and unpaid domestic work issues under the economic autonomy program.

INAMU's incursion in areas of science and technology—mostly based on the Santo Domingo Consensus of 2013, the agreement of the Economic Commission for Latin America and the Caribbean's Twelfth

Regional Conference on Women from Latin America and the Caribbean, dedicated that year to ICTs and STEM—was reinforced in 2016 with the work of Mauren Navarro Castillo, a specialist in public policy at the Institute. In our interview in 2019 she noted that with the looming advance of automation, "institutions have started to run, like the MICITT, who has seen the need for labor in which women must play an important role, and obviously this has to do with women, so the INAMU has had to remain relevant regarding this issue." Navarro Castillo has a holistic perspective on digital technologies that follows "humanistic" (a term she prefers to "feminist") principles based on ecological awareness and solidarity. She is fiercely opposed to the US-based capitalist models of technological design, distribution, and adoption. I asked Navarro Castillo what it meant for her to incorporate women in STEM:

> Firuzeh: But when we think that we want women in the field of science and technology, what do we want women to do? What do we want women to contribute?
>
> Mauren Navarro Castillo: Of course, yes, yes, their abilities obviously, in the development of a country, I would say, this . . . responsibly, responsibly, right? And that implies understanding that I can develop something that has a positive impact on my society and in my country and that implies talking about the environment, about projects and products that do not affect childhood, putting them more like zombies or affecting their emotional part of cognitive development. . . . With products that positively impact the abilities of women. We are talking about health, medicine, and others, and obviously I see them producing, being recognized for their scope, for their capabilities. Not simply because it is fashionable.

Navarro Castillo's perpsective offers a glimpse into the contradictory nature of the state. There is not a homogeneous policy or discourse on women, ICTs, and STEM. This opens multiple possiblities, although the major focus is financial inclusion.

In an interview in 2015, for instance, Alejandra Mora, the head of the National Institute of Women at the time, commented that in today's world, women had to learn digital skills to become "competitive" in the corporate world, as microentrepreneurs, and in the political sphere.

Mora emphasized the need for more education, training, and financing to support women in STEM at all levels. She commented that the funds disbursed through the FOMUJERES program were aimed at securing public investment in fostering an understanding that if women "have an aggregated value, their product will be better, their competitiveness will be better, which places them in a different [economic] sector." These entrepreneurial and inclusionary policies and discourses are overwhelmingly individually based and focus on women "making it" in state, national, and global private sector spheres. In the context of prevalent state and transnational emphasis on making women into neoliberal, technologically savvy figures to advance economic development, in what ways is it possible to reimagine the Third World Technological Woman?

Decolonial and Feminist Entrepreneurship?

"Decolonization also crosses through entrepreneurship," Kemly told me during one of our many conversations about Sulá Batsú's focus on entrepreneurship. In Sulá Batsú, "entrepreneurship" is something of a hybrid, encapsulating a blend of market-based and feminist strategies. Activists envision entrepreneurship as a form of cooperative politics that will offer possibilities of solidarity among women. The organization believes in feminist interventions in technological production, community building, and political participation, as well as local economic development. This is not simply paying lip service to developmental discourses that use practically the same language and concepts. Kemly has imprinted on la coope her converging beliefs in feminist principles of horizontality, economic justice, and community making with an entrepreneurial philosophy because "we are a business; that's clear." She explained her vision of feminist entrepreneurship this way:

> We promote that women should be associative, networked, it may be with men, no one is saying the contrary, but led by women. We have realized that neither men nor women are prepared for entrepreneurship after college, much less prepared to develop projects that address social problems. This is all part of our feminist approach. Working together in association, to solve social problems, but also generate wealth—women also have to eat. They have no power to resist the

draw of these large companies that will offer five times more money, but if they succumb, they will not be the owners of their own companies.

This sentiment resonates with official state, United Nations, and corporate discourse on digital technologies and women. Sulá Batsú reproduces the technological entrepreneurial model, with the woman as technological producer who will have a multiplier effect on her family, community, and society.

But I find that the co-op's everyday praxis is about much more. In their analysis of what they consider oversimplified feminist critiques of co-optation and selling out, Catherine Eschle and Bice Maiguashca insist that "a movement cannot earn the title of progressive if its agents and agenda are worthy, but its practices unjustifiable."[33] As feminist scholars, we must examine the ways in which feminist endeavors are entangled with power. We must also look at organizational process and implementation to understand numerous forms of political agency.[34] It is important for Sulá Batsú activists to support women to be financially independent and make money but also to foster principles based on solidarity and social justice. Outcomes are important, but their projects focus on process. They must comply with the reporting requirements of funders and offer tangible evidence of change through hard numbers; quantification remains a requirement. But for the activists, this is mostly an administrative transaction. The process of collectivization is central to both their structure as a cooperative as well as their working philosophy, evidenced, as I have described, through their collective salaries, shared tasks, and joint conceptualization and implementation of projects.

Marcela, a former long-term staff member of la coope, told me about one isolated fishing community in the south of Costa Rica, where she offered a series of workshops on how to use computers. They used a solar battery to power one computer. The fishers wanted to learn how to use technology for selling their products in local markets. The workshop was done in the community. Marcela hoped the workshop would have long-term social effects beyond helping them with their emerging business. She hoped that the skills learned and the collective use of the only computer in the village could strengthen community ties and solidarity.

Marcela told participants that their pencils, pens, and papers were also technologies, just like the computer and the internet, in terms of being tools and spaces that could help them. Establishing this sense of closeness, familiarity, and demystification of technology is one of Sulá Batsú's strategies in working on entrepreneurship. Technology is envisioned as an affective process through which women and other oppressed communities can achieve both individual and collective transformation. Technology thus opens the possibilities of collaboration and creation.

Sulá Batsú's use and promotion of free and open-source software and free copyright also contests corporate forms of hierarchical and proprietary knowledge production in what could be interpreted as a manifestation of a feminist politics of the commons.[35] Beyond the ways in which the technical system functions, free software also reflects a set of political, ethical, and moral norms, values, and commitments that embody Sulá Batsú's organizational philosophy and work.[36] Late anthropologist Jeffrey Juris described it as "a powerful model for (re)organizing society based on horizontal collaboration, participatory democracy, and coordination through autonomy and diversity."[37]

The concept of the commons, central in the literature on the internet, has been theorized as mainly a "space" in which communities share and exchange goods and labor and affect subverting capitalist market-based relations.[38] Silvia Federici argues that international development institutions have appropriated the language of the commons and "put it at the service of privatization."[39] Development institutions have found that the market can sustain itself efficiently only through the circulation of nonmonetary relationships in the form of trust and confidence (and, yes, care). But the boundaries between collective forms of organization and capitalist market-based relations may sometimes be tenuous. Sulá Batsú is a case in point. In an email conversation I had with Kemly about the objectives of the co-op, she pointed out repeatedly that Sulá Batsú was "disruptive" because it proposes the disruption of traditional cultural norms and socioeconomic approaches that maintain women's inequality in science and technology. It is focused on creating a feminist commons of cooperation, knowledge, and skills. Kemly explained: "The basis are the networks of mutual support; we must build technology that is sustained in the encounter, in mutual support that confronts technological development based on the competition of the best, in the pursuit of success understood as the entrepreneur who has a startup and sells it to make money. Our approach to the construction of technology is based on the encounter of multiplicities. Exchange and collective construction will create the technological solutions that the world requires."

At the same time, Kemly insists that "entrepreneurship is not a bad word." The co-op has been reimagining what a feminist model of entrepreneurship could look like. "To be able to be independent," she says, "we women have to create and build businesses that are different from tech businesses. There is another rupture here that I am emphasizing: What does it mean to build a feminist tech-based business? What does it mean that it be headed by women? What makes it different? How is it organized differently? What is its market? What services does it offer? Above all, Firu, what is its business model? Is it impossible to build a business model that does not practice data surveillance and violates people's privacy?"

Sulá Batsú embraces entrepreneurship as a form of success and does not engage in radical feminist and anticapitalist politics, yet its commitment to collectivization and solidarity also challenges neoliberal rationalities based on self-reliance and personal responsibility. Would international development institutions approve of its work? They would, and they have. The co-op reproduces ideas on the importance of entrepreneurship for women's and communities' well-being and success. These discourses obscure the historical and contemporary political and economic structures that have produced the inequalities that the Technological Woman is supposed to overcome. And yet, although the co-op defines itself fundamentally as a "development organization," I contend that it is also immersed in postdevelopmental imaginaries and practices, as J. K. Gibson-Graham astutely argues: "The aim of post-development theorizing about local and regional development does not preclude involvement of people and places with capitalist enterprise, wage labor, formal markets or mainstream financial institutions."[40]

Sulá Batsú instills principles of horizontality, solidarity, collective struggle, and economic redistribution—through love, trust, and deep affective bonds—that are a far cry from individualistic neoliberal politics. Is this a form of overt and planned resistance? Perhaps not. Yet Sulá

Batsú's collective politics contrast with the basis of neoliberal development discourse.

Living the World You Imagine

It would be impossible to understand Sulá Batsú's work without understanding its relationships.[41] Its members' bonds, income and knowledge collectivization, horizontality, and solidarity are deeply connected with their work on technology. They enact a form of prefigurative politics, which means that they practice the world they envision: nonhierarchical, horizontal, collective, and affectionate.[42] The office in Barrio Escalante is organized as an open space, full of natural light, where everyone can look at each other. Every day at 3:00 p.m. we had coffee together, an almost sacred daily bonding ritual. They work, talk, and laugh, and also move through conflicts regarding differences in approaches, styles, and objectives. They have arguments on issues that range from funding sources to religion and sexuality. Marcela told me that it had taken her a while to understand the horizontal structure of la coope, but "that is the idea of la coope. With Kemly we can sit down to talk about different aspects of la coope, and we can also have very strong discussions. With a lot of love and respect, we also fight. With respect and love, we can also say *mae*, I am sorry."

These affective bonds as coworkers, friends, and entrepreneurs extend to the communities they work with. Lila explained that this work was about more than teaching individuals how to use technologies: "The organization has given me a vision of thinking that if these things [the relationships we have at la coope] happen, I must replicate them with the people we work with. When we work in a community, we go with some specific goal: to offer information, knowledge, the use of technologies. Although this is our mission, there is always space to talk to them. . . . the possibility of transmitting all the knowledge I have gained not in a classroom, but over the years of working in this organization."

When I arrived at Sulá Batsú back in the summer of 2015, there was something happening that I could not articulate at first. Since the beginning of my fieldwork, I was already trying to understand the meanings of solidarity for the co-op's organizational rhythm and relationships among its members and others. There was a rhythm that did not follow a linear, progressive development. They move organically, collectively, with unstructured schedules. Sometimes they document their projects, but other times there is no paper trail—some initiatives are impossible to articulate in sentences with commas and periods. Other times, they simply do not have the time or resources. Their projects in communities do have to abide by specific procedures of grants and funders, with clear objectives, assessments, reports, statistics, and lists of outcomes. And yet there is also an emphasis on process, on experimentation, on learning from mistakes that goes beyond "collecting data."

Its members' most treasured goal is to sustain relationships of care among themselves and with the communities they work with. There continues to be an emphasis on joy, dreaming the impossible, and returning to the drawing board as many times as necessary. They make space to start over, reflect, and regret. They make time for long conversations on work-related and personal problems and hopes. Thus their vision is precisely about creating and imagining "technologies of feeling," as imagined by the Indigenous Cabécar and Bribri women. Andrea told me: "Here, we are allowed to be and to make, which is different from many other businesses. Here we can all grow together." And Samuel remarked: "I do not exactly see my job at la coope as a job, but as what I can contribute to la coope. I can be working the entire morning at la coope, stop at 2:00 p.m., do a personal errand, and then continue working at la coope. A lot of us do that here, but we all know that our priority is what we can contribute. It is another rhythm of work."

None of this means that work is not being done; the key is to understand who defines what work looks like. The Sulá Batsú collective work when loving, caring for each other, and sharing coffee with *natilla*, guava jam, and fresh bread every day. They work when they talk about their lives, heartbreaks, mistakes, and regrets. They work during those long conversations in the van traveling around Costa Rica, while Juan drives from north to south, from the Caribbean to the Pacific coast, and back. They are also working when they interrupt everything to help a coworker who is depressed. This is all part of the everyday labor at la coope. Emotions and reason are imbricated, seamlessly woven into each other, against modernist dualist ways of thinking and being.

In her quest to disengage from modern/colonial epistemologies and ways of producing knowledge, Leanne Betasamosake Simpson says that at first she did not fully appreciate how the Nishnaabeg—her own community in Canada—produced theory through practice. She writes: "It became clear to me that *how* we live, *how* we organize, *how* we engage in the world—the process—not only frames the outcome, it is the transformation. *How* molds and then gives birth. The *how* changes us. *How* is the theoretical intervention."[43] It has been precisely Sulá Batsú's *how* that alerted me to the meanings of a feminist technopolitics of care. A politics of solidarity that is expansive but not without conflicts, heartbreaks, and negotiations.

During my early days of fieldwork, I noticed that much of what made this project feminist was an everyday praxis based on solidarity. This manifests in numerous ways: in how the activists feel about each other, in how they feel about their work and mission, and in the experiences of workshop and training participants. "I cannot imagine not being part of this organization," longtime associate Lila said. "I do not see it as part of my job. I see it as an extension of my life." And Marcela described the motor of their work: "It's part of the learning process that we realized at some point that passion is what drives the loyalty of our associates and ourselves with the *cooperativa*. For me, this is key. If there is no passion and love for the *cooperativa*, people leave because it is exhausting for people and it requires an investment of the heart, of time and life that must be very strong." During my fieldwork I often heard phrases such as "This place is my life," "We love each other," "We support each other."

Kemly explained how their vision of entrepreneurship is connected to experimentation and accepting that they will make mistakes:

> For us the pleasure of going to work should be part of business management; love, affection among your *compañeros* should be part of entrepreneurship. When you analyze business theory, this is never discussed or considered. They speak of profitability, marketing, commercialization. The main bastion of our work is passion. For us, passion is part of entrepreneurship, fun, laughter. And the other thing that we always consider as part of our work is the ability of *meter las patas* [to make mistakes], without malicious intent obviously. This is also part of entrepreneurship. This is our model of a solidarity-based economy.

The most important work of la coope lies in its micropolitics: in how its members weave relationships in each space in which they move, between the team, with communities, with the technologies that they design, think, and imagine, with a politics of care of solidarity and hope in building the world they dream of. That world of shared knowledges, as their slogan says. In other words, the revolution is in how they do what they do. But relationships are also ridden with difficulties, which affect how they do what they do.

Conflicts and Negotiations

The co-op is not perfect, nor its story a fairytale. Its members have confronted internal fissures, conflicts, and irreconcilable differences, and their relationships are constantly being negotiated. People have left la coope for numerous reasons: new job opportunities, changes in personal circumstances, or moving to another country. But there have also been bitter disagreements about the co-op's mission, structure, and procedures, personal conflicts among activists, a lack of understanding of how a cooperative works, and the very real need to earn a higher and more secure income than the co-op can provide. Often these departures have been interpreted as betrayals, ending what had been close friendships.

Every time someone has left la coope, it has implied an "affective rupture," Kemly explained to me: "Contrary to traditional business theory, in which everyone is considered disposable and replaceable, everyone here is indispensable. Every single person who has belonged to la coope has been indispensable, and when they leave, la coope goes through a profound restructuring process. La coope will never be the same organization after that person left. We have always reorganized, restructured, and changed, but the organization that emerges is different every single time. There is both an organizational transformation and an affective rupture." In my interviews, this idea of an "affective rupture" was repeated over and over, albeit in different forms. Marina, one of the founders of the co-op, told me that it was "exhausting" to see so many people given a platform for "growing," "yet, once they grow, they leave, but at what cost?" And Juan said that some of these departures have been "very painful," but that they come with the organization's commitment to maintaining joint worker-management control (*autogestión* in Spanish). One of the co-op's most recent members, Pabru, told me that the co-op did not operate like a regular business, where everyone is disposable: "At la coope, everyone's value is incalculable. Every time someone enters or leaves la coope, the dynamic changes, the vision changes. The new person who comes starts to interact with everyone else and offers a different perspective. This process is so enriching, and la coope values this so much."

Cycles of financial turmoil have caused many people to leave the co-op. In addition to producing tremendous emotional upheaval among the activists, these partings temporarily destabilize the flow of the organization. Activists develop certain skills, make contacts, and create networks and then take these elsewhere. One of the major challenges of Sulá Batsú since its foundation has been to attain financial sustainability—the same stability they work to promote in the communities they serve. The balance between maintaining the joint worker-management control of the organization—with streams of "individual" income being distributed among the collective—has been very challenging. Juan and Gabriel—two of the founders of the co-op who have survived various cycles of financial crisis—told me in separate interviews that throughout the years, they have advocated for the co-op to obtain a fixed stream of income from more "commercial" contracts. Gabriel spoke at length to me about the challenges of running an organization that is so "emotional" and solidarity-based, while having to make compromises to be able to survive financially.

Like many other grassroots organizations, Sulá Batsú constantly has to balance its solidarity-centered model based on collectivization and social justice with the material conditions it needs to do its work (an issue I discuss in-depth in chapter 4). Gabriel feels conflicted because on the one hand, he wants the organization to preserve its commitment to affect and relationships, but on the other hand, he believes that the organization must make some sacrifices, such as decreasing its core staff and contract-hiring experts for specific projects. He explained that "people say how beautiful this project is and then want to stay, and this is unsustainable. . . . Everything I am saying seems contradictory to what we believe in, right?" These unresolvable contradictions and dilemmas are a structuring part of organizational life.

One of la coope's most difficult financial crises was in 2013. Kemly, along with other associates, proposed the unimaginable: to launch Casa Batsú, a cultural community center that would house la coope, the associates' external projects, and other organizations, while also providing collective spaces for events such as art exhibitions, dance lessons, music concerts, conferences, and workshops. Kemly and her then partner, who has worked in the cooperative field in Costa Rica for decades and was an associate of la coope, laughed while they remembered how this disagreement almost cost them their relationship. At the moment he thought that the idea of opening Casa Batsú was a huge mistake because it would drain their already scarce economic resources. La coope was split. There were discussions, fights, resentment, and misunderstandings. Kemly told me, "For me it was either we do this one big thing that we had dreamed about, or it was over." They finally voted and approved Casa Batsú.

During my fieldwork trip to Costa Rica in the summer of 2019, the organization was going through another very trying financial situation. Grants have become more competitive and donors more selective; international development agencies have turned to countries considered much less privileged than Costa Rica; and selling services is more difficult in the context of national and global economies in crisis, growing inequality and violence, and continued slashing of social protections due to neoliberal policies. And this has only gotten worse during the COVID-19 pandemic. Already in 2019, some activists were worn out; after working for months without income, exhausted, desperate, some of them felt hopeless. Laughter, fun, and solidarity continued to permeate their space and everyday interactions, but something had changed. La coope is much more than a job; it is a way of living. Amid the crisis, Kemly had told the team and repeated to me numerous times, "If we must close, we will do it with a celebration, a big party. This is also part of our experimentation. If it must be, we will celebrate." Knowledge is also produced in this act, in this "how," while our lives are shaped and reshaped.

Some of the activists were showing signs of exhaustion due to the challenging financial situation that the co-op was facing. Pabru, for instance, told me that "passion and love" continued to characterize la coope, but that unfortunately, the economic precarity was affecting the organization: "As a cooperative, we have not managed to generate the resources to satisfy the material needs of the people who constitute it, so there is a delicate, super-delicate issue there. But I personally, since I've been dealing with this all my life, I'm actually used to it, so to speak. If you have to eat only rice, you eat only rice." Clara told me that she was very sad with the economic situation—many of them had not received any income for months—because the "objective of la coope is to work from a place happiness." But, she added, "obviously we live in a capitalist system that reduces every possibility to what is convenient to the system. We are one of those things that can be reduced to the minimum when there is a crisis."

A moment that foregrounds the co-op's messy textures of care was exemplified in one of their staff meetings. Kemly was critical of the work of a coworker who was not at the meeting. She was disappointed and frustrated because this person had not completed some very urgent tasks. Other staff members defended their coworker. Kemly later told me: "They defended her, and that is exactly what they had to do." This speaking up for the other, talking back, and risking confrontation and conflict are also part of their collective politics and constant reflexivity. The content goes hand in hand with the structure of the organization. Talking about their cooperative model, Kemly remarked: "This has not been easy. But if we change this, we change who we are. The other option is that everyone earns his or her own salary. But this is not what we want. I mean, if we get to that point, we would rather dissolve the organization." And another associate, Alejandra, said that "many people simply cannot understand" the model and leave, while Marcela believes that generally women have understood their collective philosophy better than men. Alejandra gave a clear description of the cooperative's dynamics:

> Imagine that there is a pot and we'll do the roast together, the soup together. You put in the water, I put in the potatoes, someone else the meat. We all eat the soup. In the end, although the water is the cheapest ingredient of the soup, you had to go get the water, and the soup cannot be cooked without water. Then you'll eat a bowl of soup just like mine, and I was the one who brought the meat. In that sense everything is shared equally. Some people have not understood

this model and leave. They say, "*Púchica* [damn], I brought this big project, huge, which brings in so many thousands of dollars, and my wages did not increase, and everyone is eating my money." Well, that is the way it is. Someday you're not going to be bringing in the money, and someone else will work so you can eat. So when people do not understand this model, they tend to leave.

During a meeting in the summer of 2019, Kemly asked me to share some of my reflections about la coope with the activists. I was a bit hesitant, but she insisted. She said that I knew and loved la coope, but that I had also been critical of their work. As a researcher, I was an outsider and simultaneously an insider, someone who felt a deep *cariño* for the activists and the organization. My reflections sparked a lively conversation—sometimes sad, other times tinted with anger and frustration. They all agreed that something had to change and were immersed in that very process that has continued, even though they have mostly worked remotely since 2020 because of the pandemic. This is a snapshot of the reflections I shared that day:

> During my visits in 2015 and 2016, the coope was a different organization. There were other people, fewer men, different projects. There was a tremendous enthusiasm for the work you do, a collective rooted in justice and solidarity. Today, the coope is going through a difficult time, and that, understandably, also affects everyone. I find some signs of disappointment and exhaustion, of questioning the model and the content, of stagnation, of a certain nostalgia for the past. But I also see that many of you feel that it is a moment of reinvention, of repositioning, of reorganization.
>
> I see that solidarity, tenderness, and affection remain the fundamental axes of the work, but there is also a need for something to happen, for something to change. There is a prevailing expectation. There are some people who also have a longer institutional memory and have seen these cycles come and go. . . . More of you also position the coope as a feminist and political organization. It is interesting for me to see how your work, the daily practice of the coope, its relationships, the work with the communities, the vision of the world may have influenced this more explicit politicization.
>
> Several of you have also told me that the coope is better positioned than ever at the national, regional, and global levels, and that it is

necessary to take advantage of this moment to rethink the organization and strengthen that international image. Finally, I want to say
that several of you mentioned joy, emotion, and passion as engines of
the cooperative, and that is something you must continue to build on.

And so, their relationships remain always in construction.

Conclusion

"Not one of us would have been able to do any of this alone," remarked
Kemly during a session with la coope where I presented my research.
We were discussing what it meant to them to be part of a collective, to
share knowledge, tasks, time, space, and income as well as affection,
solidaridad, conflict and disagreements. Their work on technology is
bonded with their caring relationships and organizational praxis. It is
in this "how" that technology is produced and reimagined. This is what
makes a "technology of feelings" possible, and this technology of feelings is most importantly a technology of justice. A technology that facilitates, creates, and supports sustaining life with dignity in the midst of
death and violence. A technology that is permanently being negotiated
through care and solidarity, pain and anger, individual and collective
struggle, precarity and abundance.

Development plans for the virtuous Third World Technological
Woman encounter challenges, sometimes even unbeknownst to the
actors. Sulá Batsú is not necessarily an anticapitalist organization. Members affirm that "women cannot be afraid of the market" and that la
coope is an "enterprise." Yet their project also challenges market logics
based on individualism, self-sufficiency, and personal responsibility as
solutions to inequality, even when they operate within those same dynamics. Sulá Batsú reproduces the entrepreneurial framework in their
work with women. At the same time, Sulá Batsú challenges this dominant development paradigm through principles of horizontality, redistribution, knowledge exchange, and care. The emotional relationships
embedded in their organizational process embody a feminist praxis. The
co-op both reproduces and subverts the entrepreneurial model.

While Sulá Batsú may center aspects of an ideal Technological

99

Woman, their feminist practice—enabled by a politics of care—contests mainstream development agendas. "The defense of life" is crucial in a world in which colonial-capitalist policies, which govern most of our technologies, increasingly thrive on the extraction, exploitation, and dispossession of life, human and nonhuman.[44] And that is what la coope does: they defend life, forging a "politics of connections," as Segato says. These relationships of solidarity not only *denounce*, and here is the key, but they also *announce* the possibility of more just worlds, where everyone, the land, animals, and objects—why not?—can flourish together.[45]

THREE

Pleasure

When we think about a politics of care, we rarely think about pleasure or joy. And yet pleasure is a fundamental dimension of care: of caring about ourselves, others, the planet, the nonhuman. What is care without pleasure? We can clearly see care without pleasure in the gendered and racialized figure of self-sacrifice, exhaustion, and exploitative, precarious, and unvalued labor. If we start thinking about care and caring as a vital individual and collective praxis of creating relationships that build better worlds and sustain life in all its forms, then pleasure is central. This is also—or *should* also be—the image of care. Feminist philosopher Graciela Hierro argues that pleasure is a feminist ethical project central to feminist liberation: "the duty is to reach pleasure, pleasure is survival, vitality, authenticity, laughter, happiness, sociability, eroticism and love, in sum, everything that constitutes the *buenvivir* [good living]."[1]

We should also be able to feel pleasure in caring. But in our world, particularly for historically oppressed communities, pleasure is elusive and persistently denied. Just in 2021, there were a series of direct attacks on online sexuality. Apple and Google launched policies regulating sexual content, under the guise of protecting children and combatting sexual trafficking, which particularly affects queer communities and sex workers.[2] An international coalition of organizations, including the Association for Progressive Communications (APC), signed an open letter calling on Apple to abandon its plan to build surveillance capabilities in its products to "protect children."[3] Also in 2021, the website OnlyFans said that it would eliminate pornography and sexually explicit content from its platform, a decision it reversed after the outrage of sex workers and other communities who had contributed to the site's fame and profit.[4]

In the global South, mechanisms of control both through the regulation of sexuality and through science and technology have been inherent to colonial-capitalist and development policies.[5] Technologies have been deployed for economic development, environmental destruction, biotechnical interventions through forced sterilization, mapping and segregation, and militarism.[6] Scholars have identified the dangerous trends in the South of biometric surveillance and informational capitalism as well as data colonialism through the extraction of personal data for profit.[7] Digital violence is not an isolated phenomenon but rather part of the violence intrinsic to the capitalist-colonial order, which, as Silvia Federici argues, has been a war consistently waged on women's and feminized bodies.[8] The commoditization of violence, as feminist philosopher Sayak Valencia calls the increasing profitability of death in the Third World, particularly affects women and other oppressed communities in the South and North, both online and offline.[9] Ironically, international development largely construes digital technologies as saving the Third World, making what I call the Third World Technological Woman an exemplary modern neoliberal subject.[10] Examining collective strategies of technopolitical agency thus becomes an urgent task.

There are different ways to think about what a politics of care might look like in relation to our digital technologies—for example, the Cabécar Indigenous women's integration of collective and ancestral knowledges and emotions in the creation of technology (analyzed in chapter 2), Sasha Costanza-Shock's work on design justice, Yasnaya Elena Aguilar's powerful concept "tequiology" that emphasizes the collaborative creation of technologies as a common good, or Safiya Umoja Noble's research on algorithmic racism and how to transform the making of our technologies.[11] I explore a politics of care that flourishes in the forms of pleasure, joy, and desire amid online gender-based violence by looking at the feminist activism of APC's Women's Rights Programme (WRP).

At the center of this feminist insistence on pleasure lies the body—specifically, women's and feminized bodies. Care is also an embodied practice. APC WRP activists view the internet as an embodied space where desire should flourish. And this is a subversive practice. Federici claims that "our struggle then must begin with the reappropriation of our body, the revaluation and rediscovery of its capacity for resistance, and expansion and celebration of its powers, individual and collective."[12] APC WRP activists celebrate pleasure as one of their strategies to contest online gender-based violence through a series of transnational projects that include the Feminist Principles of the Internet and the EROTICS[13] project. Although APC WRP's global and local campaign against online gender-based violence Take Back the Tech (running since 2006) provides evidence for its emphasis on agency, in this chapter I focus on the Feminist Principles of the Internet initiative and the EROTICS Project because of their emphasis on pleasure.

APC WRP activists problematize online violence through two main strategies: (1) by using activism against online violence to advocate for online sexual agency and pleasure, and (2) by anchoring themselves in a Southern epistemology that makes explicit the connections between online gender-based violence and broader social, historical, and political histories and contexts. APC WRP advocates for pleasure together with the use of open-source software and noncorporate platforms, cybersecurity, data privacy and consent, and state, transnational, and corporate internet regulations, policies, and governance.[14]

A History of the Women's Rights Programme of the Association for Progressive Communications

The APC, founded in 1990 as a global "network of networks," is both a transnational network and a nongovernmental organization with consultative status with the United Nations that works on internet rights advocacy and policy on local, state, and suprastate levels as well as with grassroots organizations. As of 2021, the APC comprised fifty-seven organizational members and thirty-three individual members in seventy-three countries, the majority from the global South. The APC is a decentralized virtual network with a small staff using the internet to work and communicate. APC members—known as "nodes"—focus on connecting the nonprofit sector and social movements around the world (working much like internet service providers today): "APC pioneered the use of ICTs by civil society. In many countries where they operated, APC nodes (computer centers which simply picked up e-mail, forwarded it, and offered related services) were often the first providers of access to the internet."[15] The APC has played a vital role in connecting grassroots organizations and activists in the global South with numerous UN events since 1990 via online communication. As the internet has expanded and become commercialized, the APC has become more focused on internet rights, policy and activism, with three program areas: communications and information policy, women's rights, and the use of technology and capacity building.

Founded in 1993 as the Women's Networking Support Programme, the WRP initiated advocacy against online violence in the global South in 2005. Financed through the APC, support for specific projects has come from the Ford Foundation, the Dutch Ministry of Foreign Affairs, the International Development Research Centre (IDRC), and the Swedish International Development Cooperation Agency (SIDA), among others. The WRP works at the intersection of research, policy advocacy, movement building, and on-the-ground grassroots capacity building and training. It has issued hundreds of papers, briefs, and reports on violence against women online and regularly participates in local, national, and global conferences on internet rights and women's rights, including UN events such as the annual Committee on the Status of Women (CSW).

The twelve activists I interviewed between 2015 and 2021 are from Argentina, Bosnia and Herzegovina, Canada, Lebanon, Malaysia, South Africa, and the United States, and they live all over the world. Some of them are part of the core staff; others work through contracts. They participate in the annual APC meetings in South Africa and communicate frequently as a group via email, using open-source video-conferencing applications and other digital platforms, since there are no physical headquarters. They are open-software users and promoters. APC

WRP is known among the global feminist community for its trailblazing work organizing the online communication and networking at the 1995 Fourth World Conference on Women in Beijing. The organization provides key insights into the transnational context of the intersection of gender, feminism, and technology.[16]

Pleasure, Embodiment, and Care

Activists' politics redefine the Third World Technological Woman overflowing the containers imposed by marketization, extraction, surveillance, and violence by insisting on the power of pleasure. Scholar-activist adrienne maree brown defines pleasure as "a measure of freedom" and a "feeling of happy satisfaction and enjoyment."[17] Hierro conceptualizes pleasure as an ethical feminist principle. These scholars nurture my definition of pleasure as an element of freedom and feminist justice and as the ability to express and feel joy. In talking about online sexual pleasure, I am mostly referring to expressions of sexuality using technologies as vehicles and spaces, such as sexting, sharing erotic videos, sex cams, and online dating and hooking up, but also to expansive forms of joy such as connecting with others.[18] This technopolitical strategy asserts the importance of marginalized communities' freedom to express pleasure amid online attacks aimed at inhibiting their desires. I argue that the feminist defense of online pleasure forms part of a "politics of connections"—a micropolitical strategy that announces life in the face of violence.[19]

Fostering pleasure is a subversive feminist tactic, and yet any strategy of resistance or strategy that advances ways to re-exist is complicated. Activists have important concerns about the implications of harm and trauma, lack of support and safety, and the conflicts that arise in advocacy that leads to criminalization. And increasingly during the past years, numerous UN agencies have co-opted radical activism around online gender-based violence and even pleasure in their discourses. We thus need to understand what a feminist perspective from the global South reveals about online gender-based violence. Moreover, in what ways do embodiment and pleasure represent a feminist technopolitics of care? Below, I examine these connections and insurrections.

I have two important clarifications. First, I am not arguing that APC WRP activists are advancing an unbridled form of sexual agency or that accessing "agency" is uncomplicated.[20] Sexual agency is a complex concept and practice for many communities across race, class, sexuality, religion, and ability. Pleasure is also "a regulatory regime" that is "subjective and contextual," as sociologist Angela Jones argues in her study of "camming" and the online sex industry.[21] Maggie Nelson explains, for instance, that "there is no world in which 'agency' or 'free will' exist apart from webs of relationality, which includes relations of power."[22] Nonetheless, I believe that expanding the spaces (to use Nelson's phrase) in which pleasure is a collective liberatory endeavor is a key feminist undertaking.

Second, I am not theorizing women's online pleasure in the image of some kind of animal-machine (biological-technological) sociopolitical and material imaginary, akin to Donna Haraway's cyborg.[23] Although important in transgressing dichotomies of nature/culture, the cyborg—a product of a specific historical context during the conservative 1980s Cold War era of President Ronald Reagan—holds a certain techno-optimistic impulse that activists contest even when they appropriate these technologies. I envision pleasure as a feminist technopolitical tactic that, as Federici states, "does not ignore the constraints that technologies place on our lives and their increasing use as a means of social control as well as the ecological cost of their production."[24] With this awareness, APC WRP activist Max argued in our interview in 2015 that there is a need for an anticapitalist approach to technology:

> Capitalism is a driver of technology because we want to know how to make our lives more efficient. And so, our feminist understanding of technology has to be coupled with a Marxist understanding of capitalism and of where technology wants to take us, who owns it, who produces it, who designs it, who has control over it. So when we say that women should take back the tech, it's also about taking collective control of these private technological advancements. Which is why I'm not as hopeful about social networks as I was anymore. And I'm a bit scared about technological advancements that support surveillance, support regulation, support control, and are privately owned versus technology that actually brings an end to the capitalist models and bring more equality and more justice.

A feminist technopolitics of pleasure is grounded in contesting—and aiming to transform—the numerous webs of capitalist violence in which technologies are produced, distributed, designed, administered, discarded, and used.

Insurgent Sexualities from the South

Julia, who has been closely involved with APC WRP's activism against online gender-based violence since 2009, told me:

> The idea of the global South is that we are starving. If the idea is that women in the global South are innovating, that we are doing amazing things, experimenting, and playing, it does not fit into the development discourse. Funders do not want to fund happy Black women. No one is going to give you money if you are smiling and have a beautiful set of teeth, no! That is why it has been hard not only to talk about it [our work], but to get donors to see it as an important agenda—it does not fit into that narrative. We are talking about accessing the internet as a catalyst, as something to enable a range of other rights.

This quote captures many of the strands of APC WRP's activism, situated in the global South, on issues of pleasure and development. Feminist activists continue to contend with having to fit poor women in the global South into the narrative of victimhood so that they will be considered "worthy" development subjects. When digital technologies—ultimate markers of neoliberal economic prosperity—are added to this mix, it becomes even more difficult to introduce different imaginaries, such as women who feel pleasure in all its vast dimensions. APC WRP's activism provides a gateway to discuss how digital technologies can open a range of possibilities for women and other oppressed communities. Julia says that their work on online violence advances more complex narratives about women and technology in the global South: "This work is changing how we understand who we are in this world, our bodies, what happens between the body and the technology. It is shifting what privacy means, it is blurring the line between our age-old arguments of what is public and what is private, to the fundamentals of feminism. And I realized, 'Oh shit, why is no one talking about this at all?' even in the spaces we were working in. Some people said, 'What is the point? We have no computers, no electricity.'"

107

APC WRP's work on violence, sexuality, and pleasure posits technology not as a tool for market-based economic advancement or a magic bullet to end poverty but rather as a complex sociotechnical system. For feminist activist Min, a former APC WRP member, the strategy comes in stages, with the goal to present a more complete landscape:

> In the first stage, you maybe need to understand this as poverty alleviation. And then you need to understand this as STEM. And then you need to understand this as intervening in actual women's lives and bodies. And that's where APC comes in. But eventually, hopefully, they all start to come together and give a fuller picture and see this in the kind of more integrated human rights of women . . . in all of the human rights from freedom of expression to right to public participation, gainful employment, family life, information, health, so on and so forth. So, that is what I think we're kind of working to do.

Images of victimization continue to pervade global South imaginaries, decades after Chandra Mohanty's groundbreaking analysis on how Western scholars represented women in the Third World.[25] Still today, feminist activists struggle against these representations in their work. Images of pleasure and joy are still uncomfortable and threatening. Julia told me that her vision for APC WRP's activism was "that women are playing with tech; we are not using it to make more money or learn how to code, maybe to learn how to bake a cake—something that is not so functional or seen as important. Pleasure is political." In the same vein, Wendy Harcourt argues that "body politics has been at the core of political struggles around gender equality, human rights, and public health" in grassroots and institutional development spheres alike, adding that this "corporeal, fleshly, material existence of bodies is deeply embedded in political relations, from historical colonialism and agricultural practices to population control policies and the contemporary bio-politics of migration and war."[26]

Beyond calls for individuals from oppressed communities to become designers and climb the STEM ladder—which is important and yet also a neoliberal project in many ways—APC WRP feminist activists foster a pleasure-based politics that reinvents historical tropes on Third World women's victimization and misery as well as their purported heroism.[27]

They engage in tactics that produce liberatory frames around women's and queer sexuality and pleasure online (figure 2). I thus examine not what online violence forecloses but what activism against online violence—anchored in a Southern perspective—creates. Narratives of play, fun, and pleasure constitute an "insurgent decolonial practice" that "creates hope . . . in spite of violence."[28] The EROTICS Project and the Feminist Principles of the Internet illustrate the activists' work on technology and sexuality.

The EROTICS Project

The APC's Women's Rights Programme has been critical in promoting a "feminist internet" and internet gender rights in the global South. One of its central initiatives is the EROTICS Project: An Exploratory Research on Sexuality and the Internet, a global research effort collecting data on the experiences of feminist scholars and sexual rights

FIGURE 2. "Free the Nipple" by Flor de Fuego launched during APC WRP's 2018 global Take Back the Tech campaign. Courtesy: APC WRP. Reprinted with permission.

activists—including young women, individuals self-identified as working on LGBTQI+ issues—with the internet since 2008. These scholars and activists aim to defend the rights of sexual rights activists to use the internet to express themselves and to work freely and safely. EROTICS is a multiphase, multicountry project combining survey research, capacity building, advocacy, and movement building. The project partners with local organizations in the countries under study. For phase one (2008–11), APC WRP surveyed sexual rights activists in Brazil, India, Lebanon, South Africa, and the United States. Phase two (2012–14) covered Indonesia, Turkey, and India. Between 2016 and 2018, APC WRP expanded the EROTICS Project to foster networks of organizations working on sexual internet rights in Bangladesh, India, Nepal, and Sri Lanka. And in 2019 it expanded the EROTICS network in South Asia with a two-year project that included activists who did not identify as sexual rights activists.

EROTICS research consistently finds that activists use the internet for outreach, community-building, advocacy, and sexual expression of women and queer experiences of pleasure and desire. It finds that state and nonstate (i.e., religious institutions, corporations) content regulation, surveillance, and censorship harm activists by curtailing their online expression and policing their sexuality and sexual rights under the guise of protecting morality. So-called protection may take the form of blocks, filtering, take-downs, and banning of domain names. Sexual rights activists thus find themselves in a dilemma: the internet is a fundamental space for work and life and, at the same time, it has become a space where they are increasingly under threat. A 2017 global survey report, for example, found that respondents are avid users of email (especially Gmail), social networks (especially Facebook), and instant messaging (especially WhatsApp). Yet participants also feel unsafe online, particularly on Facebook with its lack of transparency on personal data use. Sexual rights activists, mostly LGBTQI+ respondents, are wary about state and nonstate regulations, for instance, against pornography, prostitution, and other "harmful content" that construct women, nonbinary individuals, and children as vulnerable and helpless under a veil of morality that acts "as a strategic argument to justify interference with the online activities of groups already discriminated against offline."[29]

In the introduction to the report *EROTICS South Asia Exploratory Research: Sex, Rights and the Internet,* hvale vale explains the importance of the right to sexuality online: "The right to sexuality in_on [*sic*] the internet is a way of expressing the self and represents at the same time exploration, affirmation, resistance and transformation. We all need to understand it and stand by it. Support should not be denied and should be the political practice of any advocate."[30] Their approach to sexuality is grounded in intersectionality. Max, one of the coordinators of the first phase of the EROTICS Project, told me that the project seeks to support insurgent sexualities: non-normative and dissident sexual practices and ways of being considered abject by cis-heteronormativity, white supremacy, religion, and empire:

> The research looked at women's usage of the internet; it looked at sexual expression, particularly at marginalized sexual expression. I remember in Brazil there was research around the BDSM community [bondage and discipline, sadism and masochism]; in Lebanon it was the LGBTQ community; in India it was young women in urban areas using the internet to talk about their sexuality; in South Africa it was looking at lesbians and chat rooms. We found through the research that actually sexual minorities and women and young people were using the internet to explore questions around their sexual identities and their desires.

Max confirms the need to do work on sexuality, pleasure, and technology that goes beyond policing and regulation. EROTICS thus delivers a potent transnational collection of data, analysis, and strategies not on the need to protect "vulnerable" subjects but rather on the right to express pleasure online as a fundamental human right. It unveils a sexual politic anchored in the global South that builds on the internet as a vital sexual dimension of people's lives.

The Feminist Principles of the Internet

APC WRP's Feminist Principles of the Internet (FPIs) is an evolving set of ideas, values, and principles "that offer a gender and sexual rights lens on critical internet-related rights" to #imagineafeministinternet. The document—an outcome of EROTICS research—is an invaluable road map to imagine a feminist internet critical of the capitalist dynamics

111

driving technologies—racism, cis- and heteronormativity, ableism, and misogyny—that contributes to movement building. The goal is to offer a framework for women's movements to explore the intersection of technology and power. These principles are less palatable to mainstream development and funding agencies because of their feminist radical vision, yet true to APC WRP's politics. Fifty activists collectively authored the Feminist Principles at APC's Global Meeting on Gender, Sexuality, and the Internet in Malaysia in 2014, which were expanded at subsequent meetings in Malaysia in 2015, 2017, and 2022.

The principles are a step toward integrating activism on online violence with a powerful intersectional perspective. APC WRP's idea of a feminist internet is one that "works towards empowering more women and queer persons—in all our diversities—to fully enjoy our rights, engage in pleasure and play, and dismantle patriarchy. This integrates our different realities, contexts and specificities including age, disabilities, sexualities, gender identities and expressions, socioeconomic locations, political and religious beliefs, ethnic origins, and racial markers."[31] The FPIs cover a range of issues. The document includes seventeen principles, organized into five major clusters: Access, Movements, Economy, Expression, and Embodiment.[32] In each cluster are a series of related principles, such as resistance, open source, pornography, consent, privacy and data, and violence. The principles are critical of "the capitalist logic that drives technology" and embrace the internet as a "transformative political space" for feminist movement building and resistance.[33] The clusters Expression and Embodiment specifically address women's and queer pleasure and desire as fundamental internet rights.

Embodiment

What does "embodiment" mean as a feminist tactic of resistance in the context of online activism from the global South? The internet has been generally considered as a disembodied and deterritorialized space. The possibility of disembodiment on the internet has provided individuals and historically marginalized communities opportunities to express themselves freely.[34] But viewing the internet as a uniquely disembodied space can also obscure how bodies are affected throughout the production, maintenance, moderation, consumption, uses, and disposal of technologies. Individuals engage in labor at every stage in these processes—overwhelmingly precarious, exploitative, and extractive labor.[35] APC WRP proposes that the internet in itself is a space of embodiment (which should not be conflated with the right to remain anonymous online, one of the FPIs). Both bodies and territories are traversed and affected by technologies.

APC WRP's principle of embodiment states: "The feminist principles on embodiment looks at our diverse experiences and relationships as human beings embodying multiple identities and realities in 'disembodied' online spaces." On the internet, which is intervened by a series of transnational corporate, state, and individual practices, bodies are also targets of violence, surveillance, and data extraction. The embodiment cluster has six principles having to do with consent, privacy and data, memory, anonymity, children, and violence. In an article on APC WRP's website, genderit.org, activist Shivani Lal explains how, after participating in a workshop in Malaysia about the FPIs, they were enthralled with the idea of embodiment vis-à-vis the ways in which the internet has been theorized as a disembodied space:

> We had a session on movement building, and one of the participants said, "Organising and resistance is about relationships"—it's about feeling, sensing and processing emotions. When a troll threatens me online, I physically feel scared. When I see art and poetry by protesters online, I feel a sense of power and I get goosebumps. When I retweet and someone tells me that's "slacktivism," I feel rage. We also talked about the importance of self-care and taking a break and reflecting on our needs as a group and as individuals, to recharge to get back at it again. It's important to acknowledge our embodiment—and this too is an act of resistance, especially when the rest of the world tells you otherwise.[36]

Saldroite, a Cairo-based writer, editor, and researcher, writes on genderit.org in a post titled "Queer Lust and Internet Orgasms" about their embodied experiences of pleasure in their journey of experimentation with alt-porn online: "I was navigating the internet like I was navigating life with so much passion and hunger for knowledge and pleasure. . . . I didn't know the possibilities of Tumblr until I joined it. I thought I was doing it for my writing, but I was fascinated by the politics, the queerness, the sex, the anonymity of queer lovers struggling in their poly-amory relationships and their queerness."[37]

Lal's and Saldroite's testimonies on online pleasure and embodiment speak to the ways in which bodies—mostly Indigenous, Black, Brown, poor, disabled, LGBTQI+, women's, and feminized—have historically been at the center of violence, struggle, and resistance. State and nonstate actors engage in practices of material and symbolic dispossession and extraction of these bodies in the name of progress, development, and modernity. Gender-based violence is intrinsic to modernity/coloniality, in what María Lugones defines as the "coloniality of gender," which is not to deny that patriarchal relations existed in other forms in precolonial times.[38]

Indigenous community feminists in Latin America—called Abya Yala by some Indigenous peoples—have been making the body-territory connection for many years now.[39] Lorena Cabnal explains that "the oppressions of the patriarchal, colonial, and racist system have been built on bodies," but "the body is also the source of the vital energy of emancipation, rebelliousness, transgression, resistances, of eroticism as a vital energy."[40] In her groundbreaking book *Feminismos diversos: El feminismo comunitario*, Cabnal explains the Xinca-Mayan feminist epistemology of the body-territory and the importance of "recovering the body" as a site of Indigenous political struggle and pleasure:

> Recovering and defending the body also involves consciously provoking the dismantling of the male pacts with which we coexist; it implies questioning and provoking the dismantling of our female bodies for their freedom. It is an approach that invites us to recover the body to promote life in dignity from a specific place, to recognize its historical resistance and its dimensions of transgressive, transforming, and creative power. Part of the recovery of the cosmic body memory of the ancestors, to gradually weave their own history from their particular body memory, and how they decide to relate to others. To feel, think, decide, and act from internalizing new practices such as autoeroticism, the enjoyment of the sexual dimension in freedom, pleasure, art, words, leisure, and rest, inner healing, rebellion, joy.[41]

Bodies—axes of thoughts, emotions, memories, and materiality—are interwoven with the internet and digital technologies as sites of struggle, and these experiences are lived in particular ways because these bodies are intersected by race, gender, class, sexuality, and ability. The feminist and race digital sociologist Jesse Daniels found that "the impact of digital technologies on self-identified women's lives is grounded in materiality and embodiment."[42]

The focus on embodiment is central to APC WRP's positionality as thinking from the global South, from a particular standpoint that it considers has been persistently made invisible in technology conversations in the North. When asked what a "Southern perspective" means in the WRP's work, Changeling (one of the activists who works closely with the EROTICS Project) told me in a June 3, 2019, email:

> It is about recognizing the importance of embodiment where the practice of intersectionality is the lived experience of structural discriminations that women and gender plural subjects experience every day. It is the practice of decolonizing and decentralizing vs. the centrality of Silicon Valley's technology overwhelming white man discourse. It is about naming privilege and whiteness, making spaces for a collaborative self instead of a competitive one. It is about empathy and recognition of vulnerability as a condition of activism but also solidarity as a response and a practice of political engagement.

Sexualities are embodied experiences, and this does not conflict with embracing social constructionist and performative frameworks of feminist and liberatory politics. Sexualities in all their manifestations (but, again, mostly non-normative and dissident sexualities) have borne the brunt of stigmatization and dispossession. Disciplining sexualities, controlling their reproduction, and the labor of these bodies has been often central to colonial-capitalist projects as well as to mainstream development agendas.[43]

Amid the incessant attempts to destroy bodies, Sayak Valencia calls for a resurgence of new forms of resistance amid violence that produces "new methods for the use of the body, power, and desire."[44] I propose that a "method"—not necessarily new but reenvisioned—for thriving amid violence is fostering pleasure and joy. Being able to feel and enjoy pleasure—as eroticism as well as spirituality, connection, joy, and even rage—is a threat to racist, misogynist, LGBTQI+-phobic forms of power and violence. Pleasure is a political framework that mobilizes embodied ways of being and thinking, remaking the possibilities of life in the midst of socioeconomic and ecological crises. Pleasure is crucial for that "politics of connections" that Rita Laura Segato argues is the key to build better worlds.[45] In a phone interview in 2020, APC WRP activist Camelia stressed that the importance of embodiment is the impetus behind the principles:

> The struggle is not one-sided nor simply reactive in the sense of women not suffering online VAW [violence against women] or VAW—the fight is about women living empowered and in plenitude. This entails owning and unapologetically exercising practices that position us as sexual beings, with desires, needs and deserving pleasure and fun as well. It is about us women moving ourselves from our reproductive place and claiming back what is ours: starting with our very own bodies! That is why the feminist internet framework is comprehensive and brings together all these facets.

Changeling argues that APC WRP's feminist politics and initiatives centralize the importance of creativity, rather than uniquely "responding to threats." Nevertheless, Changeling explains that feminists have had to devote most of their time and energies responding to violence amid the absence of institutional and social support. And yet, as Changeling wrote in a June 3, 2019, email, they are optimistic: "Movements like #metoo push the agenda. At the same time the internet remains a place of exploration and the awareness of the many selves, the understanding of the powers of the internet make activists, WHRD [women human rights defenders], feminists, continue their work of naming and creating. Building memories, and providing discourses and narratives that are not a response to a threat but the collective and continuous displaying of the many realities we all inhabit, and we all share, and constantly re-invent."

APC WRP's emphasis on pleasure, also a deeply embodied experience, is an act of defiance that "resists disappearance," as gender theorist Judith Butler argues in their analysis of the body as protest: "These bodies exist still, which is to say that they persist under conditions in which their very power to persist is systematically undermined."[46] Placing the body at the center of our technologies is thus also part of defending life. Silvia Federici explains that capitalism has historically dispossessed women's bodies and knowledges and exploited the gendered labor of the reproduction of life.[47] Digital technologies are increasingly part of this system that thrives on both the destruction and exploitation of life. Thus, according to Raquel Gutiérrez Aguilar, the "defense of life is an intransigent refusal of the negation of dignified life and a rejection of the death imposed by the destruction of the necessary conditions for—human and nonhuman—reproduction, caused by the intensified cycles of capital accumulation."[48]

The defense of life is in conflict with capitalism, and yet (not surprisingly) we continue to see that state and transnational institutions focus on technology as a tool for life via capitalist economic growth. Julia commented on this emphasis: "I know I am going to sound like a raging radical feminist, but this particular approach of economic empowerment is supporting a very particular world order of neoliberalism. This is not a surprise. Tech is changing women's lives. Look at them. They have more money, they are continuing to support an economic model that keeps them in the same place. . . . Why aren't we talking about entrepreneurialism on a different scale? Because this all fits in a capitalistic logic. I didn't want to say that!" Fostering online sexuality and pleasure advances imaginaries and visions that create an *otherwise*. APC WRP, along with many other feminist organizations in the global South, contests the numerous forms of social, political, and economic violence percolating the sociotechnical realm. In a "reversal" of the Northern, male-dominated technological gaze, APC WRP activists reappropriate technological spaces to support non-normative manifestations of pleasure.

Amid violence there are spaces for liberatory practices. Decolonial scholar Catherine Walsh puts forth various "contexts and spheres of collective insurgent praxis" such as life, territory, and gender.[49] I add technology to this list. Pétalo, a journalist and activist who has collaborated with APC conducting research, workshops, and trainings, told me that "to decolonize our bodies and our territories, we must empower ourselves with technology. We have to be creators. We have to understand how these tools are created because colonialism also cuts through information." The activism of APC WRP against online gender-based violence foregrounds pleasure, advancing a project of life amid violence (figure 3). I believe that its activism around sexuality, pleasure, and technology is its most radical contribution yet.

117

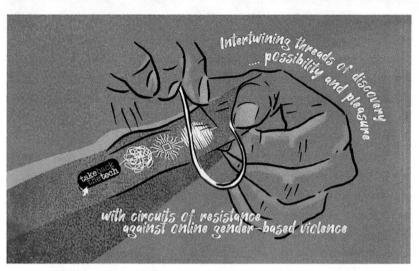

FIGURE 3. Image by Ezrena Marwan launched during APC WRP's 2020 global Take Back the Tech campaign. Courtesy: APC WRP. Reprinted with permission.

Connecting the Dots: Looking at Online Gender-Based Violence from the South

Online gender-based violence is generally viewed as an isolated act perpetrated by (mostly) abusive men as partners, ex-partners, trolls, and mobs, among other configurations. But the contention that intimate violence is interconnected with other structures of power has been a fundamental feminist argument in the study of violence: theorizing intimate forms of violence must include examining the numerous webs of violence in which intimacy is embedded.[50] The feminist slogan "The personal is political" evokes that what happens in our lives—be it in our homes, communities, or workplaces, or on the streets—is a political issue that must concern the state and other institutions. A Southern epistemology exposes the connections of intimate violence to colonial and capitalist logics. APC WRP's global and grassroots activism against online violence connects the intimate to the structural, aiming to shift narratives, "discourses, norms," as Min explained.

A Southern perspective moves beyond simplistic narratives of digital inclusion. Many activists instead follow a multidimensional framework, contextualizing online gender-based violence within institutional violence, speaking about power, misogyny, racism, ableism, and LGBTQI+ phobia.[51] They situate violence within transnational, corporate, and state spheres, thus breaking with individually focused and cultural explanations. By referring to the myriad of social, political, and affective relationships between women, queer people, and digital technologies, APC WRP activists move beyond the figure of the caring/economic Third World Technological Woman. In an interview, Max described the typical global North and liberal narrative:

> Usually, a lot of the discourse is about white women who are getting harassed. And liberal approaches to dealing with the problem, as if it's isolated cases, as if it's not structural, as if it's not connected, as if patriarchy is not connected to racism, or to colonialism, or to heteronormativity. So, both at the level of analysis and at the level of solutions, we find some problematic ways of dealing with these solutions. And then the fact that they're not really interested in women of the global South, who are the majority of women dealing with these issues. They mostly seem to be focused on Northern women experiencing violence.

Max told me that UN Women and other state and transnational actors started paying attention to online gender-based violence recently, but the focus is always "neoliberal" and market-oriented. "So, when it's not an approach that challenges capitalist models of economy online," Max said, "it doesn't get to the root of the problem. For example, having to deal with social network companies like Facebook, Twitter, and Google, whose primary concern is always profit, it becomes different to ask them to reform their policies so that women don't experience violence. Usually, it benefits white women."

Max is critical of focusing on the criminal legal system as a space for accountability or playing into the scripts of protection and victimhood of states and corporations. Max explained APC WRP's multilayered analysis of online gender-based violence anchored in the global South:

> Sometimes activism around gender-based violence is done in a way that is convenient to governments and corporations and to religious institutions. These are three huge structures that are very patriarchal and very capitalist and very hegemonic, you know? So, the sort of activism that doesn't disrupt these structures, or challenge them, is very

liberal, reformist activism that doesn't get to the root of the problem. So, I think the value of APC's work is that it's always grounded in the global South; it's grounded in our own contexts, which are all postcolonial contexts, struggling economies, dictatorships, war areas. And these are the contexts in which women are also struggling with this familiar but new problem of online violence against women.

Max's arguments speak to how Gutiérrez Aguilar explains that violence against women is a part of the "triangular amalgam" of "expropriation, exploitation, and domination" that "weaves together patriarchy, capitalism, and colonialism."[52] This web of violence does not preclude the fact that most of these forms of violence are perpetrated by men.[53] But making these connections visible and central to feminist struggles condemns the increasingly vicious violence against women's and feminized bodies, particularly on Black, Indigenous, and nonbinary and trans bodies, while also denouncing the responsibility of a vast web of capitalist-colonial violence.

Similarly, feminist political theorist and activist Verónica Gago argues that the feminist coalitional politics that have emerged during the strikes and protests in Argentina since 2017 have made the threads of violence visible, "pluralizing" the "meanings of sexist violence by mapping its *simultaneity* and its *interrelation*" and transcending liberal politics of recognition, inclusion, and rights.[54] Gago's analysis of violence is expansive, linking the disintegration of the home with the dispossession of land, the wage gap, and invisibilized domestic work with austerity policies and financial exploitation through debt, state repression, and persecution of migrants with the imprisonment of women who have abortions, and the increasingly vicious nature of violence against women's and feminized bodies, in a vast web where each has a "racist imprint."[55] Colonialism and capitalism are deeply gendered, misogynist, and racist projects.

The global North dominates conversations on online gender-based violence mostly committed through US-based corporate social media platforms such as Twitter and Facebook. APC WRP challenges that narrative, according to Amelia, former Take Back the Tech coordinator:

120

It is great that it's turning into a big conversation, but it's still very dominated by North America and Western Europe. And part of that is these major platforms. That's where they're located; that's where they're headquartered; that's where they can be held accountable. But then that just means that the stories that come out tend to revolve around people in that part of the world. And what we know is that of course women in the global South are experiencing this too, sometimes at higher rates and sometimes in different ways than women in the North are experiencing.

APC WRP is thus emphatic on maintaining a perspective anchored in the South. Camelia stressed the interrelated elements constituting online gender-based violence particular to the South:

> Our focus is the global South, and it is part of a political institutional-wide approach. When it comes to online GBV, we consider this problematic in the context of many others we work with also focused in the global South: access to the internet (not only connectivity but also addressing language barriers, sociocultural background, digital literacy, etc.), internet governance, internet rights, use and development, etc.—all built around and within the feminist internet framework. We can't consider all these in isolation, but as a very complex and interrelated compendium of issues that influence one another.

The exploitation of women's bodies, knowledges, and labor is intrinsic to the advancement of capitalism, according to Federici, replacing the commons (common lands) after being privatized in the transition from feudalism to capitalism in Europe in the 1600s.[56] Women's bodies have been "the primary ground of exploitation and resistance in capitalism."[57] The incessant need to accumulate capital at all costs has only grown, entering into what Segato calls an "apocalyptic phase of capitalism."[58] In this phase, again, women's bodies are marked—literally, according to Segato—as sites of increasingly cruel forms of violence.[59] Corporatized digital technologies form part of this interconnected network of violence. For decades, communities as well as activists have been denouncing how the private sector profits from death, violence, and misinformation. In the big tech sector, the revelations of the ways in

121

which Meta literally profits from violence are only the most recent confirmation of a long list of how online violence is commoditized.[60]

Of course, this does not mean that online gender-based violence is uniquely connected to technocapitalism, but rather that it is inherently connected to technocapitalism. As Segato emphatically states: "We have to withdraw the problem of women from the ghetto, and rather think about it as interwoven, as the foundation and elementary pedagogy of all other forms of power and subordination: racial, imperial, colonial, of center-periphery relationships, of eurocentrism with other civilizations, of class relationships."[61] Feminist anti-racist and decolonial scholar-activists such as Ochy Curiel and Yuderkys Espinosa Miñoso have amply theorized the imbrication of gender, race, and colonialism in Latin America and the Caribbean.[62] I posit that these analyses are also crucial for comprehending and approaching digital violence.

What Is Online Gender-Based Violence?

Violence that happens online is particularly interesting because it's an exaggerated form of patriarchy, so you can see some of the things people no longer say, you know, in real life . . . [they] find some freedom to say it online. And I think that's good and it's interesting, although it can be harmful. Because it helps us sort of look at patriarchy under a magnifying glass.

—MAX, APC WRP ACTIVIST

APC WRP defines online gender-based violence as "online harassment, cyber stalking, attacks on [people's] sexuality, exposure of personal information, threats based on morality or religion, manipulation of images, nonconsensual distribution of intimate images or distribution 'sex videos' that are used for blackmail and can result in repeated trauma every time they are reposted online" that can be an extension of social, economic, and political forms of gender discrimination as well as of intimate partner violence."[63] Until 2015 the organization used the term *technology-related violence* to convey that digital violence can affect women even if they are not online. But it decided to change the term— for the moment, as all these concepts are constantly evolving—to *online*

122

gender-based violence to "communicate our intersectional understand-ing of violence against women which considers race, class, sexuality, age and other locations." The change in terminology also reflects the find-ings of its research on sexuality and the internet and has become more commonly used.[64] But online-gender based violence includes technology-facilitated violence that abusers deploy, such as "stalkerware" (software used to spy and torment victims).[65] Gender-based violence is not new, of course, but technology facilitates and amplifies its searchability, scal-ability, replicability, and permanence.

Online gender-based violence consistently targets the most margin-alized women: Black, LGBTQI+, disabled, and young women.[66] And online misogyny mostly consists of sexual attacks, targeting women for being women, Black women for being Black women, and so on in an endless assault on historically marginalized identities and bodies.[67] It can be perpetrated by individuals or take the form of "networked ha-rassment."[68] Online gender-based violence is a global problem according to the data available across countries.[69] Various global and local reports have found that journalists, human rights defenders, many of whom are Indigenous defenders of the land, and political candidates who identify as women are increasingly targets of online gender-based violence.[70] Online violence has only increased during the COVID-19 pandemic that started in late 2019, as have gender violence and femicide in general.[71]

Feminist activists and scholars alike have insisted on the importance of dismantling the online/offline binary, revealing the ways online vio-lence affects the lives of survivors and how it is part of a continuum of the misogynistic practices that structure our societies.[72] In the literature on online violence, specifically, dismantling the online/offline binary emphasizes the importance of acknowledging that online gender-based violence is real, that the online often quite literally harms people's lives offline, and that its origins and consequences are part and parcel of the pervasive violence against women and girls in the world. Yet I argue that dismantling the online/offline binary must go beyond this analysis. Online gender-based violence is also part of a sociotechnical capitalist-colonial apparatus that preys on life. APC WRP's perspective anchored in the South opens up these layers of analysis, as I detail below.

123

Recognizing the harm that online gender-based violence causes is fundamental for understanding its consequences in victim's lives. Advancing pleasure as a political framework does not mean to "set up pleasure as a new standard either, and space must be provided for trauma and tears."[73] APC WRP mentions some forms of harm that participants have disclosed in its research, such as psychological/emotional harm (depression, anxiety, suicidal thoughts), social isolation (withdrawing from public life, family, and friends due to feelings of shame and humiliation), economic loss (losing jobs), limited mobility (not feeling they can engage in online/offline activities), and self-censorship/chilling freedom of expression in fear of further victimization. APC WRP makes a series of recommendations to states and transnational actors, such as the United Nations—which in recent years has exponentially increased the number of resolutions against online gender-based violence—and to the private sector, mostly corporate internet intermediaries and social media platforms like Meta, Twitter, and Google.[74]

Its recommendations, detailed in its submission to the United Nations Special Rapporteur on Violence against Women in 2018, include, for states, developing a comprehensive and accurate definition of online gender-based violence, passing adequate legislation that protects women's freedom of expression and affirms their bodily autonomy and self-determination, supporting anonymity and encryption, promoting means of swift redress and reparations, and training for members of the law enforcement and judiciary system. For internet intermediaries, it recommends ensuring data security and privacy "by design" and preventing online gender-based violence.[75]

Opposing harms, threats, and danger is part of APC WRP's advocacy, and yet Julia explained to me in an interview in 2015 that agency is what should be centered:

> Our responsibility is to go back to the early thinking around technology around TBTT [Take Back the Tech], which is yes, we need to address VAW [violence against women], but in a way that centralizes women's agency and freedom and the transformative potential of technology. That is the shift—discursively that is how we need to shift the conversation; that needs to be the entry point.

Not the internet is a bad place, not tech makes everything worse for women, the dark side. . . . For me politically, we are at a moment in our work where we have an obligation to reinsert this into the conversation because we have been responsible for shaping the conversation. We have the obligation now to adjust this, to talk about freedoms, possibilities, and transformation outside of violence against women.

Pleasure and agency often lie at the edge of violence, harm, and trauma. Feminist technopolitics of care are irremediably entangled with violence in one way or another, as well as with the consequences of violence, one of which is criminalization.

The Dilemma of Criminalization

APC WRP, like scholars, organizations, and activists working against online gender-based violence in the global South and North alike, considers some thorny issues in its recommendations to state and nonstate institutions, such as anonymity and freedom of expression. Both principles are at the forefront of APC WRP's activism, but these rights have also been deployed to protect perpetrators. I consider here a specific and crucial challenge: advancing legislation that criminalizes online gender-based violence.[76] I focus on this issue due to the important feminist critiques, particularly from abolitionist Black women and women of color in the United States and the global South, of the ways in which feminist antiviolence movements have dovetailed with feeding the prison industrial complex and furthering racist neoliberal politics, while neglecting an intersectional analysis and praxis that attends to the socioeconomic and political structures that enable and produce violence against women, transwomen, and feminized bodies.[77] The result has led to high rates of incarceration of mostly poor Black and Brown men and women, the decimation of the fabric of entire communities, and the individualization (mostly through targeting individual men) of a much broader structural-political problem.[78]

In recent years, numerous countries in Europe, as well as Australia, Canada, Israel, Japan, and the Philippines, have passed laws specifically against online gender-based violence, mostly criminalizing the nonconsensual distribution of intimate images or image-based abuse, generally called by the misnomer "revenge porn."[79] In the United States forty-eight states and Washington, DC, and Guam have passed legislation against the nonconsensual distribution of intimate images, and the first federal law against "nonconsensual pornography" awaited voting in the Senate in 2022 after being passed by the House of Representatives as part of the Violence Against Women Reauthorization Act of 2021.[80] In Latin America there is a wealth of jurisprudence on the issue as well as bills under consideration.[81] Peru, El Salvador, Ecuador, Dominican Republic, Puerto Rico, and Mexico have passed specific legislation against "revenge porn."[82] In Mexico the "Olympia Law," named after a victim of online violence, was first passed in the state of Mexico in 2019, then in twenty-nine more states, and in 2021 it became a federal law.[83] Recently, in the absence of state response, other forms of accountability have emerged through social media, such as online lists of perpetrators often accused anonymously. Scholars such as Segato and Gutiérrez Aguilar have been debating the consequences of these lists and what it means for feminists to practice models of justice that are punitive, like those of the state.[84]

Many activists have advocated for criminalization, but they have also pointed out serious problems: the lack of state preventative strategies such as education, the focus on punitive measures instead of remedies and reparations and a holistic vision against violence, the limited access to justice for the most marginalized individuals, the general reigning of impunity, the dangers of state protectionism and intervention, and the fact that many states already have laws that could be used to punish online gender-based violence.[85] And yet legislation is advancing globally, and calls for broader, stronger, and more coherent laws to criminalize online gender-based violence continue.[86] In an interview via Zoom in 2021, longtime APC WRP activist Keila told me that criminalization has been one of the "unintended consequences" of their work against online gender-based violence, when their objective has always been to show that "online gender-based violence does not happen in a fucking vacuum!"

This conflict is particularly challenging for APC WRP, an organization that has consistently framed online gender-based violence within what sociologist Patricia Hill Collins calls a "matrix of oppression" moving away from quick fixes to profound problems.[87] APC WRP has also taken a stance against state interventions in the internet, which often curtail freedoms and opportunities for self-determination under the guise of protection. In its submission to the UN Special Rapporteur on Violence against Women, the organization states: "Given patriarchal and racist judicial systems where impunity is more common than justice, there is the possibility of new laws being used against those vulnerable communities it was designed to protect."[88] In an interview in 2015, Max argued:

> The fact is there's no one solution to such a systemic problem. But there are solutions that women use that are very strong solutions, like bringing together a community to support someone who has suffered from this violence. Using different strategies, some people want to reply and fight back, some people want to counter the narrative with different content, some people create more projects out of these issues. Some people just ignore the violence and just carry on, you know? And I think all these approaches are solid and important. And I think from my own experiences with online violence, the thing that matters most of all is not being able to sue the perpetrator or being able to call the police or being able to block the content. All of this doesn't matter as much as feeling a sense of support from my community.

Intersectional analyses of the harms of online gender-based violence also need intersectional and transformative proposals to eradicate these harms.[89] This is sorely missing from the broader conversation on online gender-based violence.

Grassroots and community-based initiatives that support victims and survivors of online gender-based violence beyond state criminalization have flourished in Latin America, such as *líneas de ayuda y acompañamiento* (help lines, where victims find activists who support them throughout their process), trainings and workshops on "digital self-defense," online campaigns, and the creation of spaces for collective care. In recent years in Latin America, many grassroots organizations and NGOs are working on issues of online violence, safety, and care—including sexuality and pleasure—such as Coding Rights and Think Olga in Brazil; Fundación Karisma in Colombia; Luchadoras, Insubordinadas, Sursiendo, Laboratorio de Interconectividades, and La Sandía Digital in Mexico; Ciberfeministas in Guatemala; Enredadas in Nicaragua; Acoso.online and the NGO Amaranta in Chile; Tédic in Paraguay (an APC member); Hiperderecho in Perú; and the regional network Ciberseguras. In 2021, the Transfeminist Digital Care Network of Brazil created Gincana Monstra, a beautiful collective online convening for mostly Black cis and trans women and non-binary individuals that enabled a "deeper exploration of feminist digital safety methodologies and infrastructures of care." The hands-on card deck Oracle for Transfeminist Technologies is another speculative feminist project that envisions more caring digital futures.[90] Feminist servers and infrastructures are emerging, such as María Lab and Vendeta in Brazil and Kéfir in Mexico. Feminist scholar-activists Joanna Varon and Paz Peña have proposed "consent" as a framework to center women and queer agency online both on issues of data.[91] There have been numerous strategies that seek justice for victims, both online and offline, some of them associated with the #MeToo movement, by using powerful hashtags in what has been called "hashtag activism."[92] Research on activism against "non-consensual pornography" in the United States found that consciousness raising, an ethics of care between activists and in their advocacy, and a shared sense of place provided the strongest bases of their activism, even when it is policy-focused.[93] Creating infrastructures of care could lead to feminist models of justice beyond criminalization.

UN Discourse on Online Gender-Based Violence

In an interview during the 59th Commission on the Status of Women (CSW) in March 2015 in New York City, a UN official warned me that she would not talk about the "whole violence against women online" issue because they still did not have an official stance—this, in spite of the fact that the 59th CSW had numerous high-level and side events on online violence against women. In recent years there has been an increase in focusing on the dangers—the "dark side"—that technology poses for women and other marginalized communities, such as online gender-based violence, surveillance, data privacy, AI biases, the platform economy, and the threats of automation for labor rights in reports, publications, and resolutions.[94] The dark side of technology is increasingly prevalent, while development institutions continue to advance market-based economic growth agendas that hinge upon the very violence they are denouncing. Violence and profit flourish in tandem. Thus this question lingers: What are we leading women into? The life of the entrepreneurial and tech-savvy Third World Technological Woman suddenly seems less rosy. The ideal entrepreneurial subject is set forth and then reclaimed; one of the many paradoxes of capitalism is this constant making and unmaking.

The 1995 Beijing Platform of Action does mention the misrepresentation, objectification, and discrimination against women in the media.[95] But with the informational technological shift in the first decade of the 2000s, the intersection between violence and digital technologies was mostly mentioned in tandem with trafficking and sexual exploitation enabled by technology, with some reports addressing online sexual harassment and cyberbullying.[96] The "trafficking-technology nexus" particularly buys into moral panics that often rely on dubious data, pigeonhole women as victims, advance a carceral punitive agenda, and cause a chilling effect for sexual agency.[97] The UN launched its first full report on violence against women online in September 2015, titled *Cyberviolence Against Women and Girls: A World-Wide Wake-Up Call.*[98] It was immediately criticized by some high-profile victims of online violence, such as game developer Zoe Quinn, mostly for its faulty research, for conflating trafficking with sex work and pornography; overemphasizing legal remedies, criminalization, and policing; and for being vague and superficial in its recommendations.[99] The report included citations from APC's work and collaborations with some well-known experts such as Nancy Hafkin. The UN apologized for "several errors" and "poorly sourced material" in the report, and it was taken offline (the executive summary is available on the Broadband Commission's publi-

129

cations website).[100] Hesitancy about the now mainstream issue of online gender-based violence was evident.

Tensions around activism against online violence were palpable during my research. In one interview, a veteran feminist and technology activist told me, "The whole violence online thing scares women away, just when we want them to embrace technology." Another activist said, "The violence issue is important, but I think it scares women off," adding, "This is not an issue for all of us [working on gender and technology]." Within APC WRP there is concern about the inclusion and framing of online gender-based violence in UN discourse. And there is also ambivalence: inclusion can make an important issue visible, while simultaneously depoliticizing it. Activists are proud that they have been able to advance discourse and policy related to online violence. However, some are uneasy with increasing cooptation of their work by development institutions and corporations and the creation of a singular discourse on violence against women online. They worry about the absence in public discourse of fun, play, curiosity, and freedom as other possibilities at the intersection of gender and technology.

Julia, a crucial figure in APC WRP's activism on violence against women online, was very honest in our interview:

> In the last two years, I have been increasingly worried that we have overprivileged VAWO [violence against women online] as an issue in the context of technology. And that overprivilege has resulted in a few things, like we see in this meeting [the 59th CSW], the interest around tech is violence, not around transformation and freedoms, which is what we talk about when we talk about tech. We are also responsible for this. If I can claim that VAWO is on the agenda because of us, I also have to claim that freedom and transformation through tech are not on the agenda because that is a decision that we made.

Julia believes that APC WRP "overprivileged" online gender-based violence when its intent was to open a range of conversations around technology, feminism, and social justice. Its advocacy against online violence initiated transnational conversations around gender and technology beyond simplistic economic and market-oriented frameworks. Yet inclusion in the "mainstream" leaves out the socioeconomic, political,

130

and historical contexts that APC WRP has centralized. Julia hits on an important point when she says that online misogyny blends comfortably into global activism against violence against women: "In hindsight, I don't think we should have done anything different, but I think the overprivileging of VAWO is not only about tech but about feminism and the women's movement, because it's always there, not only in the North or South, but generally. It is always being privileged and we have done exactly the same thing."

Julia argues that the future of APC WRP is to continue to work on violence against women and online gender-based violence, "but in a way that centralizes women's agency and freedom and the transformative potential of technology." This is the shift that needs to be the "entry point," she adds. There comes a moment when organizations that want to remain radical have to revise their objectives. Speaking to this dilemma, Min told me that she was very proud of their activism against online violence, emphasizing that it is about women "reclaiming power" over the internet and technology. But back in 2015, she had started to worry that violence would dominate public discussions on gender and technology:

> We started this work in 2005, so it's taken ten years for it to get the kind of formal recognition that it has now. And the work isn't over. I mean you only have some mention of it in policy documents here and there . . . but you still don't have this kind of overview of saying, actually, online violence against women is part of the larger rubric of violence against women. . . . So, in that sense it's still something that's slowly, that's starting to be visible. And starting to have recognition. And starting to have some serious responses. And I think that is a good thing. But it cannot be the only thing.

When institutions tackle issues around violence, they often treat it as an isolated category that becomes decontextualized, depoliticized, and even spectacularized to further particular agendas. In an interview at the 59th Commission on the Status of Women in 2015, APC WRP's project associate, Laura, said that "focusing just on violence is unproductive." She said that although it seems that its focus has been on online violence, it centered voice, the power of storytelling, and the transforma tion of unequal power relationships. APC WRP activists are very proud of their activism, while also recognizing the limitations and unintended consequences.

What will happen if the UN incorporates pleasure as a technopolitical framework? This is an open question. The capacity of capitalism to "include" under the guise of social justice and transformation is constant and endless. Thus the making, unmaking, and remaking of the Third World Technological Woman is always in process.

Conclusion

In the midst of increasing violence, APC WRP is reimagining the internet as a feminist space that enables different ways of thinking and being. The emphasis on fun, pleasure, and play forms a vital part of its commitment to transform bodies, relationships, and technologies. Pleasure as a feminist technopolitical strategy against online gender-based violence manifests through two of its main projects: the EROTICS Project and the evolving Feminist Principles of the Internet initiative. APC WRP's commitment against online violence is expansive, connecting the intimate to the structural, anchored in a Southern perspective that makes these threads visible and concrete. The body—intersected by race, class, sexuality, ability, geopolitics, and ability—lies at a central site of its activism. It is difficult to think about pleasure—or about violence—without considering embodiment. Moreover, bodies, mostly dissident and historically oppressed, are entwined with the internet and digital technologies as locations of struggle.

Pleasure as a feminist technopolitical tactic turns "the knowledge of the body into power" through a "politics of connections" that defies violence.[101] But pleasure is also entangled with violence, danger, and risk, thus exposing the tensions that feminist activists navigate. Part of the technopolitical work of pleasure—and care—is understanding the differential experiences, the power relations, and the harms, while breaking away from tropes of victimization, in what Payal Arora and Rumman Chowdhury call part of a "cross-cultural femtech framework."[102] The feminist work of pleasure is to confront these power relationships as well as expand the spaces in which pleasure can be truly liberatory.

Violence is extremely complex. Struggles against violence are never straightforward, easy, or simple. The state—as well as some social movements—has deployed criminalization, incarceration, and punitive measures as policies and tactics against "crime." This has not produced safer or more peaceful societies. For years, Black and Brown scholars and activists have analyzed the devastating effects that punishment and incarceration have had on oppressed communities. They have led the way in proposing alternatives that can transform victims, perpetrators, and communities without feeding into the neoliberal frenzy of mass incarceration of Black and Brown people. APC WRP has had to face the dilemma of advocating against online gender-based violence through punitive global and local policies and laws, while at the same time focusing on community-based solutions. This is a prevalent tension in feminist digital activism that requires further reflection and debate.

FOUR

Uneasy Alliances

During a meeting of feminist digital activists and scholars of Latin America, the organizers asked us to write on a sticky note the name of a technology-focused organization we admired and put it on the wall. We were then asked to sift through the sticky notes and make comments on them if we wished. I was surprised when I saw that on my sticky note—on which I had written the name of the feminist cooperative Sulá Batsú—someone had written: "We do not like Sulá Batsú because they receive money from Google." I felt confused and frustrated. Having studied Sulá Batsú since 2015, I knew it was a feminist organization with a deep commitment to social justice, even with its contradictions.

That moment sparked the idea of writing this chapter on the negotiations feminist activists make to be able to do their work. These choices, which are also shaped by broader institutional and structural forces, are riddled with conflict and constitute what Ann Shola Orloff, Raka Ray, and Evren Savci have called "uneasy alliances."[1] This chapter considers questions such as, What would feminist justice look like if we transcend binaries between autonomy and co-optation, the feminist and the non-feminist? How do feminist activists cultivate a politics of care and connections when having to depend on problematic funding to sustain their work? The Third World Technological Woman is also made and unmade in decisions about funding.

134

For decades, scholars and activists have had debates on the role of non-governmental organizations (NGOs) in social movements and liberatory politics.[2] The meteoric rise of NGOs in the 1980s and 1990s provided an ideal organizational structure for the global advancement of neoliberal policies with the withdrawal of vital state protections, leaving the most oppressed communities even more vulnerable. NGOs were to replace these protections with services. Organizations transformed from more grassroots, horizontal, and organic forms into professionalized, hierarchical, and managerial structures in which labor was increasingly bureaucratized and focused on outcomes, rapid solutions, and evidence of results. Influenced by state and corporate funding, many organizations distanced themselves from more radical politics and the communities that they were supposed to serve.

Powerful concepts such as the "NGO-ization of resistance," as Arundhati Roy called this phenomenon, the "NGO boom," as Sonia Alvarez named it in Latin America, and the "nonprofit industrial complex," as the organization INCITE! called it have provoked invaluable critiques of co-optation, while questioning whether NGOs are able to enact radical politics focused on systemic change.[3] These pointed critiques often also recognize the contradictions, spaces of resistance, and ruptures within NGOs, leading to nuanced analyses that have increased throughout time.[4]

It is certainly both a paradox and an unfortunate consequence when feminist struggles and claims dovetail neatly with neoliberal rationalities.[5] And we have seen plenty of this, overwhelmingly in white liberal feminism's inattention to and complicity with the dismissal of issues around race and economic justice. But the organizational landscape is complex. As anthropologists Victoria Bernal and Inderpal Grewal contend: "Neoliberalism may . . . create a recognizably homogenous framework for contemporary NGOs working on women's issues, but it does not control all the practices and agendas of these organizations."[6] The boundaries between autonomy and co-optation and resistance and domination are porous, and these ambiguities have surfaced before and beyond the NGO-ization of feminist movements. In a fascinating inter-

135

view with sociologist Srila Roy about the "co-optation of feminisms," Grewal argues that various institutions co-opt feminist ideas, such as corporations, NGOs, the state, and communities, "but there was no point at which feminism was unattached to some kind of institution or organization. It was always the state, the empire, the market—so it's hard to sustain the idea of feminism as an autonomous movement."[7] Grewal contends that the focus on co-optation has also "de-authorized" certain manifestations of feminism, such as activism against sexual assault on US campuses, and interrogates judging what is classified as feminist or not. But where are the boundaries traced? How do activists negotiate? What do they simply refuse? To answer these questions it is vital to examine on-the-ground feminist politics.

Ann Shola Orloff and Talia Schiff call for contextual analyses of women's and feminist endeavors.[8] And in their examination of critiques of feminism and co-optation, Catherine Eschle and Bice Maiguashca similarly underline that "no practice should be assumed to be progressive—or not—in advance of empirical study."[9] Although Eschle and Maiguashca argue that progressive politics would be "best served" by a radical political agenda focused on systemic change, they refuse to use radicality as the only measure of feminist politics and believe that reforms could also lead to "feminist futures." In addition, we have witnessed in recent years, particularly in Latin America, the emergence of feminist radical grassroots, coalitional, and intersectional mobilizations in the streets, in assemblies, and in communities that have led to historical gains in reproductive rights and opposition to gender-based violence.[10] Thus NGO-ization has not eradicated radical and massive feminist mobilization.

NGOs and social justice organizations in general must indeed continue to be carefully scrutinized and open to critique, while we recognize and explore the cracks and possibilities within them. As scholars, it is important to examine how feminist endeavors are entangled with power as well as look at organizational practices to understand various forms of political agency.[11] I argue that there are opportunities for feminist disobedience against, within, *and* beyond neoliberal structures even when anticapitalist commitments are at the core of feminist endeavors, as this book shows. Within these complexities and ambiguities, feminist organizations contend and negotiate with an increasingly corporatized funding landscape that both presents serious ethical dilemmas as well as providing a site for creative appropriations.

The Corporatization of Development

In the past decades, particularly since the 2008 global financial crisis, there has been a shift in development financing, with increasing emphasis on public-private partnerships and more funding from the private sector, including corporations (and the expansion of "corporate social responsibility" practices), philanthropic institutions and individuals, and private foundations. These are the so-called new actors of development financing. The traditional actors are state institutions, bilateral and multilateral agencies, and some large international nongovernmental organizations (INGOs). This shift—also part of the consecration of neoliberalism as a dominant socioeconomic and political model—impacts grassroots and nonprofit organizations, particularly in the global South, as well as state policies and agendas and global governance structures such as the UN.[12] These new and old development actors are not static—some private foundations have also been traditional financers—nor monolithic. I am not presenting a binary between traditional development funders and new ones. There are tensions, negotiations, and problems with both. What is important is to understand the shifting terrain of the macro-landscapes of development financing and the ways in which activists negotiate these transformations in the face of numerous political, socioeconomic, and ecological crises.

The Association for Women's Rights in Development (AWID), a global feminist, member-based organization founded in 1982, has been conducting research since 2005—the tenth anniversary of the Beijing Conference—on the landscape of development funding and the impact on women's organizations with the project "Where Is the Money for Women's Rights?" The series of reports found that the corporatization of development has indeed shaped the administrative structures of many feminist grassroots and nonprofit organizations, imposing a limiting result-based approach to monitoring and evaluation that emphasizes narrow, individually based solutions to profound structural problems.[13]

The model follows a neoliberal results-focused approach that can be quantified and neatly categorized to the detriment of practices that center process, relationships, and the needs of communities.

The paradigmatic shift toward corporatization represents fundamentally "a change in emphasis from aid to investment."[14] It is thus unsurprising that a 2013 survey of 170 private initiatives involved in funding women's project found that most of the funded initiatives, 35 percent, focused on "women's economic empowerment and entrepreneurship," with 44 percent disbursed for "training and technical assistance."[15] But only around 27 percent of these 170 initiatives partnered with women's organizations, and only 9 percent directly funded them, instead privileging large NGOs.[16]

Although women and girls have increasingly become the face of development, a minimal amount of funds reach feminist and women-led organizations. For instance, in 2021, AWID found that 99 percent of aid and foundation grants do not reach women's rights and feminist organizations, especially affecting those for LGBTQI+ people, Indigenous people, young women, workers, refugees, and undocumented migrants in the global South.[17] In 2019, 48 percent of women's organizations in the database of the major funding organization Global Funds for Women reported that their annual budgets were US$30,000, a "moderate yet insufficient" increase from AWID's 2013 report that found that the annual median budget was US$20,000.[18] Meanwhile, funding for "anti-gender," conservative, and fundamentalist groups has steadily increased in the past years, with over US$3.7 billion in funding, more than triple what LGBTQI+ organizations received globally. The funding for women's organizations was already meager before the global "anti-gender backlash" against sexual and reproductive rights, the privatization of essential public services, union busting, tax avoidance, environmental pollution, and the extraction of natural reserves, and it has only decreased during COVID-19.[19]

In the AWID report titled *Challenging Corporate Power: Struggles for Women's Rights, Economic and Gender Justice*, Rachel Moussié argues that corporate intervention manifests in multifaceted ways: through formal institutionalized power on national policies; through "shadow power," which is not institutionalized yet impacts policies through, for example, lobbying; and through the more pernicious "invisible power" that shapes cultural norms, values, and beliefs "rooted in colonialism and imperialism" and in "white supremacy, capitalism, and patriarchy."[20] In this landscape Moussié states that "women and oppressed groups in both the global North and South feel the brunt of corporate power through deplorable working conditions, the appropriation of their land and natural resources, a lack of access to quality public services, and the invisibility of their unpaid and low paid informal work."[21]

This is the terrible bind that so many feminist organization find themselves in. On the one hand, they need funds to be able to do their work. On the other, they must negotiate beliefs when these same funders are the ones dismantling everything they are seeking to rebuild. From data extraction for profit to ecological devastation, land grabbing, dispossession and displacement, funding for reactionary policies and groups, and the predatory practices of big corporations such as Google and Meta or Exxon Mobile and Coca-Cola and of foundations such as the Bill and Melinda Gates Foundation—a major funder of the United Nations—their sources of wealth are well-known.[22] So, for example, although Melinda Gates, cochair of the Gates Foundation, pledged US$1 billion in 2019 over the ten years to "gender equality" and co-leads the UN Secretary-General's expert panel on digital transformation, the foundation's focus on techno-solutionism and population control in its health and agricultural programs undermines the socioeconomic and ecological conditions necessary for "gender equality."[23]

Private Funding of the UN

The UN system is funded through mandatory (also called "assessed") and voluntary contributions. Mandatory contributions are paid by member states in amounts decided by the General Assembly in proportion to the country's population and wealth, and voluntary contributions are from countries and other donors. In the past, voluntary contributions have steadily increased, including funding from the corporate and philanthropic sectors. All mandatory funds are for "core" contributions, which are unrestricted funds linked to multilateral mandates and strategic plans. However, and this is a vital point, voluntary contributions can be either core or non-core, meaning that they can be restricted to uses determined by the donor. The increase of voluntary contributions started in the early 1990s, and in 1997 non-core funding surpassed core contributions for the first time, "limiting the flexibility that UN entities have on the use of the funds they receive."[24]

The trend toward more voluntary contributions was heightened with the 2000–15 Millennium Development Goals and enshrined in the 2015–30 Sustainable Development Goals' emphasis on public-private partnerships framed by the Third International Conference on Financing for Development, held in Addis Ababa in July 2015. The shift to voluntary, restricted contributions was caused primarily by chronic underfunding of the UN system by traditional member states and governments, the adoption of neoliberal market-based solutions to development such as privatization and deregulation, and the 2008 global financial crisis.[25] To be clear, the largest amount of funding of the UN still comes from national governments, which can be in the form of mandatory or voluntary contributions. In 2020, according to the UN System's Financial Statistics office, the total amount of revenue for all UN institutions and entities was US$62.6 billion. Of that total, the largest amount, $38.80 billion, was from voluntary non-core contributions; $13.68 billion from assessed contributions; $5.31 billion from "revenue from other activities"; and $4.82 billion from voluntary core contributions.[26]

As a comparison, in 2010, for the total UN budget of $39.64 billion, $20.3 billion came from voluntary non-core contributions and $13.2 billion from assessed contributions, reflecting an incredible growth in restricted funds and stagnancy in the flow of unrestricted funds. In 2020, of the total of $42.3 billion revenue from governments, assessed contributions were $13.6 billion, with the United States as the largest contributor, followed by China and Japan. The voluntary core contributions totaled $3.7 billion, with Germany as the major contributor, trailed by Sweden and the United States. And voluntary non-core contributions were $24.9 billion, with the United States as the major contributor, followed by the UK and Japan. In stark comparison, in 2010, government-based voluntary non-core contributions had totaled $12.5 billion.

Between 2010 and 2020, revenue from "nongovernment donors," such as the European Union, UN interagency pooled funds, and International Financial Institutions, as well as funding from NGOs, public-private partnerships, foundations, and academic and research institutions increased from $2.26 billion to $10.46 billion. In 2020 this sector was led by the European Union, followed by the Global Fund and the United Nations Secretariat Office for the Coordination of Humanitarian Affairs. Unspecified "private donors" were in the sixth position and the Bill and Melinda Gates Foundation in the eighth position of the ten major nonstate funders that year. One of the most feared results of the increasing corporate financing of the UN system is the way in which it influences global governance, multilateralism, and power relationships between the global North and South.[27]

Private financing of development initiatives impacts macro-, meso-, and microspheres from global systems such as the UN to states and state-level institutions, to grassroots organizations. This is the background and the reality that activists have to navigate.

Tensions, Negotiations, and Boundaries
Sulá Batsú

Conversations about funding are always uncomfortable. After years of collaborating with activists, I have realized that trust—gained with time and resulting in relationships based on honesty—is indispensable for being able to talk about such a complicated issue. This chapter does not portray an either-or relationship between feminist activism and funding, but rather my aim is to explore the tensions and negotiations activists must navigate to be able to do their work. In our many conversations about funding, Kemly, Sulá Batsú's coordinator, has defended the autonomy of the co-op in the face of both public and private funding streams. She is ardent in her defense of la coope, while also knowing that other organizations criticize it precisely for being open to receiving corporate funding.

"Honestly, with the experiences that we have had," Kemly says, "we have been able to do totally alternative things. And some of our most alternative projects have been funded by these companies." She is referring to various TIC-as projects that have been financed by Google. Kemly insists that Sulá Batsú does not accept any "conditions," which is its "only condition." She immediately says that in this case Google did not impose any conditions, "the only one being, perhaps, that we had to allow them to mention our program, for instance, in their press releases. That is the concession we had to make." She adds that the Silicon Valley tech company "didn't even ask us to use their logo." Kemly admits that this has been a learning process. The co-op was founded over fifteen years ago, and its members have learned how to navigate funding while holding on to their principles and practices. She insists that it's important to acknowledge that the corporate sector is not monolithic: "For me it is very important to say something; it is not fair to demonize all private companies. Obviously, the business models of Google and Facebook are terrible business models and are based on the exploitation of people at the highest level. We are clear about that. But it seems to me that there is a demonization of private companies. . . . We are a private company!"

Although a cooperative and far from being part of the "corporate sector," Sulá Batsú navigates the line between identifying as a business and as a grassroots organization. Technically, it is considered a business, but its organizational practices defy mainstream business models. Kemly thus believes that piling up the many types of initiatives under a single umbrella is problematic. Although funders might try to influence the projects they give money to, she argues that the organization must acknowledge the ways in which grassroots organizations can use and have used these funds for efforts that advance social justice. In sum, funding can be employed for purposes unintended by the funders. So, while many of these companies work directly against many of Sulá Batsú's principles and goals, the organization also uses those funds in ways that dismantle corporate extractive and exploitative practices. An example is the co-op's La voz de las chicas del Centro de América financed by Google. The project's goal is to support marginalized young women from Central America in developing their voice and critical thinking through the intersection of art and technology. "Google never intervened," Kemly explains, "and this is an alternative, antiestablishment project."

Kemly is adamant in emphasizing that receiving funding from states and international development institutions can also be problematic: "Google can place conditions when they disburse funds, and so can the Dutch development cooperation agency. I really don't see the difference. Development cooperation institutions all talk in the name of the poor, and they need poverty to be able to do their work. If poverty ceases to exist, all of them would disappear. Everyone has their agenda. . . . Aren't the funds that come from developed countries also an attempt at colonizing us?" In line with this critique and in accord with her insistence on recognizing the agency of organizations, Kemly sees the relationship between funders and civil society initiatives as part of a dialectical process of sorts. She explains that, for example, certain topics suddenly become "sexy" and receive a flush of funding. But in time, these issues fall out of the spotlight and are consequently underfunded. Which comes first? She explains: "At one point it was 'gender and technology,' which is already declining and no longer a priority. So right now, hundreds of these organizations that work on gender and technology issues are going to start working with Indigenous people, for example, which is the next hot issue, or with technology and the environment. Then the organization goes from one thing to the other. I think this is such a bad practice and so determined by capital, because that's the truth."

Sulá Batsú has been working with Indigenous women and technology, as well as on the intersection of climate justice and technology, for quite some years now, but it is not planning on letting go of its pivotal work on gender and technology. Instead of focusing on funders, Kemly argues, the key is remaining fiercely independent, knowing when and where to draw the line. "We are a self-managed cooperative, and that is part of our freedom," she says. Boundaries are drawn, and some things are simply unacceptable and nonnegotiable. For example, over the years Sulá Batsú has consistently rejected funds from Coca-Cola as well as from corporations that own the cultivation of pineapples in Costa Rica. Kemly says, "The pineapple companies, in all the regions where we have worked, have told us, 'We want to do this with you; we will give you thousands of dollars so you can develop training projects' in the communities where we work. Really, huge amounts of *colones* or hundreds of dollars to work with pineapple companies. We have also said no to them." Activists draw boundaries and delimit what is nonnegotiable for them.

APC WRP has a distinct funding structure. The WRP receives funding its parent organization, the APC, from membership quotas of organizations, and from state and nonstate sources, and it also offers small grants for feminist organizations in the global South. As a transnational organization working in the global South, the APC is registered in the United States, which limits it from some funding for the "developing" world. Julia, who has been working with APC WRP for over ten years, explains that a decade ago it was difficult to convey the relevance of projects working at the intersection of technology, social justice, and feminism. The idea that technology was a woman's human right had barely started emerging. APC WRP sought to access funds directed at two major intertwined themes: women's rights and internet/digital rights.

Thus it had to make two arguments: Why does technology matter for women's rights? And why do women's rights matter for technology? This is an important point, because APC WRP centered technology as a feminist issue, which was both innovative and challenging in terms of framing and accessing funds. Julia recalls: "There was a moment of a deliberate decision to say, 'Look, our work is located within the women's rights movement, and we need to be more explicit about what this means.' Also, in terms of where we access resources from, and so one of our grants was the Millennium Development Goal 3 [MDG3] Fund,[28] which really was around technology and violence against women, and I think that that was a very important moment for this very deliberate framing of ourselves as part of the women's movement." Because online gender-based violence was very new at the moment, framing it as part of violence against women was more appealing to funders.

In a previous conversation, Keila, a longtime feminist and tech activist who has been very involved with the APC WRP's Take Back the Tech campaign, said that since the Feminist Principles of the Internet is "a more positive frame of the way you want to carry out the work, . . . I think that's a really hard thing to fund sometimes—maybe I'm wrong." She added: "If you look at those principles, it's a more positive frame of the way you want to carry out the work. You're not starting out from the negative, from the prevention point—you either cross your arms, cross your legs, protect yourself—you're not from a defensive pose. And so that's the type of work we'd really like to be doing. But I think that's a really hard thing to fund sometimes."

A lot has happened in the past decade. There is now more awareness about the interconnections of women's and digital rights, similar to issues around climate and racial justice. APC WRP has historically received funds from the Dutch Ministry of Foreign Affairs, the International Development Research Centre (IDRC), the Swedish International Development Cooperation Agency (SIDA), and more recently from the Ford Foundation and private philanthropic organizations whose names Julia could not disclose. There has definitely been an increase in private funding in the past years, she notes. But although this can be problematic in terms of influencing agendas, Julia considers that the newfound understanding of the private sector, mostly of philanthropic foundations, is "a really positive development." Julia emphasizes that many of the themes feminist digital organizations are working on are actually historical issues—such as the intersections of gender with violence, poverty, labor, racism, and sexuality—but they have acquired new meanings and framings with the advances of online gender based violence, the digital economy, electronic surveillance, and automation, to name a few.

In addition, Julia believes that the donor community has a much more intersectional perspective which understands that these issues are inseparable. There are definitely waves of interest from funders, she agrees, but these cycles have become more interconnected. "There was a time when there was a lot of focus on gender-based violence," she recalls, "and in some way that's still there, but it's much more integrated. . . . It almost feels like it's become commonplace when you're talking about online gender-based violence, you are also talking about violence against women. This standard is a kind of norm setting that has been happening over the course of the last few years. Definitely big things now are climate justice, automation, and artificial intelligence. But in AI there's a big piece around race and diversity."

Like Sulá Batsú, APC WRP also draws boundaries. Julia explains that APC WRP has rejected seeking funding from big tech corporations such as Meta: "Accepting funding from big tech companies just doesn't sit right with us, with the kind of politics we want to have. . . . Our role is to maintain . . . accountability of big tech companies, because we can have a relationship outside of those contractual worlds." But APC WRP's policy of not accepting certain funds is not a "blanket" decision, she adds. For instance, the organization has a position on the regional advisory board for Meta in Africa, which is looking at women's rights and information and communication technologies in the continent. She says that many feminists who they have worked with are now part of Meta, and these relationships continue to be important for them. "How do we support that allyship as part of our activism if we constantly say, 'We actually want to have nothing to do with you,'" she questions.

At the same time, Julia emphasizes that there are many regional, political, socioeconomic, and historical contexts that must be taken into consideration when grassroots organizations, as well as APC WRP member organizations, decide to accept funding from corporations with problematic agendas. She explains that since APC WRP is a membership organization, it is driven by the needs, feelings, and perspectives of the members, which are vastly different across regions: "Many of our members in Latin America, for example, will not touch certain resources. . . . Some of our members in Africa may actually have very different opinions." For Julia, beyond the critique of big tech, it is crucial to think about the possibilities that lie outside this enormous structure. Although the critique is necessary, it can limit imagining the creation of better worlds. "If we are able to imagine something outside of this, then what would that be?" she asks. "Our imaginations are under such stress because we live with such precariousness all the time. Where is the room for this kind of creativity? Where is the room for this kind of experimentation?" A lot of this experimentation is currently happening within grassroots, decentralized, and informally structured organizations. These are not the organizations being funded by either state or private donors, which seek out projects that have formal hierarchical administrative, bureaucratic, and financial structures. These organizations are less tied to the neoliberal requirements of assessments, evaluations, evidence, and outcomes.

This is why APC WRP—which also disburses small grants—is currently focused on funding these kinds of organizations with grants between $1,000 and $2,500. Julia believes that some of the most imaginative work on the intersection of feminism, technology, and social justice is happening in these collectives within a changing activism landscape. She told me:

> That's a really big piece of our work right now, as a woman's program, to make sure that smaller organizations, people, and networks that might not be able to qualify for big resources, are able to receive resources through us. . . . Donors need to pay attention to this fact that maybe the NGO is not going to be the vehicle through which the kind of change that we want to have happen is going to happen, because the world is changing and organizing is changing and movements are changing, and technology is a big part of this change.

And, yet, if donors eventually catch on to these innovative and important transformations, activists might find themselves once again having to negotiate their principles and values to be able to survive, thrive, and do the work.

Conclusion

The corporatization of development initiatives has increased over the past decades, impacting macro-, meso-, and micropolitics. This has put many activists in a difficult position between accepting funds they need and having to navigate—both internally within the organization as well as externally with activist communities—the tenuous and complicated journey of remaining true to themselves. In this process, organizations sometimes form "uneasy alliances" that advance their work even when they have to make certain compromises, although they also draw boundaries and engage in refusal. Broad-brush critiques of the politics of funding serve no one. Analyses of funding must be case-based and contextual. There should always be space for critique and scrutiny, while also moving beyond simplistic arguments about co-optation.

I agree with Eschle and Maiguashca that organizational politics must be examined empirically, because they are constituted by shifting relationships, commitments, conflicts, and negotiations that defy facile explanations.[29] One might immediately deduce that an organization that runs a project funded by, say, Google is a servant of said corporation.

But only close, empirical study can reveal the nuances of these relationships. Organizations are evolving entities with their own agency and decision-making processes that are contingent upon numerous historical, political, cultural, and socioeconomic factors. In an ideal world, feminist organizations would be able to flourish with absolute autonomy. This is not the world we are living in. Yet.

There are vast differences between resource-constrained and grassroots organizations and more formal NGOs, state-level and global institutions such as the UN. Each sphere merits close examination to understand how corporate funding is influencing its agendas. The UN, for instance, wields a form of power that can shape the lives and livelihoods of millions of people. Thus it is worrisome that the UN—along with other powerful institutions—is receiving more funding from the private sector. This should continue to be closely examined.

A Feminist Technological Otherwise

In the fall of 2021, former Facebook employee turned whistleblower Frances Haugen leaked a trove of the company's internal documents that revealed—or, rather, confirmed what activists and scholars had known for some time—that Facebook profited from harm and violence. In an interview with the news program *60 Minutes*, Haugen said, quite disingenuously: "The thing I saw at Facebook over and over again was there were conflicts of interest between what was good for the public and what was good for Facebook. And Facebook, over and over again, chose to optimize for its own interests, like making more money."[1] "What was good for Facebook," as it turns out, was disinformation, ethnic violence, and numerous forms of hate and harassment including online gender-based violence (among other forms of harm).[2] Again, this was not a surprise for many, yet the massive evidence constitutes an invaluable source. Tech reporter Karen Hao found that Facebook not only profited from violence—by spreading disinformation—but that together with Google, it funded the disinformation.[3] The marriage between capitalism, technology, and violence was crudely evident, once again.

The "Facebook Papers" confirms just one of the various manifestations of the coupling of capitalism and technologies in the current era. This does not mean that technology is good or bad, but rather that technologies are political artifacts.[4] And how they are mobilized is also political. The global development apparatus participates in this technocapitalist complex in many ways, one of which specifically targets women in the global South by preying on tropes of care and selflessness in building a worthy neoliberal subject that will be the very motor and promise of the technological future. The emphasis on inclusion enfolds numerous forms of exclusion and violence. The insistence on digital inclusion neglects the roots of the socioeconomic sufferings imposed upon marginalized communities. The discourse suffocates imagining transformation beyond techno-solutionist strategies. The discourse is fixated on a race against time. It is within this context that feminist digital activists anchored in the global South build, negotiate, and reimagine a world in which technologies thrive not on inclusion but on justice. Enacting a feminist praxis rooted in solidarity and pleasure, digital activists contest neoliberal prescriptions on how women and other oppressed individuals and communities in the global South are supposed to interact with digital technologies. Solidarity and pleasure present women in their "complex personhood" a persistent yet always incomplete task for those who have to prove their humanity over and over again.[5] Solidarity and pleasure are intrinsic to a "politics of connections" that represent "spheres of insurrection" amid the increasing commoditization of our relationships, particularly facilitated by technological ubiquity.

In Sulá Batsú a politics of care based on solidarity is imbricated in its practice as a feminist development, technology-focused cooperative that works with marginalized communities in Costa Rica and Central America and in the very fabric of the organization. Sulá Batsú has fomented an entrepreneurial model that both conforms to and rejects the ideal, individualistic, neoliberal figure that we have come to expect from numerous state and nonstate institutions. Its technological entrepreneurial project is conceived as a collective alliance that is place-based and focused on process rather than outcomes, in a "hybrid" constellation that blends market-based and feminist principles of horizontality and redistribution. Sulá Batsú embraces entrepreneurship as a possible avenue for success, yet its commitment to collectivization also contests neoliberal logics based on self-reliance, self-discipline, and personal responsibility.

Sulá Batsú's entrepreneurial undertaking represents a "politics of connections" not as a site to be financially preyed upon but rather as a site for creating relationships that are bounded with technology while decentering its preeminence. Its projects, such as TIC-as and the hackathons, with mostly women and people from rural and Indigenous communities, are primarily built on creating strong and long-lasting relationships of reciprocity and solidarity. This is what has preeminence. In Sulá Batsú, relationships with and through technology are really about care; technology is localized, collectivized, and felt. The organizational fabric of la coope is built upon care. Its members enact a form of "prefigurative politics" in which their everyday organizational practices resemble the world they are building. They are living the world they imagine, and this is a deeply feminist praxis. At the same time, activists identify the co-op as a "business" and as "part of the market," and they have to abide by specific procedures required by grants and funders, with clear objectives, assessments, reports, data, and outcomes.

Their caring relationships are also riddled with conflict and dissension, which are woven into how the organization and the activists have evolved over time. Since its foundation almost two decades ago, la coope has confronted numerous financial, organizational, and affective crises. People have come and gone, sometimes causing resentment. Precarity has led to exhaustion and disenchantment at times, and different visions and goals have collided. The emphasis on experimentation and joy can be exhilarating, but it can also instill tremendous uncertainty. These are just some of the trade-offs when activists attempt to live and work in ways that dismantle hierarchical, linear, and exploitative organizational structures. The COVID-19 pandemic has caused both financial and emotional turmoil in the co-op. The economic effects have been well documented, but what are the implications for members of organizations that are built on affective ties? Not being able to share their physical space, kiss and hug each other, drink coffee every day at 3:00 p.m., or travel together to collaborate with communities across the country has had its toll.

It is precisely within these contexts that Sulá Batsú has been undergoing a radical change, veering toward a more critical praxis and vision of the problematic politics of inclusion in a systematically exclusionary system, more specifically related to its projects on women and STEM.

151

Albeit indirectly, Sulá Batsú's work with the Indigenous Cabécar women has revealed the problems of some of their long-held projects, such as women's inclusion in STEM, and how state and corporate institutions parade women they have trained to demonstrate "diversity and equity" while leaving structural inequality intact. Sulá Batsú's work with the Cabécar women represents a pivotal moment of transformation for la coope in understanding how technologies, knowledges, and feelings can converge toward a politics of care over violence.

In the Women's Rights Programme of the Association for Progressive Communication (APC WRP)—a global forerunner in activism against online-based gender violence—activists practice an ethics of care by mobilizing pleasure as a technopolitical strategy anchored in a Southern political perspective. The internet is conceived as a space for embodiment in which desire should also be able to flourish. In the global South the control and regulation of nonnormative bodies, sexualities, and genders have been intrinsic to the colonial-capitalist order for centuries. These practices continue to be prevalent in online and offline realms. Violence—including online gender-based violence—both constitutes and fuels the capitalist-technology complex, which is intertwined with white supremacy and heternormativity. Adopting political strategies around pleasure, joy, and play thus represents an important site of contestation. Instead of calling on Indigenous, Black, Brown, poor, disabled, and LGBTQI+/non-binary people, and women to be more restrained online, these activists are calling for online rebellion. Through some of their transnational initiatives, such as the Feminist Principles of the Internet and the EROTICS Project, APC WRP problematizes online violence by anchoring itself in a Southern epistemology that makes evident the connections between online gender-based violence and broader social, historical, and political histories. The feminist defense of pleasure forms part of a "politics of connections"—a strategy that announces life in the face of violence.[6]

But fostering pleasure as a feminist technopolitical tactic is complicated. In the context of online gender-based violence, there are important concerns around the implications of harm and trauma; the lack of support and safety; the complexities of sexual agency intersected by race, class, religion, age, and ability; and the conflicts in pursuing criminalization as a solution to online violence. Sexual agency is not an unbridled strategy in response to online gender-based violence. Harm and trauma can augment in response to acts of pleasure and joy, especially when demonstrated by those whose pleasure has been consistently negated. Although crucial, emphases on cybersecurity and technical strategies to protect online data will not dismantle the structures that foster and enable gender-based violence. Not everyone will feel drawn by a call to enact sexual pleasure contingent to their social locations. The proliferation of laws against online violence may resolve imminent dangers caused by individual perpetrators but leaves systems of injustice intact while potentially furthering racist and classist politics. These issues continue to be at the center of APC WRP's reflections. But giving up on the subversive capacities of pleasure and joy as an individual and collective project would also mean giving in to technocapitalist dictums and prescriptions.

Funding is another important part of the puzzle of care. The corporatization of development affects global and local macro-, meso-, and microspheres of politics. This includes the surge of private funding of the United Nations—an institution that both Sulá Batsú and APC WRP interact with in different forms—affecting state and nonstate policies and discourses on the role of digital technologies in our societies. Although women are increasingly the face of development, feminist organizations in the global South continue to be chronically underfunded, while funding for "anti-gender" initiatives is on the rise. In this challenging funding landscape, both Sulá Batsú and APC WRP have to contend with "uneasy alliances" with funders while trying to remain true to their missions, principles, and values, often built precisely on a profound critique of corporate interests. But these are not either-or relationships. Upon close examination and study, we understand the compromises, negotiations, refusals, and boundaries that activists draw with funders. These moments are tied to how activists build projects and relationships of care. We can hope for a world in which social justice activists can flourish economically with absolute autonomy, while we explore the complexities that they currently contend with.

International development is yet another realm in which care is mobilized in the path toward digital inclusion. The pairing of technology and capitalism—which is not new, yet is reconfigured and presented in renewed ways amid globalization and successive socioeconomic and ecological crises—has permeated development discourse in ways that aim to economize the most intimate spaces of life. The connections that allow for these spaces to flourish are gendered and racialized—it is overwhelmingly women and Black, Brown, Indigenous, and feminized individuals who have sustained these realms. Capitalism has always needed and exploited what happens in these spaces to be able to thrive; this has been well studied, theorized, and lived. Digital technologies provide ideal vehicles for preying on these connections for national, supranational, and corporate growth and interests. The recent surge of the fintech industry is only a part of how numerous institutions and markets are trying to capitalize intimate realms of life.

It is in this context that an ideal Third World Technological Woman appears as a particular savior. This figure can be digitalized in ways that make these connections legible to feed into ever-growing demands of profit and market expansion. The technological future—and present—needs women but not only as workers, both paid and unpaid. It needs what these women represent: nurturance, selflessness, self-sacrifice—women as unlimited sources of care. But including this woman in this brave new world brings numerous forms of harm, such as increasingly vicious violence, economic precarity, displacement and dispossession, and ecological devastation, in addition to enhanced modes of data extraction, surveillance, and online violence. Many of the very institutions priming women for the digital society are contributing to—and benefiting from—the violence that besieges them, their families, and communities. This is the impossible paradox of the Third World Technological Woman.

The critique of inclusion, and digital inclusion in particular, is tricky. It is, after all, "what one cannot not want."[7] Inclusion has its benefits. Being included can have, and certainly has had, fruitful and positive results. In this book I have shown, for example, the ways feminist activists work within, against, and beyond various forms of inclusion—digital, financial, institutional, and so on. To suggest that the refusal of inclusion is the path to liberation can stem from a position of privilege: for those who are already included, recommending refusal can be paternalistic and trite. The right to refusal is indeed fundamental, as many Black, Brown, and Indigenous scholars and activists have contended.[8] So is understanding that technologies will not solve complex social problems.[9] I do believe that practicing solidarity, pleasure, and joy are forms of refusal. But I am not suggesting refusal or any form of contestation in particular—that is not my place. These strategies should come—and have come—both from activists and the communities themselves.

What I am suggesting is that we remain attentive to the politics of inclusion in the current systems we are living within. We are surrounded by policies, practices, and discourses that capture dreams and hopes of inclusion while being simultaneously invested in extraction and dispossession. And who are the ones set to be included? Those who have been historically excluded, as part of a "technology of governance" that brings in "those who have been recognized as strangers . . . but also of making strangers into subjects," as Sara Ahmed argues.[10] Amid endless social, economic, and ecological crises, we must continue to interrogate the goals and the consequences of inclusion in systems that are persistently unjust and racist, misogynistic, transphobic, classist, and ableist—systems that "include" while simultaneously dispossessing, extracting, and exploiting. We should continue to be attentive to the imaginaries being mobilized and weaponized to lure people to want to be included. Digitalization—in its many forms as a state, global, developmental, and corporate project—is one of these realms that depend on inclusion: inclusion of bodies, workers, lands, infrastructures, data, consumers, users, designers, expertise, creativity, care, relationships, and intimacies.

A wealth of people around the world are reinventing the digital society—like Sulá Batsú and APC WRP—from community internet networks, hackerspaces, platform cooperatives, and design justice nodes to feminist, queer, climate justice, antiracist, Indigenous, and abolitionist grassroots organizations and coalitions; unions fighting for decent wages and working conditions; movements for better health care, housing, and education; and community-based webs of mutual aid. Solidarity and pleasure are already intrinsic to many of these projects. These may not be perfect—nor are they supposed to be—yet I believe that this is where the most thrilling visions and practices for social justice are unfolding. After all, as abolitionist scholar and activist Mariame Kaba argues, "Hope is a discipline and . . . we have to practice it every single day."[11]

On Methods

When I was a reporter in my homeland Puerto Rico, I made an attempt every day to guide my work by these words from the legendary journalist Ryszard Kapuściński:

> It's important to keep in mind that we work with the most delicate matter in this world: people. With our words, with what we write about them, we can destroy their lives. Our jobs take us for one day, maybe five hours, to a place that we leave after our work is done. We will surely never return to that place, but the people who helped us will stay, and their neighbors will read what we have written about them. If what we write puts these people in danger, maybe they will not be able to live there anymore, and who knows if there is another place where they will be able to go to.[1]

I remembered Kapuściński's words when I sat in the newsroom to write the story of a survivor of domestic violence or sexual assault, of a poor community trying to live and thrive amid institutional violence and extreme precariousness, of an immigrant who had to endure horrors to obtain a better life only to be revictimized by racist and xenophobic violence upon her arrival, of a transwoman who had fought tirelessly to be treated with a minimum of dignity.

When I started graduate school in the United States, I learned about

157

the long and painful history of scholars (mostly white, mostly from the global North) extracting information from the communities they studied, distorting, stigmatizing, and misrepresenting their lives while gaining recognition and material advancement from the people who had opened their lives to them. They would not share their analyses with these communities in at least an attempt to seek their feedback and offer something constructive, edifying, inspiring. This happened—and still happens—even when the researcher's words could destroy these communities. Harm can come in many forms.[2] I thus started my career as a researcher holding Kapuściński's words close to my heart and pen. My voyage as a researcher has also been nourished by decades of fierce feminist, Indigenous, and Black scholarship on the complexities of methodological praxis that has offered invaluable insights on how to navigate this fulfilling, uncomfortable, and joyful process.[3]

I do not claim to have found the solution to any of the dilemmas inherent to research methodologies—in fact, I think this is impossible. I have learned to make honest attempts at bridging the power asymmetries between myself and the activist communities I study, and in this journey I have made mistakes, dealt with regrets, and wrestled with many demons. Even as I write this methodological appendix, I question its meanings and implications. On the one hand, it is a fundamental piece—as all accounts of methods are—that (I hope) demonstrates intellectual honesty, reflexivity, and accountability. On the other, it is designed to be a separate section at the end of the book, as if methods could be relegated to a discrete space. Our methodological philosophies and practices are intertwined with every single part of our research: fieldwork, theoretical frameworks, empirical findings, arguments, analyses, and conclusions. Yet I still think it has value.

In Defense of Solidarity and Pleasure studies three main sites: Sulá Batsú, APC-WRP, and discourse produced by the United Nations. I engaged with George Marcus's ethnographic "multi-sited" approach by traveling both literally and figuratively over countries and documents "following the metaphor" to understand the making, unmaking, and remaking of what I have termed the Third World Technological Woman.[4] Following the metaphor helped me explore what sociologist Millie Thayer calls the "cracks between discourses and practices."[5] These are the fractures, ruptures, resistances, and negotiations of feminist organizational practices, and the labor, experiences, and lives of feminist digital activists. May these pages shed light on my journey writing this book, and most important, on the relationships it has shaped.

Gathering Voices, Experiences, Discourses

I came to this topic in 2014, after years of thinking about the implications of digital technologies for social movements, especially for feminist movements. As a journalist in Puerto Rico, I had lived the digital revolution in the newsroom and seen the impact it had on journalism, leading to the erosion of traditional media's authority. Activists and other underrepresented communities were increasingly using digital spaces and tools to communicate, distribute their messages and claims, and make the media and other institutions accountable. The feminist movement in Puerto Rico was one of many political actors that embraced digital technologies. This led me to study the digital media strategies of the feminist movement in Puerto Rico for my master's thesis in journalism. The project that was ultimately to become this book took me back to communities of feminist activists in the global South to understand the ways in which they are working in the present to create a liberatory future.

I conducted preliminary and informal phone interviews in 2014 with ten feminist digital activists as well as gender and technology experts in Latin America and the Caribbean. I read dozens of international development and corporate reports on gender and technology. These conversations led me to Sulá Batsú and APC WRP as important actors in the emerging feminist digital movement both in Latin America and on a transnational scale, yet anchored in the global South. Sulá Batsú is a local development cooperative in Costa Rica, whereas APC WRP is a transnational organization and network; both offer distinct yet comparable missions, visions, and trajectories. During the span of this project, 2014 through 2022, I conducted a total of seventy-six in-depth semistructured interviews in addition to twelve follow-up interviews with Sulá Batsú and APC WRP activists between 2019 and 2022.

Since 2015, I have been in touch with Sulá Batsú and APC WRP activists through hundreds of texts messages via email and video/voice/

159

text applications, such as Skype, Zoom, Jitsi, WhatsApp, Telegram, and Signal. I regularly review their websites to keep up with their latest projects and papers. Most of my interviews were with Sulá Batsú and APC WRP members (n = 29; table 1) since organizations are the unit of analysis in the book, but I also interviewed feminist digital activists working in other groups in Latin America (26) to obtain a broader landscape of feminist digital activism in the region. I conducted interviews with participants of Sulá Batsú's TIC-as project (5) as well as representatives from the United Nations (ITU, UN Women, and Cátedra UNESCO in Argentina) (5), state agencies specializing in women's rights or technology and science in Costa Rica (INAMU and MICITT) (3), gender and technology scholars from the higher education institutions Tecnológico de Costa Rica in San Carlos and the University of Costa Rica (2), the nonprofits Alliance for an Affordable Internet (A4AI) and World Pulse (2), and foundations and corporations (the Bill and Melinda Gates Foundation, Intel, and the Omidyar Network) (4). I coded all interview transcripts thematically, grouped under topics that emerged from the texts. These topics started to form the patterns that I analyze throughout the book. I wrote numerous analytical memos during fieldwork and the coding process.

I did fieldwork in San José, Costa Rica, during the summers of 2015, 2016, and 2019. During these research trips, I was embedded in Sulá Batsú and in the lives of the activists. I spent every weekday at their office

TABLE 1 (OPPOSITE). Sulá Batsú and APC WRP research participants.

In total, 29 individuals from Sulá Batsú and APC WRP completed the survey, though not all survey respondents answered each question.

Race/Ethnicity. Respondents answered questions about race/ethnicity via open ended questions, and were given latitude to self-identify. Owing to the complicated and value-driven nature of questions about race and ethnicity, just 22 individuals chose to answer the question at all, and responses were varied—no two answers were the same. One individual identified as Black, while several individuals identified as Latina, Latin American, Mestizo/mestiza, Mezclada (mixed), and Morena.

Position in Organization. Again, individuals were asked about their organizational role via open-ended questions. The range of professions and skill sets of respondents is wide, and we collected information from people who identify as software engineers, graphic designers, lobbyists, activists, journalists and communications professionals, archaeologists, anthropologists, and sociologists. In total, 23 individuals provided information about their organizational status.

Respondent information	Category	Sulá Batsú	APC WRP
Total respondents		17	12
Nationality (N=27)	South African	0	2
	Argentinian	0	3
	Canadian	0	1
	USA	0	2
	Malaysia	0	2
	Lebanon	0	1
	Costa Rica	16	0
	Other or no answer	1	1
Gender (N=27)	F	12	9
	M	4	0
	Other or no answer	1	3
Class (N=23)	Middle class	7	9
	Middle upper class	2	0
	Working class	5	0
	Upper class	0	0
	Other or no answer	3	3
Years in organization (N=21)	Under 1 year	2	0
	1 year–4 years	5	2
	5–9 years	3	2
	10–19 years	6	1
	20+ years	0	0
	Other or no answer	1	7
Level of study completed (N=23)	Student/up to HS grad	0	0
	Bachelor's degree	7	4
	Licentiate (+1 year Bachelor's)	4	0
	Graduate degree	3	5
	Other or no answer	3	3

in San José, conducting interviews, talking informally with activists and staff, participating in their meetings and events, and collaborating with voluntary work mostly on internet and social media strategies and with translations from Spanish to English. I attended their trainings, workshops, and events throughout the country. I tried as much as possible to become a part of the co-op while I was there.

The nature of APC WRP as a transnational network without a physical location made fieldwork more challenging. Since 2015, I conducted most interviews with APC WRP activists online (through video or audio). I had periodic online conversations with some of them, particularly those living and working in Latin America. In March 2015, I conducted one week of fieldwork at the UN Women's 59th Commission on the Status of Women (CSW) meeting in New York City, focused on the twentieth anniversary of Beijing's Platform for Action. During this event I shadowed and interviewed three APC WRP activists. I attended the panels in which APC WRP was participating, in addition to many others on issues of gender and digital information and communication technologies.

The third research site is constituted by texts produced between 1995 and 2022 by the United Nations or under the auspices of the UN, the UN Economic Commission for Latin America and the Caribbean (ECLAC), technology corporations, philanthropic foundations, and international NGOs mostly focused on the intersection of gender and digital technologies. In total, I analyzed 203 texts. This analysis was supplemented by organizational literature from APC, APC WRP, and Sulá Batsú, including hundreds of reports, briefs, working papers, research studies, flyers, blog posts, presentations, and guides. The majority of my textual analysis is focused on UN and ECLAC texts.

The UN has an extremely complex system of documentation, with many different types of texts.[6] There are "documents" (resolutions, decisions, reports), "publications," and "official records." Resolutions, formal expressions of UN organs, and decisions, often formal actions taken by UN organs about procedural issues, have equal legal standing. "Resolutions" are particularly important because they "reflect the view of the member states; provide policy recommendations; assign mandates to the UN Secretariat and the subsidiary bodies of the General Assembly, and decide on all questions regarding the UN budget."[7] Implementing the recommendations contained in resolutions is not binding (with some exceptions), and implementing the policies is the responsibility of each member state. "Reports," which are very common across the UN, are the texts that most UN bodies offer about their work.[8] "Publications" are any kind of written materials for the general public issued by the UN, and "official records" are printed publications on proceedings of the main organs of UN conferences.[9]

Feminist digital activists engage with many of these texts, particularly regarding ones adopted by the Human Rights Council that address human rights in the digital realm.[10] I mostly examined what the UN defines as resolutions, publications, and reports across funds and programs, and other entities under the General Assembly (particularly UN Women); functional and regional commissions under the Economic and Social Council (ECOSOC); and specialized agencies such as ITU and UNESCO. Besides using Google to find relevant texts, I searched through the following UN online archives: Official Document System, UN Digital Library, UN iLibrary, UN News Portal, UN Meetings Coverage and Press Releases, and ECLAC's digital repository using a combination of such keywords as "women," "gender," "technology," "digital technology," "development," "financing," "online violence," and "internet." I periodically examined specific websites, mostly those belonging to UN Women, ITU, and UNESCO, to gather the most recent information and news on their gender and technology projects. I was also in touch via email with librarians at the UN Archives and Records Management Section in New York City.

In the process of data analysis and coding, I identified numerous configurations of the "Third World Technological Woman" and uncovered consistencies and contradictions. Many actors conceptualize international development texts, including state representatives, development officials and practitioners, members of the private sector, and activists. These texts are not the sole product of technocrats locked away in offices, and they are not monolithic. There often are discrepancies and variations within the same texts or series of texts.[11] My analysis is not a critique of individual authors of UN texts but rather a way of examining how "social reality is produced and made real through discourses" because "social interactions cannot be fully understood without reference to the discourses that give them meaning."[12]

It is often difficult to separate these discourses from feminist claims, since they are the product of negotiations that take place through a series of global and local meetings and conferences.[13]There are feminists in the "UN orbit"—embedded in these institutions—and some of those same feminists have been involved in grassroots movements and organizations.[14] Various UN conferences, events, declarations, and treaties have opened important "programmatic and discursive" spaces for women's movements worldwide.[15] That said, activists from the global South continue to be excluded along intersections of race, class, sexuality, and ability, along other divides.[16] In Latin America and the Caribbean, for example, there have been tensions between feminist activism at UN conferences and the more grassroots, decentralized, and regional *Encuentros*.[17] Some feminist scholars and activists have also questioned the relevance of the UN for feminists.[18] However, international development agencies continue to produce knowledge and shape policies that influence activists' struggles and state practices. Most important for this book, APC WRP and Sulá Batsú have been active in development circles, particularly at the UN and the ECLAC, as well as some technology corporations, as advocates or by way of funding.

Honesty and Accountability

There is still a long way to go, but nowadays it is common to read academic texts—especially in certain fields in the social sciences—that contain some form of reflection on the social location, power, and privilege of the researcher vis-à-vis "the researched." And yet these forewarnings have been interrogated as lacking material and institutional heft.[19] Feminist scholars have moreover warned that practicing solidarity and "empathy" with participants can be deceitful, and even more exploitative because the power relationship remains unequal.[20] Reflexivity can harm minoritized scholars, reinforcing long-standing stereotypes because of the ways in which privilege works. It makes privileged scholars look transparent and honest, while marginalized scholars seem biased and less rigorous.[21] These are all profound dilemmas, but what is the alternative? The liberatory project of solidarity intertwined with accountability and struggle cannot be abandoned because of its challenges.[22]

As a Puerto Rican and Caribbean woman raised in Puerto Rico, with an Iranian father, middle-class, with white skin, a single mother (now of a beautiful young woman), working in US academia, I am at the intersection of many privileges as well as oppressions. Upon entering the field, I fathomed myself as an insider in the spaces I studied with activists from the global South, but I was sharply reminded that the insider/outsider binary is porous and fluid. The relationships I made in the field—and continue to maintain—are constantly being constructed and negotiated. In some ways I didn't "study up" or "study oppressed people" but studied the "similar" in terms of class and racial/ethnic identity. Yet in many other ways, I studied the dissimilar in terms of cultural background, life experiences, politics, religious beliefs, and worldviews.

Since I started this project in 2014, I have attempted to bridge the power relationships between myself and the organizations and activists studied. The process has been both fulfilling and difficult, and I have learned to work through and negotiate the permanent discomfort of attempting to do justice to the people who have shared their time, space, knowledge, and feelings with me. I spent the most time with the activists of Sulá Batsú, with many of whom I have formed beautiful relationships as a *compañera*, as in *acompañar* ("to accompany"). In Spanish, *compañero* or *compañera* can mean many things: a lover, a partner, a comrade, a friend. In my relationships with la coope, it is meant in its most literal translation: a companion. Beyond being with them in their office at Casa Batsú in San José, we shared lunches, dinners, coffees, working trips throughout the country, and many conversations. Although I have physically "left the field," we have always stayed in touch. I have presented my work to the group during different stages of research. I have shared drafts of chapters and articles as well as transcripts of our interviews. They have invited me to present my work at online and offline events they have organized.

In June 2022, the co-op's coordinator, Kemly Camacho, and I presented on the challenges and joys of our relationship as researcher and collaborator at the Ninth Latin American and Caribbean Conference of Social Sciences—one of the largest and most important social science and humanities conferences in the world—organized by the Latin American Council of Social Sciences (CLACSO in Spanish) in Mexico City. Our presentation at CLACSO was an exhilarating reminder of the possibilities of feminist research practices and methods—and, most important, of the relationships it can nourish. All this has been part of my becoming a *companion* to Sulá Batsú's activists and their practice and vision of social justice, and yet none of this means that my work has not been critical of the organization.

Moreover, the co-op has also been critical of my work. We have disagreed on issues concerning the significance of entrepreneurship or feminist politics, for example. I have worked through these critiques in conversations with la coope—mostly with Kemly, my principal participant and collaborator—and also in essays published in academic journals and conference presentations. Some tensions have been resolved, and we have learned to live with others. It is fundamental that we as sociologists break away from modern-colonial constructs of "the objective observer" as the only path toward academic rigor. Why can't we be critical, thorough, and meticulous while acting with care and solidarity? "I refuse the split," as Cherríe Moraga memorably said in relation to imposed boundaries of identity.[23]

A feminist methodological praxis built on solidarity has transformed me, shaped my relationships with participants, and transgressed traditional paradigms of the production of knowledge in Euro-US academia, such as imposing the rule of the academic expert, undermining local knowledges and practices, and repressing emotion in research. Beyond the value of reciprocity or "giving back," it has been of utmost importance to me that my analyses, observations, and critiques enrich and serve the activists and organizations. It has filled me with happiness to learn that my work has helped them reflect on their own work, look at themselves differently, and, in the case of Sulá Batsú, even redefine themselves as a feminist organization after years of conversations about what feminism is, or can be.

APC WRP does not have a physical location, and activists live in countries around the world, which means that the nature of my relationships with them has been different. Our communication has mostly been online via email and video/text/voice apps. I have developed relationships with various activists, particularly those living in Latin America, but not being able to spend in-person time with them has presented its difficulties. Online relationships can indeed be very profound, yet not being able to have quality face-to-face encounters, together with the vast times zones between us, has limited the possibility of forming deeper bonds. Nonetheless, APC WRP activists were generous with their time and responsive to my numerous requests via emails and text messages. They have invited me to write for their online gender and technology website (genderit.org), interviewed me about my research, and cited my work in their own investigations and white papers. I have shared drafts of articles and chapters with them throughout the years and have received substantive feedback and valuable insights. It has been thrilling to see the ways in which online-based research can lead to such rich intellectual exchanges and conversations as the ones I have had with the APC WRP activists.

A constant reminder of the ways in which methods remain entangled in academic colonial structures has been the issue of language. Sociologist Sylvanna Falcón proposes multilingualism as a principle and a criterion for engaging in decolonial feminist transnational methodology.[24] Multilingualism may take numerous forms, such as translating our work, expanding citational politics, and adhering to the meanings given by the communities we collaborate with. My research with la coope is entirely in Spanish, which is my native language: the interviews, conversations, and the fieldnotes. Moreover, our political and affective structures are built on Spanish. It was just in 2022, with funding from the institution where I work, that I was able to hire someone to translate my research on the co-op to Spanish (I had previously published online excerpts in Spanish). Some of the activists had noted the problem of language. Those who are not completely bilingual in English and Spanish wanted to be able to fully comprehend the research as well as share it among their networks in Central and Latin America. Feminist scholar Richa Nagar describes this dilemma when she argues that although identity-based reflexivity is important, there must be "an extension to a more material and institutional focus."[25]

The political economy of funding and the academic race for publication and labor security also shape our methodologies, challenging the possibilities of harnessing alternative models of collaboration. I have published iterations of this research in various websites, online magazines, and peer-reviewed academic journals, and I have presented at academic and activist conferences both in the United States and internationally. In addition, extensive excerpts of my fieldnotes, written while doing fieldwork with Sulá Batsú, were published in an essay for the *Journal of Contemporary Ethnography.* Beyond providing me with the important opportunity to share my research with different audiences, these venues have been a critical space for demonstrating methodological honesty and accountability. My main responsibility, nonetheless, is with the communities of activists who have collaborated with me throughout the years.

I have circled back many times to Kapuściński's advice and warning. It is a reminder to always think about the lives my writing could affect in some way, in any way. Our methodological practices are always (or should be) a work in progress, a never-ending approximation to crafting research that is caring and solidary as well as critical, thorough, honest, and accountable.

NOTES

Introduction

1. Moussié, *Challenging Corporate Power*; Adams and Martens, *Fit for Whose Purpose?*; Seitz and Martens, "Philanthrolateralism."

2. Costanza-Chock, "Design Justice, A.I., and Escape from the Matrix of Domination"; Eubanks, *Automating Inequality*; Noble, *Algorithms of Oppression*; Zuboff, *Age of Surveillance Capitalism*; Couldry and Mejías, *Costs of Connection*; Benjamin, *Race after Technology*; Arora, "Bottom of the Data Pyramid"; Amrute, *Encoding Race, Encoding Class*.

3. In this book *technology* and *digital technology* mostly refer to information and communication technologies including hardware and software, mobile phones, smartphones, computers, the internet, social media, and applications (apps) in interaction with society, comprising sociotechnical systems. Moreover, *technologies* refers to ways of being and knowing in what Tressie McMillan Cottom describes as "technique, technology, and process of modern life." Since I started my research in 2015, definitions of digital technologies increasingly include big data, the internet of things, artificial intelligence (AI), and machine learning. Throughout this book I specify when *digital technologies* refer to the latter. McMillan Cottom, "Where Platform Capitalism and Racial Capitalism Meet," 441.

4. Segato, *La guerra contra las mujeres*, 30. My translation.

5. Bhattacharya, "Introduction: Mapping Social Reproduction Theory"; Fraser, "Contradictions of Capital and Care"; Federici, *Revolution at Point Zero*; James, *Our Time Is Now*.

6. There is a large and long history of literature on feminism and care; see, among many others, Held, *Ethics of Care*; Ruddick, "Care as Labor and Re-

169

lationship"; Camps, *Tiempo de cuidados*; Fisher and Tronto, "Toward a Feminist Theory of Caring"; Pateman, *Sexual Contract*; Ruddick, "Maternal Thinking."

7. Puig de la Bellacasa, "'Nothing Comes Without Its World.'"

8. Collins, *Black Feminist Thought*; Simpson, *As We Have Always Done.*

9. Anzaldúa, *Light in the Dark = Luz en lo Oscuro*; Lorde, "Uses of the Erotic"; Cabnal, *Feminismos diversos*; Segato, *La guerra contra las mujeres*; Gargallo, *Feminismos desde Abya Yala*; Paredes, "El feminismocomunitario"; Moraga and Anzaldúa, *This Bridge Called My Back*; Hull, Scott, and Smith, *But Some of Us Are Brave.*

10. Hobart and Kneese, "Radical Care," 2.

11. Gutiérrez Aguilar, "Because We Want Ourselves Alive." My emphasis.

12. Murphy, "Unsettling Care."

13. Abu-Lughod, "Do Muslim Women Really Need Saving?"

14. Cortés, "Generación Incubadora."

15. It is fundamental to point out that theories and practices of relationality have a millenary history in numerous Indigenous communities. Erasing this is yet another form of oppression, as Zoe Todd powerfully argues in "An Indigenous Feminist's Take" (16): "So it is so important to think, deeply, about how the Ontological Turn—with its breathless 'realisations' that animals, the climate, water, 'atmospheres' and non-human presences like ancestors and spirits are sentient and possess agency, that 'nature' and 'culture,' 'human' and 'animal' may not be so separate after all—is itself perpetuating the exploitation of Indigenous peoples." I incorporate aspects of Latin American Indigenous feminist thought throughout this book. See also TallBear, "Why Interspecies Thinking Needs Indigenous Standpoints."

16. Hobart and Kneese, "Radical Care," 2.

17. Foucault, *Birth of Biopolitics.*

18. Puig de la Bellacasa, "'Nothing Comes Without Its World,'" 204.

19. Ricaurte, "Mapping," 20.

20. Rolnik, *Esferas de la insurrección*, 13. My translation.

21. Gutiérrez Aguilar, "Because We Want Ourselves Alive."

22. Mohanty, *Feminism without Borders*, 7.

23. Dean, "Feminist Solidarity, Reflective Solidarity," 5.

24. It is important to note that APC WRP is not advocating for an unbridled online sexual agency. This is also why I have refrained from calling their practices "sex-positive," a concept often associated with white feminism in the global North. Manifestations of sexual pleasure are complicated and are intersected by age, race, class, gender, sexuality, disability, religion—in sum, by power and social location. I study online sexual and erotic pleasure because it stemmed from my empirical findings, but in this book pleasure is also about joy, fun, experimentation, and desire. Perhaps "sexual pleasure" is not an analytic that can be used by some communities, but pleasure, in its multiple and vast dimensions, could be, as adrienne maree brown has argued in her

book *Pleasure Activism*. For an excellent critique of US white feminist "sex positivism" and its history of equating women's sexual liberation with "empowerment" without an intersectional analysis, see Zakaria, *Against White Feminism*.

25. Foucault, *History of Sexuality*, vol. 1.

26. Nelson, *On Freedom*, 91.

27. Segato, *La guerra contra las mujeres*. My translation.

28. Segato, 27. My translation.

29. Segato, 27. My translation.

30. Segato, 29. My translation.

31. Lugones, "Heterosexualism and the Colonial/Modern Gender System."

32. Mohanty, "Under Western Eyes."

33. Segato, *La guerra contra las mujeres*, 19 (my translation).

34. Jolly, Cornwall, and Hawkins, *Women, Sexuality and the Political Power of Pleasure*.

35. Morris et al., *Researching Sex and Sexualities*; Wieringa and Sívori, *Sexual History of the Global South*; Pereira, *Changing Narratives of Sexuality*; Harcourt, "What a Gender Lens Brings to Development Studies"; Harcourt, "Gender and Development."

36. Cornwall, "Buzzwords and Fuzzwords," 480.

37. Santiago, "Lorena Cabnal."

38. Reyes, "¿Qué significa realmente el 'vivir sabroso' de Francia Márquez?" My translation.

39. López, "Lorena Cabnal."

40. "A un año del asesinato de líder indígena hondureña Berta Cáceres." My translation.

41. Lorde, *Sister Outsider*. See also brown, *Pleasure Activism*; Nash, "Black Sexualities"; Morgan, "Why We Get Off." There is also excellent scholarship that complicates the historical coupling of technology and Black victimization, such as André Brock's work on Black joy and digital practice (*Distributed Blackness*), and Catherine Knight Steele's on Black women's appropriation of technology (*Digital Black Feminism*).

42. Scholars Ana Shola Orloff, Raka Ray, and Evren Savci use the term *uneasy alliances* to explore how feminist politics can embrace agendas that are contrary to liberatory principles. Orloff, Ray, and Savci, "Introduction: Perverse Politics?"

43. Phillips and Cole, "Feminist Flows, Feminist Fault Lines," 190; Ferree and Tripp, *Global Feminism*.

44. Graeber and Grubačić, "Introduction," 23. There is a long history and a large literature on community-based cooperation and solidarity as a strategy of resistance and survival, particularly in times of crisis, in Indigenous, Black, Latinx, disabled, LGBTQI+ and non-binary communities across the world. See, for example, Spade, "Mutual Aid."

45. Puig de la Bellacasa, *Matters of Care*.

46. Escobar, *Encountering Development*.

47. Boserup, *Woman's Role in Economic Development*.

48. Scott, *Seeing Like a State*.

49. Cornwall and Rivas, "From 'Gender Equality' and 'Women's Empowerment' to Global Justice"; Roy, *Poverty Capital*; Moeller, *Gender Effect*; Bobel, *Managed Body*; Alvarez, "Ambivalent Engagements, Paradoxical Effects"; Wilson, "Towards a Radical Re-Appropriation"; Sen, Grown, and Development Alternatives with Women for a New Era (Project), *Development, Crises, and Alternative Visions*; Rodríguez Moreno, "Mujer y desarrollo."

50. Spivak, *Spivak Reader*, 10.

51. Escobar, *Encountering Development*; Cornwall, "Buzzwords and Fuzzwords"; Eade and Cornwall, *Deconstructing Development Discourse*; Sachs, *Development Dictionary*.

52. Kabeer, "Gender, Poverty, and Inequality"; Beneria, Berik, and Floro, "Gender and Development."

53. UN reports broadly define the Fourth Industrial Revolution as characterized by the dominance of emerging technologies such as artificial intelligence (AI), robotics, the internet of things, 3-D printing, quantum computing, and genetic engineering, among others.

54. The term most frequently used in both development reports and in the scholarly literature on gender, technology and development is ICT, as well as the umbrella term ICT4D (ICTs for development).

55. Williams and Artzberger, "Developing Women as ICT Users"; Zerai, *African Women, ICT and Neoliberal Politics*.

56. Gurumurthy, *A History of Feminist Engagement with Development and Digital Technologies*; Gurumurthy and Chami, "Development Justice in the Digital Paradigm"; Arora, *The Next Billion Users*; Arora and Rangaswamy, "Digital Leisure for Development"; Gajjala, "Woman and Other Women"; Gajjala and Tetteh, "Relax, You've Got M-PESA."

57. van Dijck, *The Culture of Connectivity*; Mejias and Couldry, "Datafication"; Zuboff, *The Age of Surveillance Capitalism*.

58. Escobar, *Encountering Development*; Ziai, *Exploring Post-Development*; Gibson-Graham, "Post-Development Possibilities for Local and Regional Development"; Saunders, *Feminist Post-Development Thought*; Demaria and Kothari, "Post-Development Dictionary Agenda."

59. Gibson-Graham, "Post-Development Possibilities for Local and Regional Development," 1.

60. White, "Arturo Escobar."

61. Rolnik, *Esferas de la insurrección*, 112. My translation.

62. Calkin, "Feminism, Interrupted?"; Chant and Sweetman, "Fixing Women or Fixing the World?"

63. von Schnitzler, "Citizenship Prepaid."

64. Karim, *Microfinance and Its Discontents*; Roy, *Poverty Capital*; Roy, "Subjects of Risk"; Radhakrishnan, *Making Women Pay*.

65. Roy, "Subjects of Risk," 140.

66. Foucault, *Birth of Biopolitics*, 242.

67. Foucault, 148.

68. Roy, "Subjects of Risk"; Elyachar, "Empowerment Money"; Cornwall, "Buzzwords and Fuzzwords."

69. Escobar, *Encountering Development*; Rose, *Powers of Freedom*.

70. Eisenstein, "Feminism Seduced"; Roberts, "Political Economy of 'Transnational Business Feminism'"; Roy, *Poverty Capital*.

71. Pedwell, "Affective (Self-) Transformations," 168.

72. Miller, Arutyunova, and Clark, *New Actors, New Money, New Conversations*; Moussié, *Challenging Corporate Power*.

73. Freeman, *Entrepreneurial Selves*, 213.

74. Martin, *Financialization of Daily Life*, 3.

75. KPMG Global, "Pulse of Fintech H2'21." Bateman, Duvendack, and Loubere, "Is Fin-tech the New Panacea for Poverty Alleviation and Local Development?"

76. Kemble et al., "The Dawn of the FemTech Revolution."

77. Mishra and Suresh, "Datafied Body Projects in India"; Cox, "Equity in Health Technology"; Rosas, "The Future Is Femtech"; Hendl and Jansky, "Tales of Self-Empowerment through Digital Health Technologies." See also Privacy International, "No Body's Business."

78. Schiebinger, "Harnessing Technology and Innovation."

79. Bernal and Grewal, "Introduction," 14.

80. Miller, Arutyunova, and Clark, *New Actors, New Money, New Conversations*.

81. Arutyunova and Clark, *Watering the Leaves, Starving the Roots*; Miller, Arutyunova, and Clark, *New Actors, New Money, New Conversations*.

82. The McKinsey Global Institute found that around four hundred million workers globally could be displaced by automation by 2030. McKinsey Global Institute, "AI, Automation, and the Future of Work"; McKinsey Global Institute, "Future of Women at Work." And according to the World Bank's *World Development Report 2016: Digital Dividends*, automation will be mostly affecting the "developing world."

83. ITU, *Measuring Digital Development: Facts and Figures 2021*.

84. Gurumurthy, *Gender and ICTs: Overview Report*. It is in this context that technology is conflated most with science because the stated objective of entering scientific fields is to become designers and producers of technology.

85. *UNESCO Science Report: The Race against Time for Smarter Development*; Bello et al., "To Be Smart, the Digital Revolution Will Need to Be Inclusive."

86. Brown, *Undoing the Demos*, 36.

87. I want to thank my mentor and friend, the anthropologist Nina Sylvanus, for this vital insight.

88. Federici, *Caliban and the Witch*.

89. Couldry and Mejías, *Costs of Connection*; Srnicek, *Platform Capitalism*; Zuboff, *Age of Surveillance Capitalism*; Costanza-Chock, "Design Justice, A.I., and Escape from the Matrix of Domination"; GenderIT, "Declaración: II Encuentro Internacional Ciberfeminista: Descolonizando internet"; Bouterse and Sengupta, *Decolonizing the Internet: Summary Report*; Eubanks, *Automating Inequality*; McMillan Cottom, "Where Platform Capitalism and Racial Capitalism Meet."

90. Rolnik, *Esferas de la insurrección*.

91. UN, *Report of the Secretary-General: Roadmap for Digital Cooperation*.

92. Donner and Gupta, "António Guterres Wants Gender Parity at the U.N."

93. Stake, *Multiple Case Study Analysis*.

94. Bedford, *Developing Partnerships*.

95. Prügl, "Neoliberalising Feminism," 616.

96. Connell and Dados, "Where in the World Does Neoliberalism Come From?"; Ferguson, "Uses of Neoliberalism"; Callison and Manfredi, *Mutant Neoliberalism*.

97. Bernstein and Jakobsen, *Paradoxes of Neoliberalism*.

98. Brown, *Undoing the Demos*.

99. Harvey, *Brief History of Neoliberalism*.

100. Callison and Manfredi, "Introduction: Theorizing Mutant Neoliberalism."

101. Gutiérrez Aguilar, "Women's Struggle against All Violence in Mexico"; Gago, "Is There a War 'on' the Body of Women?"; Segato, *La guerra contra las mujeres*.

102. Dados and Connell, "Global South," 13.

103. Milan and Treré, "Big Data from the South(s)," 321.

104. Medina, Marques, and Holmes, "Introduction: Beyond Imported Magic," 2. For important studies on the failures of techno-solutionism in eradicating inequality, see Daniel Greene, *Promise of Access*, on technology and poverty in the United States; and Morgan G. Ames, *Charisma Machine*, on the unfulfilled promises of the One Laptop per Child project in Latin America.

105. hooks, "Marginality as a Site of Resistance."

106. In her excellent study on feminist and antiracist activism at the UN, sociologist Sylvanna Falcón notes that antiracism forums were much more open to intersectional analysis, whereas the general UN agenda on women has been "dominated by Western-centric ideologies" that erase differences and treat women as a homogenous group. Falcón, *Power Interrupted*, 8.

107. There is currently an important transformation in the field of ICT4D from uncritical frameworks that approach ICTs' inclusion in development

processes that were not questioned to problematizing both technologies and the project of development. See, among others, Masiero, "Should We Still Be Doing ICT4D Research?"; Walsham, "ICT4D Research"; Avgerou, "Theoretical Framing of ICT4D Research." Richard Heeks, for example, has called for shifting paradigms from "digital divide" to "digital justice" and reframing concerns about exclusion to examine "adverse digital incorporation," a concept I examine in chapter 1. Heeks, "From the Digital Divide to Digital Justice in the Global South"; Heeks, "From Digital Divide to Digital Justice in the Global South: Conceptualising Adverse Digital Incorporation."

108. Daniels, Gregory, and Cottom, *Digital Sociologies*, xxiii.

109. I use the term *colonial* throughout this book (rarely *decolonial*, sometimes *anticolonial*). The trajectories of and debates about *colonial, decolonial*, and *postcolonial*—also in relation to feminism—are long, tumultuous, and outside the scope of this book. I can only speak to what *colonial* means to me. I am from a country, Puerto Rico, that has lived under colonial rule since 1493, first under the Spanish and then, since 1898, under the United States. In Puerto Rico, colonialism manifests through epistemic, symbolic, and material violence. It is about the genocide of Indigenous peoples, the enslavement of Africans, and the continuous dispossession and theft of our lands. It is about a process of persistent economic exploitation and corruption that has left us in bankruptcy and debt. But colonialism is also about how this project of violence has aimed to capture our intimate, social, and cultural spaces as well as our imaginations. "Aimed to capture" because colonialism in Puerto Rico has always encountered fierce resistance in many forms—sometimes as pleasure, sometimes as solidarity. This is my perspective, and where my definition of the *colonial* comes from. The corporate development digital technology machinery is colonialist as a settler project that steals, extracts, and exploits land, with a capitalist agenda based on making profit at all costs that aims to capture intimate spaces of our everyday lives with different implications intersected by race, class, gender, sexuality, and ability.

For some critical debates on *coloniality* and *decolonizing*, see Tuck and Yang, "Decolonization Is Not a Metaphor"; Rivera Cusicanqui, "Ch'ixinakax Utxiwa"; Cabnal, *Feminismos diversos*; Espinosa Miñoso, *De por qué es necesario un feminism descolonial*; Curiel, *Descolonizando el feminismo*; Mignolo, *Local Histories/Global Designs*; Quijano, "Coloniality and Modernity/Rationality"; Lugones, "Toward a Decolonial Feminism"; Segato, "Género y colonialidad"

110. Environmental scientist and scholar Max Liboiron (in *Pollution Is Colonialism*, 3) rightly argues that leaving white or settler scholars unmarked while marking all others "re-centers settlers and whiteness as an unexceptional norm, while deviations have to be marked and named." In this book I try as much as possible to avoid marking scholars or activist's nationalities or race. It is important to state that many of the authors I build upon are feminist

scholars and activists from Latin America, where racial categories have specific and distinct sociopolitical histories. This does not conflict with the fact that there is rampant racism—particularly anti-Black and anti-Indigenous—in the region, as well as a persistent history of settler colonialism and dispossession.

111. Ahmed, *Living a Feminist Life*, 15.

112. Connell, *Southern Theory*; Connell, "Meeting at the Edge of Fear"; Connell, "Decolonizing Sociology"; Banerjee and Connell, "Gender Theory as Southern Theory."

113. My friend and colleague, the historian Seçil Yilmaz, offered important feedback on the issue of harm.

114. Haraway, *Staying with the Trouble*, 1.

Chapter 1

1. Action Coalition on Technology and Innovation for Gender Equality, https://techforgenerationequality.org/about/.

2. Federici, *Revolution at Point Zero*; Fraser, "Contradictions of Capital and Care"; Dalla Costa and James, *Power of Women and the Subversion of the Community*; James, *Our Time Is Now*.

3. The UN is a massive institution that is far from cohesive. In the corpus of discourse under study, there are gestures toward transformation that are not necessarily extractive or focused on financialization. I have pointed to some of the patterns that undercut other important UN proposals, such as the universal right to health care, housing, decent work, and climate change and ecological responsibility, among others. In the methodological appendix I analyze this polyvalence, explain how texts were selected, and clarify the complex UN classification system of documents.

4. Van Waeyenberge, "Post-Washington Consensus," 205. In line with the increasing corporatization of development, economist Daniela Gabor has called the current moment the "Wall Street Consensus," focused on guaranteeing private financial investments of state-led development interventions through mechanisms such as private-public partnerships (PPPs). Gabor, "The Wall Street Consensus."

5. UN Secretary-General, "The Age of Digital Interdependence"; UNESCO, "Artificial Intelligence and Gender Equality"; UN, *Our Common Agenda*.

6. UN General Assembly, "A/RES/70/1 Transforming Our World." The phrase "leaving no one behind" is reminiscent of the "No Child Left Behind" law signed in 2002 by US president George W. Bush that imposed standardized testing to measure academic performance and narrow the "achievement gap" in schools. A wealth of research has found that the law actually left many children behind, particularly low-income and minoritized students, due to its strict focus on testing.

7. Bello et al., "To Be Smart, the Digital Revolution Will Need to Be Inclusive."

8. Heeks, "Digital Inequality beyond the Digital Divide."

9. McMillan Cottom, "Where Platform Capitalism and Racial Capitalism Meet," 443.

10. Rankin, "Governing Development."

11. Care Collective, *Care Manifesto*, 4.

12. Pérez Orozco, *Feminist Subversion of the Economy*.

13. Foucault, *Birth of Biopolitics*, 148.

14. Elyachar, *Markets of Dispossession*, 27.

15. West, Kraut, and Chew, *I'd Blush If I Could*, 27.

16. UNDP, *Gender Equality Strategy 2022–2025*; UN Women and UNDP, *Government Responses to COVID-19*.

17. UN Women, *SDG Monitoring Report*, 216.

18. UN Women, 101.

19. Bergeron and Healy, "Beyond the 'Business Case,'" 9.

20. Bergeron and Healy, 9.

21. Spivak, *Spivak Reader*e

22. UNDAW and UNESCO, *Gender, Science Technology Expert Group Report*, 18.

23. Huyer and Mitter, "ICTs, Globalisation and Poverty Reduction."

24. Since I started my research in 2015, Intel seems to have moved closer to working with young women and ICTs in the United States instead. Intel's website for She Will Connect announces three projects geared at digital literacy education for girls in the United States. Along the same lines, in 2019 Melinda Gates announced that she was committing US$1 billion to "expanding women's power and influence in the United States." Gates, "Melinda Gates."

25. West, Kraut, and Chew, *I'd Blush If I Could*, 27.

26. Molinier, *Leveraging Digital Finance for Gender Equality and Women's Empowerment*, 46.

27. Demirgüç-Kunt et al., *Global Findex Database 2017*; Molinier, *Leveraging Digital Finance for Gender Equality and Women's Empowerment*; Task Force on Digital Financing of the SDGs, *People's Money*.

28. FIGI—Financial Inclusion Global Initiative, accessed October 21, 2022, https://figi.itu.int/.

29. Financial Inclusion Global Initiative (FIGI) Symposium, accessed October 21, 2022, www.itu.int/en/ITU-T/extcoop/figisymposium/Pages/default.aspx. My emphasis.

30. Greene, *Promise of Access*, 2.

31. "The Global Findex Database 2021: Financial Inclusion, Digital Payments, and Resilience in the Age of COVID-19," accessed October 21, 2022, https://globalfindex.worldbank.org/#about_focus.

32. Demirgüç-Kunt et al., *Global Findex Database 2021*.

33. Gates, "Digital Tech Is Turning the Unbanked into the Banked."

34. Demirgüç-Kunt et al., *Global Findex Database 2021*, 10.

35. UN, "Inequality in a Rapidly Changing World," 76.

36. See Masiero, "Biometric Infrastructures and the Indian Public Distribution System"; Masiero and Shakthi, "Grappling with Aadhaar"; Masiero and Das, "Datafying Anti-Poverty Programmes."

37. Gabor and Brooks, "Digital Revolution in Financial Inclusion," 3.

38. Cavallero, Gago, and Perosino, "¿De qué se trata la inclusión financiera?"

39. This is an important document as it has set the agenda for multistakeholder priorities for financing for development.

40. Doha NGO Group on Financing for Development, "Declaration from Doha Civil Society on Financing for Development," 11.

41. Per the UN's own findings, as well as those from other sources, emerging data confirms that violence against women increased during COVID-19 and that global poverty increased for the first time in twenty years. See UN Women, *Measuring the Shadow Pandemic*; *Lancet*, "Violence against Women"; UN, *Sustainable Development Goals Report 2021*.

42. See Malala, "Law and Regulation," for an analysis on the regulatory and legal issues surrounding the implementation of M-Pesa in Kenya.

43. Suri and Jack, "The Long-Run Poverty and Gender Impacts"; Bateman, Duvendack, and Loubere, "Is Fin-tech the New Panacea?"

44. Gajjala and Tetteh, "Relax, You've Got M-PESA."

45. Wajcman, *Feminism Confronts Technology*; Arora, *Next Billion Users*.

46. UN Inter-agency Task Force on Financing for Development, "Financing for Sustainable Development 2022."

47. UN Secretary-General, *UN Secretary-General's Strategy on New Technologies*.

48. UN Secretary-General, 16.

49. UN Secretary-General, 10.

50. Irani, *Chasing Innovation*, 3.

51. Moeller, *Gender Effect*; Bobel, *Managed Body*; Chant and Sweetman, "Fixing Women or Fixing the World?"; Roy, *Poverty Capital*; Roy, "Subjects of Risk"; Wilson, "Towards a Radical Re-Appropriation"; Murphy, *Economization of Life*; Roberts, "Political Economy of 'Transnational Business Feminism'"; Radhakrishnan, *Making Women Pay*; Altan-Olcay, "Entrepreneurial Subjectivities and Gendered Complexities"; Karim, *Microfinance and Its Discontents*; Rankin, "Governing Development"; Rankin, "Social Capital, Microfinance, and the Politics of Development."

52. Wilson, "Towards a Radical Re-Appropriation."

53. Roy, "Subjects of Risk," 149.

54. Cavallero and Gago, *Una lectura feminista de la deuda*, 38. Author's emphasis, my translation.

55. Roy, "Positive Side of Co-optation?," 257; Bergeron, "Post-Washington Consensus and Economic Representations of Women"; Calkin, "Feminism, Interrupted?"; Chant and Sweetman, "Fixing Women or Fixing the World?";

Cornwall, "Buzzwords and Fuzzwords"; Cornwall, "Women's Empowerment"; Cornwall and Anyidoho, "Introduction"; Cornwall, Harrison, and Whitehead, "Gender Myths and Feminist Fables"; Cornwall and Rivas, "From 'Gender Equality' and 'Women's Empowerment' to Global Justice"; Jong and Kimm, "Co-Optation of Feminisms"; Roberts, "Political Economy of 'Transnational Business Feminism'"; Roy, "Subjects of Risk"; Roy, "Enacting/Disrupting the Will to Empower"; Wilson, "Towards a Radical Re-Appropriation."

56. West, Kraut, and Chew, *I'd Blush If I Could*, 33.

57. Greene, *Promise of Access.*

58. The definition of skills is inconsistent, but there is an increasing move to define "basic" skills as those needed to send an email with an attachment, for example; "standard" or intermediate" skills as the ability to make a slide presentation; and "advanced" or "high-level" skills as those needed to participate in the tech industry. ITU, *Measuring Digital Development 2021*; UN University and EQUALS, *Taking Stock.*

59. In development studies, the concept of technological appropriation is often traced back to Schumacher's *Small Is Beautiful: Economics as If People Mattered* on the importance of communities in the developing world to create their own "appropriate" technologies. Many digital activists, particularly in Latin America, use *appropriation* to describe defiant and subversive uses of technologies.

60. Noble, *Algorithms of Oppression*, 65.

61. Evident recently when Google ousted computer scientist Tinmit Gebru. Rankin, "For 50 Years, Tech Companies Have Tried to Increase Diversity." In addition to internal DEI programs, in recent years both Meta and Google have sponsored projects focused on gender and technology, such as closing the gender data gap and increasing women's digital entrepreneurship in both the global North and South. See Women Will (website); Google Developers, Women Techmakers (website); Ravindranath, "Introducing the Inaugural Class of the Google for Startups Accelerator"; Levine, "Helping to Close the Gender Data Gap."

62. GSMA and Oslo Metropolitan University for the EQUALS Leadership Coalition, *Perceptions of Power*; UNICEF and ITU, *Towards an Equal Future*; UN University and EQUALS, *Taking Stock.*

63. UN Women, *Innovation for Gender Equality.*

64. UNCTAD, *Applying a Gender Lens to Science, Technology and Innovation*, 17.

65. Shiva, *Staying Alive*; Mies and Shiva, *Ecofeminism.*

66. UNESCO, UN Women, ITU, and Microsoft, *Girls in STEM and ICT Careers*, 3.

67. EQUALS Global Partnership (website), accessed October 21, 2022, https://www.equalsintech.org/about.

68. UN University and EQUALS, *Taking Stock*, 25.

69. UN University and EQUALS, 35.

70. UN University and EQUALS, 33.

71. UN University and EQUALS, 36. My emphasis.

72. These technologies were mostly grouped at the time under advances in the digitalization of information and communication technologies, including computers, internet, radio and television. But the report includes analog technologies.

73. Gurumurthy, *A History of Feminist Engagement*, 3.

74. The priority theme of the 67th session of the CSW in 2023 is "Innovation and technological change, and education in the digital age for achieving gender equality and the empowerment of all women and girls" (see UN Women. "CSW67, 2023," www.unwomen.org/en/csw/csw67-2023).

75. Gurumurthy, *Gender and ICTs*.

76. Gurumurthy, *A History of Feminist Engagement*, 4.

77. Lee, "UNESCO's Conceptualization of Women and Telecommunications 1970–2000."

78. Chant and Sweetman, "Fixing Women or Fixing the World?," 518.

79. Gurumurthy, *A History of Feminist Engagement*, 4.

80. "ITU World Information Society Award Ceremony."

81. Moussié, *Challenging Corporate Power*.

82. Hafkin and Taggart, "Executive Summary"; Huyer and Carr, "Information and Communication Technologies."

83. Huyer and Mitter, "ICTs, Globalisation and Poverty Reduction."

84. WSIS, organized by the UN and the ITU, was the first major multistakeholder platform for ICT issues that brought together actors from the state, civil society, and the private sector. ITU is the is the UN specialized agency for information and communication technologies.

85. "Gender in the Information Society: Emerging Issues"; Gurumurthy, *Gender and ICTs*; Gurumurthy, *A History of Feminist Engagement*.

86. Gurumurthy, *A History of Feminist Engagement*, 5; Pyati, "WSIS: Whose Vision of an Information Society?"

87. Civil Society Declaration to the World Summit on the Information Society, "Shaping Information Societies for Human Needs," 326.

88. World Summit on the Information Society, Tunis Commitment.

89. Gurumurthy, *A History of Feminist Engagement*, 6.

90. "Best Practice Forums," IGF, https://www.intgovforum.org/en/content/best-practice-forums-bpfs.

91. "Best Practice Forum on Gender and Access."

92. Gurumurthy, *A History of Feminist Engagement*, 9.

93. UN General Assembly, *2030 Agenda for Sustainable Development*.

94. "Digital Technologies to Achieve the UN SDGs," www.itu.int/en/mediacentre/backgrounders/Pages/icts-to-achieve-the-united-nations-sustainable-development-goals.aspx; UN Department of Economic and Social Affairs, Technology Facilitation Mechanism, https://sdgs.un.org/tfm.

95. Cummings, Seferiadis, and Haan, "Getting Down to Business?," 768; Weber, "Politics of 'Leaving No One Behind.'"

96. The Special Procedures of the Human Rights Council are "independent human rights experts with mandates to report and advise on human rights from a thematic or country-specific perspective" (see UN Human Rights Office of the High Commissioner, Special Procedures of the Human Rights Council (webpage), www.ohchr.org/EN/HRBodies/SP/Pages/Introduction .aspx. There are both thematic and country mandates.

97. Moolman, "Recognition of Online GBV in International Law"; Martins and Ferrari, "Human Rights Online at the Human Rights Council 47th Session."

98. Special Rapporteur on the Promotion and Protection of the Right to Freedom of Opinion and Expression, Frank LaRue, "A/HRC/17/27: Promotion and Protection of All Human Rights, Civil, Political, Economic, Social and Cultural Rights, Including the Right to Development," 7.

99. Special Rapporteur on Violence against Women, Dubravka Šimonović, *Report of the Special Rapporteur on Violence against Women*, 5.

100. Special Rapporteur on the Promotion and Protection of the Right to Freedom of Opinion and Expression, Irene Khan, *Gender Justice and Freedom of Expression*.

101. Eade and Cornwall, *Deconstructing Development Discourse*.

102. Dolker, *Where Is the Money for Feminist Organizing?*; Arutyunova and Clark, *Watering the Leaves, Starving the Roots*.

103. Generation Equality Forum, "Action Coalitions Global Acceleration Plan."

104. Generation Equality Forum, "Action Coalitions Commitment Makers," 2.

105. Generation Equality Forum, "Action Coalitions Leadership Structures."

106. UN Women, *Generation Equality Accountability Report 2022*, https://www.unwomen.org/en/digital-library/publications/2022/09/ generation-equality-accountability-report-2022.

107. Generation Equality Forum, "Action Coalitions Commitment Makers," 3.

108. Generation Equality Forum, "Action Coalitions Global Acceleration Plan," 16.

109. Generation Equality Forum, "Technology and Innovation for Gender Equality Action Coalition."

110. Downing, *Radical Media*; Riaño Alcalá, *Women in Grassroots Communication*; Rodríguez, *Fissures in the Mediascape*.

111. Cleaver, "Zapatista Effect."

112. Burch, "ALAI: A Latin American Experience in Social Networking."

113. Dependence theory is broadly defined as a theory that explains the

asymmetrical national economic development of poorer states, particularly "developing countries" in the global South, by focusing on external political, economic, and cultural influences. Sunkel, "National Development Policy and External Dependence in Latin America." To understand ECLAC's sociopolitical, theoretical, and policy-making trajectories and importance in the region, see Fajardo's excellent "The World that Latin America Created."

114. ECLAC, *Data, Algorithms and Policies*; ECLAC, *Digital Technologies for a New Future*.

115. ECLAC, *Montevideo Strategy for Implementation of the Regional Gender Agenda*; ECLAC, *Women's Autonomy in Changing Economic Scenarios*; ECLAC, *Santo Domingo Consensus*; ECLAC, *Women in the Digital Economy*; Vaca-Trigo, *Oportunidades y desafíos para la autonomía de las mujeres en el futuro escenario del trabajo*.

116. ECLAC, *Santo Domingo Consensus*.

117. For fifteen years the Bolivian feminist activist and sociologist Sonia Montaño was the head of the Division of Gender Affairs. Upon her retirement in 2015, she said that among her achievements, along with legitimizing abortion on ECLAC's agenda and linking gender to population issues and to the chain of production, had been working with the issue of ICTs: "it has been a very interesting link because before, technology, innovation, and productive development were for development experts, there was not the slightest gender perspective. Now, the division of production and business development has made a major change, and especially regarding ICTs" (my translation). Maldonado, "Sonia Montaño tras su alejamiento de Cepal."

118. CEPAL–Naciones Unidas, *Mujer y nuevas tecnologías*.

119. CEPAL–Naciones Unidas, 11.

120. Bonder, *New Information Technologies and Women*; Bonder, *El enfoque de género en el ADN de la educación científico-tecnológica*.

121. Bonder, *New Information Technologies and Women*, 50. My translation.

122. Bonder, *From Access to Appropriation*, 4. My translation.

123. The ECLAC has been involved in supporting national policies on digital development since at least 2000. The World Summit on the Information Society (in 2003 and 2005) led to the Plan of Action for the Information and Knowledge Society in Latin America and the Caribbean (eLAC in Spanish), the first of five regional action plans since 2007, in conjunction with regional ministerial conferences on the Information Society organized since 2005. "Antecedentes," www.cepal.org/es/elac2022/antecedentes.

124. Vaca-Trigo and Valenzuela, *Digitalización de las mujeres en América Latina y el Caribe*; ECLAC, *Digital Technologies for a New Future*.

125. ONU Mujeres, "Plataforma virtual conectará a más de 3,8 millones de mujeres en América Latina y el Caribe en torno a la tecnología y el emprendimiento."

126. Vera Ramírez, "El abrazo fintech del Grupo Santander."

127. ECLAC, "Women's Autonomy, Gender Equality and the Building of a Care Society."

128. Guterres, "Tackling Inequality."

129. UN, *Our Common Agenda.*

130. Bahous, "Speech."

Chapter 2

1. Instituto Nacional de Fomento Cooperativo, *Cooperativismo autogestionario.*

2. Over the years I have interviewed activists who have left the co-op who are included in the book. I use pseudonyms for the staff of Sulá Batsú, except for the co-op's director, Kemly Camacho. I use the real name of the organization because it is important to recognize their work. All the interviews were conducted in Spanish. Translations to English in this book are mine.

3. Participants in my study come from a range of socioeconomic backgrounds. At the time of this study, they all self-identified as middle-class and mestiza. In terms of education, all participants hold at least an undergraduate degree. Demographic questions were open, and I did not include income ranges or racial categories in order to be sensitive to different regional and local cultural norms and sociopolitical histories.

4. Escobar, *Designs for the Pluriverse,* 96, 21.

5. Browne, *Dark Matters.*

6. Community networks have flourished in the global South in defiance of corporate and state-controlled telecommunications. See APC and IDRC, *Global Information Society Watch 2018.*

7. Camacho, "Mercantilización del territorio y reconfiguración."

8. In 2021, Facebook (the company) was rebranded as Meta. Facebook continues to be the name of the social media platform (which is now a product under Meta). In this book, I thus use *Facebook* to refer to the social media platform (interviewees and most texts do the same as well), and *Meta* to refer to the corporation.

9. Cabnal, *Feminismos diversos*; López, "Lorena Cabnal"; Paredes and Comunidad mujeres creando comunidad, *Hilando fino*; Cabnal, "TZK'AT, red de sanadoras ancestrales del feminismo comunitario desde Iximulew-Guatemala."

10. Latour, "Where Are the Missing Masses?."

11. Segato, *La guerra contra las mujeres,* 99.

12. Noble, "A Future for Intersectional Black Feminist Technology Studies"; Weinstein, Blades, and Gleason, "Questioning Power."

13. Benjamin, *Race after Technology,* 61.

14. For the 2023 fiscal year, upper-middle-income economies are those with a GNI (gross national income) per capita between $4,256 and $13,205 (see current World Bank classifications at https://datahelpdesk.worldbank.org /knowledgebase/articles/906519).

15. CEPAL-Naciones Unidas, *El enfoque de brechas estructurales*; Banco Mundial, "Costa Rica."

16. Cupples and Larios, "A Functional Anarchy."

17. Mesa-Lago, *Market, Socialist, and Mixed Economies.*

18. Vo, "Concern for Community." Also, see the website of Costa Rica's National Cooperative Institute (INFOCOOP), at www.infocoop.go.cr/.

19. Arce Brenes, "Estudio situacional de la PYME Serie 2012–2017."

20. PROCOMER and CAMTIC, *Mapeo de tecnologías digitales 2019.*

21. PROCOMER and CAMTIC.

22. MEIC, "Política nacional de empresariedad 2019–2030."

23. MEIC, 15.

24. A4AI, *2020 Affordability Report.*

25. See Internet World Stats, at www.internetworldstats.com/stats2.htm, which collects statistics from various sources including the International Telecommunications Union (ITU), Facebook, and Nielsen Online. The website defines "internet penetration rate" as "the percentage of the total population of a given country or region that uses the Internet."

26. MICITT, *National Telecommunications Development Plan (PNDT) 2015–2021: Costa Rica: A Connected Society*, 65.

27. Costa Rica celebrated the bicentenary of its independence on September 15, 2021, together with Guatemala, Honduras, El Salvador, and Nicaragua. MICITT, "Estrategia de transformación digital del bicentenario."

28. MICITT, "Política Nacional para la Igualdad entre Mujeres y Hombres."

29. MICITT, "Política Nacional," 19.

30. MICITT, "Se oficializa la creación de la promotora costarricense de innovación e investigación."

31. "Una red global," https://sanjose.impacthub.net/sobreih/.

32. Ábrego, "La inaplazable conveniencia de las mujeres en STEM."

33. Eschle and Maiguashca, "Reclaiming Feminist Futures," 647.

34. Beck, *How Development Projects Persist*; Eschle and Maiguashca.

35. Large technology corporations, such as Microsoft, use open-source software. See Barnett, "How Corporate America Went Open-Source"; Vaughan-Nichols, "The Corporation Has Gone Open Source." This has fueled debates on the incorporation of open-source software in the corporative world. But I am referring to a specific ethos that free and open-source software activists still believe in and promote.

36. Juris, *Networking Futures.*

37. Juris, 17. Although they are often conflated in conversations, there are differences between "free" software and "open source" software. Free software is a social movement with cultural and ethical mandates, while open source is more oriented toward its practical value; see Coleman, *Coding Freedom.*

38. Hardt and Negri, *Commonwealth*; Gibson-Graham, "Post-Development Possibilities for Local and Regional Development," 12.

39. Federici, "Feminism and the Politics of the Commons"

40. Gibson-Graham, "Post-Development Possibilities for Local and Regional Development."

41. Shokooh Valle, "Moving beyond Co-optation."

42. Breines, "Community and Organization."

43. Simpson, *As We Have Always Done*, 19. Author's emphasis.

44. Gutiérrez Aguilar, "Because We Want Ourselves Alive."

45. Rolnik, *Esferas de la insurrección*.

Chapter 3

1. Hierro, *La ética del placer*, 41. My translation.

2. Nast and Rigot, "Apple and Google Still Have an LGBTQ Problem."

3. Bradford Franklin and Nojeim, "International Coalition Calls on Apple."

4. Hernandez, "Reversing a Planned Ban, Only Fans Will Allow Pornography."

5. Alexander, "Redrafting Morality"; Escobar, *Encountering Development*; Harding, "Latin American Decolonial Social Studies of Scientific Knowledge"; Medina, Marques, and Holmes, "Introduction: Beyond Imported Magic."

6. Harding, "Introduction"; Shiva, *Staying Alive*.

7. Taylor and Broeders, "In the Name of Development"; Arora, "Bottom of the Data Pyramid"; Couldry and Mejías, *Costs of Connection*; Gurumurthy and Chami, "Data"; Milan and Treré, "Big Data from the South(s)."

8. Federici, *Caliban and the Witch*; Federici, *Witches, Witch-Hunting, and Women*.

9. Valencia, *Gore Capitalism*.

10. Shokooh Valle, "Moving beyond Co-optation."

11. Costanza-Chock, *Design Justice*; Aguilar, "A Modest Proposal;" Noble, *Algorithms of Oppression*.

12. Federici, *Beyond the Periphery of the Skin*, 123.

13. APC WRP capitalizes the name.

14. Moolman, "Recognition of Online GBV in International Law."

15. Noronha and Higgs, "Internet Is a 'Radically Different' Place."

16. For a history of APC's role in the creation of "feminist and queer counterpublics" in Latin America, see Friedman, *Interpreting the Internet*.

17. brown, *Pleasure Activism*, 3.

18. APC WRP has supported the agency of sex workers. In its activism and in this book, pleasure as a feminist technopolitical tactic includes and yet also goes beyond sex work, encompassing multiple manifestations of pleasure and joy.

19. Segato, *La guerra contra las mujeres*.

20. Levey, *Sexual Harassment Online*.

21. Jones, *Camming*, 24–25.

22. Nelson, *On Freedom*, 110.

23. Haraway, *Simians, Cyborgs, and Women*.

24. Federici, *Beyond the Periphery of the Skin*, 11.

25. Mohanty, "Under Western Eyes."

26. Harcourt, "What a Gender Lens Brings to Development Studies," 369.

27. Noble, "Future for Intersectional Black Feminist Technology Studies"; Mohanty, "Under Western Eyes."

28. Walsh, "Decoloniality In/As Praxis," 35.

29. Zilli and Sívori, "Introduction," 7–8.

30. hvale vale, "Introduction," 11.

31. *Feminist Principles of the Internet*, GenderIT.org, October 3, 2016, https://genderit.org/resources/feminist-principles-internet-2016.

32. The grassroots collective Sursiendo, based in Chiapas, Mexico, and focused on liberatory digital culture, has been promoting—with the support of APC—an eighteenth feminist principle centered on environmental justice. The draft states: "A feminist internet respects life in all its forms; it does not consume it. Our proposal for a feminist internet principle in relation to the environment resignifies care towards an ethics of collective care in choices around design, extraction, production, consumption and disposal of the technologies involved." The draft is the outgrowth of the hackfeminist meeting Technology and Affections: How to Outline Policies of [Co]responsibility" held in Chiapas in 2019, convened by scholar-activists Jes Ciacci, Paula Ricaurte, and Nadia Cortés. Ciacci, "Imagining a Principle for a Feminist Internet Focusing on Environmental Justice."

33. See, for example, "Economy," https://feministinternet.org/en/principle/economy; "Movement Building," https://feministinternet.org/en/principle/movement-building.

34. Daniels, "Rethinking Cyberfeminism(s)."

35. Jarrett, "Digital Labor"; Gray and Suri, *Ghost Work*; Roberts, *Behind the Screen*; Irani, *Chasing Innovation*.

36. Lal, "How One Can Imagine Embodiment?"

37. Saldroite, "Queer Lust and Internet Orgasms."

38. Lugones, "Heterosexualism and the Colonial/Modern Gender System"; Segato and Monque, "Gender and Coloniality."

39. Community or communitarian feminism is a distinctive feminism theorized and practiced by some Indigenous feminists in Latin America. Julieta Paredes and Adriana Guzmán offer a detailed explanation of the concept in *El tejido de la rebeldia*: "Communityfeminism [as spelled in the text] is a social movement that responds to the circular form of knowledge and thought that we recover critically from our originary peoples, ways of being and thinking

that we recover, rethink, and reassert, so they can allow us to overcome ways of constructing knowledge that are fragmented, androcentric, linear, rational, and dominating of nature, incapable of relationality and of weaving forms of life so everything can live and exist" (61).

40. Santiago, "Lorena Cabnal." My translation.

41. Cabnal, *Feminismos diversos*, 22.

42. Daniels, "Rethinking Cyberfeminism(s)," 111.

43. Federici, *Caliban and the Witch*; Harcourt, "Body Politics and Postdevelopment."

44. Valencia, *Gore Capitalism*, 10.

45. Segato, *La guerra contra las mujeres*, 27.

46. Butler, "Judith Butler on Rethinking Vulnerability, Violence, Resistance."

47. Federici, *Caliban and the Witch*; Federici, *Revolution at Point Zero*.

48. Gutiérrez Aguilar, "Because We Want Ourselves Alive."

49. Walsh, "Decoloniality In/As Praxis," 35.

50. Gago, *Feminist International*; Segato, *La guerra contra las mujeres*; Gutiérrez Aguilar, "Because We Want Ourselves Alive."

51. Menjívar, *Enduring Violence*; Gago, *Feminist International*; Segato, *La guerra contra las mujeres*.

52. Gutiérrez Aguilar, "Women's Struggle against All Violence in Mexico," 675.

53. WHO, "Violence against Women."

54. Gago, *Feminist International*, 56–57. Author's emphasis.

55. Gago, 57.

56. Federici, *Caliban and the Witch*; Federici, *Witches, Witch-Hunting, and Women*.

57. Federici, *Caliban and the Witch*, 16.

58. Segato, *La guerra contra las mujeres*, 91.

59. Segato, *La escritura en el cuerpo de las mujeres asesinadas*.

60. "Facebook Files," *Wall Street Journal*; Mozur, "A Genocide Incited on Facebook"; Angwin and Grassegger, "Facebook's Secret Censorship Rules"; Taub and Fisher, "Facebook Fueled Anti-Refugee Attacks in Germany"; Ressa, "Propaganda War."

61. Segato, *La guerra contra las mujeres*, 98. My translation.

62. Curiel, *Descolonizando el feminismo*; Espinosa Miñoso, *De por qué es necesario un feminism descolonial*.

63. APC, *Online Gender-Based Violence*, 4. I use APC WRP's definitions in this book because this is the organization I have studied. I adhere to APC WRP's use of the phrase "non-consensual distribution of intimate images" instead of the misnomer "revenge porn" (Maddocks, "'Revenge Porn'"; Maddocks, "From Non-consensual Pornography to Image-Based Sexual Abuse") or other accepted terms used broadly by scholars such as "non-consensual

pornography" (Maddocks, "Feminism, Activism and Non-consensual Pornography") or "image-based sexual abuse," McGlynn and Rackley, "Research Briefing."

64. APC, *Online Gender-Based Violence*, 3.

65. Bowles, "Thermostats, Locks and Lights"; Greenberg, "Hacker Eva Galperin Has a Plan."

66. Citron, *Hate Crimes in Cyberspace*; Marwick and Miller, "Online Harassment, Defamation, and Hateful Speech"; World Wide Web Foundation, *Women's Rights Online*; Lenhart et al., "Online Harassment, Digital Abuse, and Cyberstalking"; Dunn, *Technology-Facilitated Gender-Based Violence*; Sobieraj, *Credible Threat*.

67. Jane, *Misogyny Online*; Levey, *Sexual Harassment Online*; Mantilla, "Gendertrolling"; Bailey, *Misogynoir Transformed*. Online gender-based violence of a sexual nature that may be related to the nonconsensual distribution of images—and that constitute "sexual-privacy invasions" (Citron, "Sexual Privacy")—includes digital voyeurism, sextortion, and deep-fake nude images and videos.

68. Marwick, "Morally Motivated Networked Harassment"; Marwick and Caplan, "Drinking Male Tears."

69. Citron, *Hate Crimes in Cyberspace*; World Wide Web Foundation, "Online Crisis Facing Women and Girls"; Pew Research Center and Vogels, *State of Online Harassment*; APC, *Online Gender-Based Violence*; Peña, "Violencia de género por medios digitales en Latinoamérica"; Luchadoras, *La violencia en línea contra las mujeres en México*; Ananías Soto and Vergara Sánchez, *Informe preliminar Chile y la violencia de género en internet*; APC WRP, "End Violence"; Centre for International Governance Innovation, *Non-Consensual Intimate Image Distribution*.

70. Posetti et al., "ICFJ-UNESCO Study"; Toledo, "Misoginia en internet"; Iniciativa Mesoamericana de Mujeres Defensoras de Derechos Humanos, "El Salvador"; Espinosa Gutiérrez, "Agresiones contra periodistas y defensoras de DH va en aumento"; Luchadoras, *Violencia política a través de las tecnologías*; Goldberg, "Fake Nudes and Real Threats"; Souza and Varon, *Violencia política de género en internet*.

71. UN Women, *Online and ICT Facilitated Violence against Women*; UN Women, *COVID-19 and Ending Violence against Women and Girls*; APC, *COVID-19 and the Increase of Domestic Violence against Women*.

72. Peña, "Recommendations on Technology-Related Violence Against Women (VAW) for the UN"; Gurumurthy and Chami, *Feminist Action Framework*; Kee, *Cultivating Violence through Technology?*; Shaw, "Internet Is Full of Jerks."

73. Jolly, Cornwall, and Hawkins, *Women, Sexuality and the Political Power of Pleasure*, 8.

74. Moolman, "Recognition of Online GBV in International Law"; Agu-

188

irre, "La violencia en línea contra las mujeres y las niñas (parte II)"; Aguirre, "La violencia en línea contra las mujeres y las niñas (parte I)."

75. Special Rapporteur on Violence against Women, Dubravka Šimonović, *Report of the Special Rapporteur on Violence against Women*.

76. It is important to point out that the analysis here is not about dissecting the data on how many individuals (disaggregated by race, gender) have or have not been convicted by laws against image-based abuse. The analysis centers the difficult question of feminist approaches to violence. See Schoenebeck, Haimson, and Nakamura, "Drawing from Justice Theories to Support Targets of Online Harassment" for an examination of the dilemmas of criminal legal models in content moderation of online violence in the United States.

77. Richie, "Reimagining the Movement to End Gender Violence"; Davis et al., *Abolition. Feminism. Now*; Davis, *Freedom Is a Constant Struggle*; Lang and Segato, "Justicia Feminista ante el estado ausente"; INCITE!, "Critical Resistance Statement."

78. Numerous Black women and women of color who are abolitionist scholars and activists have examined the racist politics of punishment, policing, and incarceration, providing innovative and radical visions and practices for justice, accountability, and transformation. See, among others, Kaba, *We Do This 'Til We Free Us*; Gilmore, *Golden Gulag*; Law, "Prisons Make Us Safer"; Davis, *Are Prisons Obsolete?*; Gilmore, *Change Everything*.

79. Centre for Internet and Society, "Revenge Porn Laws across the World."

80. Robertson, "Federal 'Revenge Porn' Ban"; Cyber Civil Rights Initiative, "48 States + DC + One Territory Now Have Revenge Porn Laws."

81. Peña, "Violencia de género por medios digitales en Latinoamérica."

82. Hernández Bauzá, *2010–2020: Sucesos regulatorios en materias de privacidad e internet en Latinoamérica*.

83. Gobierno de México, *Ley Olympia*.

84. Lang and Segato, "Justicia Feminista ante el estado ausente"; Gutiérrez Aguilar, "Argumentos en discusión con las ideas que sostienen Lang y Segato en su provocación."

85. APC, *Online Gender-Based Violence*; Peña, "Recommendations on Technology-Related Violence against Women (VAW) for the UN"; Luchadoras et al., "Sociedad civil insta a la Cámara de Diputados a atender violencia digital de forma integral"; Suarez Estrada, "Feminist Struggles against Criminalization of Digital Violence."

86. Citron and Franks, "Criminalizing Revenge Porn"; Franks, "Democratic Surveillance"; Citron, "Sexual Privacy"; Centre for International Governance Innovation, *Non-Consensual Intimate Image Distribution*.

87. Collins, *Black Feminist Thought*.

88. APC, *Online Gender-Based Violence*, 20.

89. Franks, "Democratic Surveillance."

90. "Digital Care," https://www.apc.org/en/digital-care-feminist-activists; "Oracle," https://www.transfeministech.codingrights.org/.

91. Padte, *Cyber Sexy*; Peña and Varon, *Consent to Our Data Bodies*.

92. In the United States, Tarana Burke founded the #MeToo movement in 2006 to address sexual violence, particularly against Black girls and women. In 2017 it became a global movement against sexual violence that spread on social media (https://metoomvmt.org/get-to-know-us/). Jackson, Bailey, and Welles, *#HashtagActivism*. In Latin America, feminist movements have used numerous hashtags to mobilize and create awareness around violence against women. Two of the most powerful hashtags against femicide have been #NiUnaMenos (#NotOneLess) and #VivasNosQueremos (#WeWantOurselves-Alive). In "Becoming an 'Intimate Publics,'" Shenila Khoja-Moolji argues that the #BringBackOurGirls social media campaign fostered a false form of public intimacy. In a fascinating commentary, Khoja-Moolji analyzes how feminist liberals based in the global North have created hashtags underscored by the impulse to save girls in the global South, such as the viral #BringBackOur-Girls, reclaiming the devolution of the hundreds of girls kidnapped by the organization Boko Haram in Nigeria.

93. Maddocks, "Feminism, Activism and Non-consensual Pornography."

94. UN University and EQUALS, *Taking Stock*; ITU and UN Women, *Action Plan to Close the Digital Gender Gap*; UN Secretary-General, *UN Secretary-General's Strategy on New Technologies*; UNCTAD, *Technology and Innovation Report 2021*; UN Women, *SDG Monitoring Report*; EQUALS Global Partnership, *10 Lessons Learnt*; West, Kraut, and Chew, *I'd Blush If I Could*; Task Force on Digital Financing of the SDGs, *People's Money*; UN, *Report of the Secretary-General: Roadmap for Digital Cooperation*; Special Rapporteur on Violence against Women, Dubravka Šimonović, *Report of the Special Rapporteur on Violence against Women*; Special Rapporteur on the Promotion and Protection of the Right to Freedom of Opinion and Expression, Irene Khan, *Gender Justice and Freedom of Expression*.

95. UN and World Conference on Women, *Beijing Declaration and Platform of Action*.

96. UNDAW, *Information and Communication Technologies and Their Impact*; Primo, *Gender Issues in the Information Society*; UNDAW and UNDESA, *Gender Equality and Empowerment of Women through ICT*; UNDAW and UNDESA, *Women2000*; Broadband Commission Working Group on Broadband and Gender, *Doubling Digital Opportunities*.

97. Musto and boyd, "Trafficking-Technology Nexus"; Mendel and Sharapov, "Human Trafficking and Online Networks."

98. Broadband Commission Working Group on Broadband and Gender, *Cyberviolence Against Women and Girls*.

99. Critiques of the report were published in the media: Singal, "The UN's Cyberharassment Report Is Really Bad"; Jeong, "'I'm Disappointed': Zoe Quinn Speaks Out on UN Cyberviolence Report."

100. Glasgow, "United Nations Apologizes for Fault-Ridden Cyberviolence Report."

101. Gago, *Feminist International*, 77.

102. Arora and Chowdhury, "Cross-Cultural Feminist Technologies," 2.

Chapter 4

1. Orloff, Ray, and Savci, "Introduction: Perverse Politics?"

2. Both Sulá Batsú and APC WRP could be technically considered NGOs. But in this book I do not refer to Sulá Batsú as such because this is not how its members define the group. Rather, they define themselves as a joint-worker-controlled (*autogestionaria*) cooperative. APC is attuned to a more mainstream NGO imaginary and practice, yet its activists also embrace nonhierarchical internal structures and grassroots politics.

3. Roy, "NGO-ization of Resistance"; Alvarez, "Advocating Feminism"; INCITE! Women of Color Against Violence, *Revolution Will Not Be Funded*.

4. Liinason, "'Drawing the Line' and Other Small-Scale Resistances"; Alvarez, "Beyond NGO-ization?"; Ismail and Kamat, "NGOs, Social Movements and the Neoliberal State"; Eschle and Maiguashca, "Reclaiming Feminist Futures"; Roy, "Indian Women's Movement"; Roy, "Positive Side of Co-optation?"; Thayer, *Making Transnational Feminism*.

5. Eisenstein, "A Dangerous Liaison?"; Fraser, *Fortunes of Feminism*.

6. Bernal and Grewal, "Introduction," 13.

7. Grewal quoted in Roy, "Positive Side of Co-optation?," 255.

8. Orloff and Shiff, "Feminism/s in Power."

9. Eschle and Maiguashca, "Reclaiming Feminist Futures," 648.

10. Gago, *Feminist International*.

11. Beck, *How Development Projects Persist*; Roy, "Enacting/Disrupting the Will to Empower."

12. Adams and Martens, *Fit for Whose Purpose?*; Seitz and Martens, "Philanthrolateralism"; Moussié, *Challenging Corporate Power*; Van Waeyenberge, "Private Turn in Development Finance."

13. Arutyunova and Clark, *Watering the Leaves, Starving the Roots*.

14. Arutyunova and Clark, 42.

15. Miller, Arutyunova, and Clark, *New Actors, New Money, New Conversations*.

16. Moussié, *Challenging Corporate Power*, 27; Miller, Arutyunova, and Clark; Alvarez, "Ambivalent Engagements, Paradoxical Effects."

17. Dolker, *Where Is the Money for Feminist Organizing?*

18. Dolker, 12.

19. Dolker.

20. Moussié, *Challenging Corporate Power*, 5, 29.

21. Moussié, 5.

22. Seitz and Martens, "Philanthrolateralism."

23. Shaw and Wilson, "Bill and Melinda Gates Foundation and the Necro-

Populationism of 'Climate-Smart' Agriculture"; Lukacs and Sicora, "Will Bill Gates and His Billionaire Friends Save the Planet?"

24. Office of ECOSOC Support and Coordination, UN-DESA, *Background Note.*

25. Leye, "UNESCO, ICT Corporations and the Passion of ICT for Development."

26. All dollar amounts, unless noted otherwise, are US dollars. UN System Chief Executives Board for Coordination, Financial Statistics (webpage), accessed September 22, 2021, https://unsceb.org/financial-statistics.

27. Adams and Martens, *Fit for Whose Purpose?*; Moussié, *Challenging Corporate Power.*

28. Since 2008, the Dutch Ministry of Foreign Affairs has offered vital funding for local and global women's organization through the Millennium Development Goal 3 (MDG3) Fund (2008–11) and then the Funding Leadership and Opportunities for Women (FLOW) Funds (2016–20). APC WRP has received funding from both streams.

29. Eschle and Maiguashca, "Reclaiming Feminist Futures."

Conclusion

1. Paul and Milmo, "Facebook Putting Profit before Public Good."

2. AP News, "Facebook Papers"; *Wall Street Journal*, "Facebook Files"; Heath, "Leaked Files Show Facebook Is in Crisis Mode."

3. Hao, "How Facebook and Google Fund Global Misinformation."

4. Winner, "Do Artifacts Have Politics?"

5. Gordon, *Ghostly Matters.*

6. Segato, *La guerra contra las mujeres.*

7. Spivak, *Spivak Reader,* 10.

8. Cifor et al., "Feminist Data Manifest-No."

9. Byrum and Benjamin, "Disrupting the Gospel of Tech Solutionism."

10. Ahmed, *On Being Included,* 163.

11. Kaba, *We Do This 'Til We Free Us,* 27.

Appendix

1. Kapuściński, *Los cinco sentidos del periodista,* 17. My translation.

2. Smith, *Decolonizing Methodologies.*

3. Nagar, *Muddying the Waters*; Mohanty, "Under Western Eyes"; Hesse-Biber and Yaiser, *Feminist Perspectives on Social Research*; Falcón, "Transnational Feminism as a Paradigm"; TallBear, "Standing with and Speaking as Faith"; Swarr and Nagar, *Critical Transnational Feminist Praxis*; Naples, *Feminism and Method*; Collins, *Black Feminist Thought*; Jaggar, "Love and Knowledge."

4. Marcus, "Ethnography in/of the World System."

5. Thayer, *Making Transnational Feminism,* 57.

6. See Administrative Instructions at https://en.wikisource.org/wiki/ Administrative_Instruction_ST/AI/189/Add.9/Rev.2.

7. Dag Hammarskjöld Library, "What Is the Difference between a Resolution and a Decision?," last updated July 20, 2022, https://ask.un.org/faq/14484.

8. Dag Hammarskjöld Library, "Types of UN Documents: Reports," accessed October 24, 2022, https://research.un.org/en/docs/reports.

9. Dag Hammarskjöld Library, "What is the difference between a UN document and a UN publication?," last updated June 10, 2022, https://ask.un.org /faq/121650.

10. Ferrari and Martins, "Notes on the 50th Session of the Human Rights Council."

11. Telleria, "Power Relations?"; Cummings, Seferiadis, and Haan, "Getting Down to Business?"

12. Phillips and Hardy, *Discourse Analysis*, 3.

13. Desai, *Gender and the Politics of Possibilities*; Falcón, *Power Interrupted*.

14. Phillips and Cole, "Feminist Flows, Feminist Fault Lines."

15. Alvarez, "Ambivalent Engagements, Paradoxical Effects," 212.

16. Falcón, *Power Interrupted*.

17. Alvarez, "Translating the Global Effects of Transnational Organizing."

18. Vargas, "International Feminisms."

19. Nagar, "Footloose Researchers, 'Traveling' Theories, and the Politics of Transnational Feminist Praxis"; Nagar and Geiger, "Reflexivity, Positionality, and Languages of Collaboration."

20. Reinharz, *Feminist Methods in Social Research*; Stacey, "Can There Be a Feminist Ethnography?"

21. Hoang, *Dealing in Desire*; Contreras, *Stickup Kids*.

22. I understand that solidarity may not be the ideal framework for other kinds of research—for example, when studying politically regressive and reactionary individuals, organizations, and institutions.

23. Moraga, "La Güera."

24. Falcón, "Transnational Feminism as a Paradigm."

25. Nagar, *Muddying the Waters*, 85.

BIBLIOGRAPHY

Ábrego, Miriet. "La inaplazable conveniencia de las mujeres en STEM," 2021. http://ticaspoderosas.com/index.php/la-inaplazable-conveniencia-de-las -mujeres-en-stem/.

Abu-Lughod, Lila. "Do Muslim Women Really Need Saving? Anthropological Reflections on Cultural Relativism and Its Others." American Anthropologist 104, no. 3 (September 1, 2002): 783–790. http://www.jstor.org/stable/3567256

Adams, Barbara, and Jens Martens. *Fit for Whose Purpose? Private Funding and Corporate Influence in the United Nations.* New York: Global Policy Forum (GPF), 2015.

Aguilar, Yasnaya Elena. "A modest proposal to save the world." Rest of the World, December 9, 2020. https://restofworld.org/2020/saving-the-world -through-tequiology/.

Aguirre, Ixchel. "La violencia en línea contra las mujeres y las niñas, preocupación de la ONU (parte I)." *Luchadoras* (blog), November 19, 2018. https://luchadoras.mx/violencia-en-linea-contra-mujeres-parte-1/.

———. "La violencia en línea contra las mujeres y las niñas, preocupación de la ONU (parte II)." *Luchadoras* (blog), November 27, 2018. https:// luchadoras.mx/violencia-en-linea-contra-mujeres-parte-2/.

Ahmed, Sara. *Living a Feminist Life.* Durham, NC: Duke University Press, 2017.

———. *On Being Included: Racism and Diversity in Institutional Life.* Durham, NC: Duke University Press Books, 2012.

Alexander, M. Jacqui. "Redrafting Morality: The Postcolonial State and the Sexual Offences Bill of Trinidad and Tobago." In *Third World Women and the Politics of Feminism,* edited by Chandra Talpade Mohanty, Ann Russo, and Lourdes Torres, 133–52. Bloomington: Indiana University Press, 1991.

195

Alexander, M. Jacqui, and Chandra Talpade Mohanty. *Feminist Genealogies, Colonial Legacies, Democratic Futures.* New York: Routledge, 1997.

Alliance for Affordable Internet (A4AI). *The 2020 Affordability Report.* Accessed September 13, 2021. https://a4ai.org/affordability-report/report/2020/.

Altan-Olcay, Özlem. "Entrepreneurial Subjectivities and Gendered Complexities: Neoliberal Citizenship in Turkey." *Feminist Economics* 20, no. 4 (October 2014): 235–59. https://doi.org/10.1080/13545701.2014.950978.

Alvarez, Sonia E. "Advocating Feminism: The Latin American Feminist NGO 'Boom.'" *International Feminist Journal of Politics* 1, no. 2 (January 1, 1999): 181–209. https://doi.org/10.1080/146167499359880.

———. "Ambivalent Engagements, Paradoxical Effects: Latin American Feminist and Women's Movements and/in/against Development." In *Under Development: Gender,* edited by Christine Verschuur, Isabelle Guérin, and Hélène Guétat-Bernard, 211–35. New York: Palgrave Macmillan, 2014.

———. "Beyond NGO-ization? Reflections from Latin America." *Development* 52, no. 2 (June 1, 2009): 175–84. https://doi.org/10.1057/dev.2009.23.

———. "Translating the Global Effects of Transnational Organizing on Local Feminist Discourses and Practices in Latin America." *Meridians* 1, no. 1 (2000): 29–67. www.jstor.org/stable/40338427.

Ames, Morgan G. *The Charisma Machine: The Life, Death, and Legacy of One Laptop per Child.* Cambridge, MA: MIT Press, 2019.

Amrute, Sareeta. *Encoding Race, Encoding Class: Indian IT Workers in Berlin.* Reprint. Durham, NC: Duke University Press Books, 2016.

Ananías Soto, Cecilia, and Karen Vergara Sánchez. *Informe preliminar Chile y la violencia de género en internet: Experiencias de mujeres cis, trans y no binaries.* Concepción, Chile: Proyecto Aurora, ONG Amaranta, 2020. https://amarantaong.files.wordpress.com/2020/08/informe-proyecto-aurora.pdf.

Angwin, Julia, and Hannes Grassegger. "Facebook's Secret Censorship Rules Protect White Men from Hate Speech but Not Black Children." *ProPublica,* June 28, 2017. www.propublica.org/article/facebook-hate-speech-censorship-internal-documents-algorithms.

Anzaldúa, Gloria. *Light in the Dark = Luz en lo Oscuro: Rewriting Identity, Spirituality, Reality,* edited by AnaLouise Keating. Durham, NC: Duke University Press, 2015.

AP News. "The Facebook Papers" (webpage). 2021. https://apnews.com/hub/the-facebook-papers.

Arce Brenes, Antonio. "Estudio situacional de la PYME serie 2012–2017." San José, Costa Rica: Ministerio de Economía, Industria y Comercio de Costa Rica, Dirección General de Apoyo a la Pequeña y Mediana Empresa, 2019. Accessed September 13, 2021. http://reventazon.meic.go.cr/informacion/estudios/2019/pyme/INF-012-19.pdf.

Arora, Payal. "Bottom of the Data Pyramid: Big Data and the Global South." *International Journal of Communication* 10, no. 0 (March 14, 2016): 19. https://ijoc.org/index.php/ijoc/article/view/4297.

———. *The Next Billion Users: Digital Life beyond the West.* Cambridge, MA: Harvard University Press, 2019.

Arora, Payal, and Rumman Chowdhury. "Cross-Cultural Feminist Technologies." *Global Perspectives* 2, no. 1 (2021): 1–13.

Arora, Payal, and Nimmi Rangaswamy. "Digital Leisure for Development: Reframing New Media Practice in the Global South." *Media, Culture & Society* 35, no. 7 (October 1, 2013): 898–905. https://doi.org/10.1177/0163 443713495508.

Arutyunova, Angelika, and Cindy Clark. *Watering the Leaves, Starving the Roots: The Status of Financing for Women's Rights Organizing and Gender Equality.* Association for Women's Rights in Development (AWID), 2013. www.awid.org/sites/default/files/atoms/files/WTL_Starving_Roots .pdf.

Association for Progressive Communications (APC). *COVID-19 and the Increase of Domestic Violence against Women: A Submission from the Association for Progressive Communications to the United Nations Special Rapporteur on Violence against Women, Its Causes and Consequences.* June 30, 2020. https://www.apc.org/en/pubs/covid-19-and-increase-domes tic-violence-against-women-apc-submission-un-special-rapporteur.

———. *Online Gender-Based Violence: A Submission from the Association for Progressive Communications to the United Nations Special Rapporteur on Violence against Women, Its Causes and Consequences.* November 2017. https://www.apc.org/sites/default/files/APCSubmission_UNSR_ VAW_GBV_0_0.pdf.

Association for Progressive Communications (APC) and International Development Research Centre (IDRC). *Global Information Society Watch 2018: Community Networks.* Melville, South Africa: APC, 2018. www.giswatch .org/2018-community-networks.

Association for Progressive Communications (APC) WRP. "End Violence: Women's Rights and Safety Online." APC, 2015. https://genderit.org/on linevaw/.

"A un año del asesinato de líder indígena hondureña Berta Cáceres." Indigenous Rights Radio, March 3, 2017. https://derechos.culturalsurvival.org/ un-ano-del-asesinato-de-lider-indigena-hondurena-berta-caceres.

Avgerou, Chrisanthi. "Theoretical Framing of ICT4D Research." In *Information and Communication Technologies for Development*, edited by Jyoti Choudrie, M. Sirajul Islam, Fathul Wahid, Julian M. Bass, and Johanes Eka Priyatma, 10–23. IFIP Advances in Information and Communication Technology. Cham: Springer International Publishing, 2017. https://doi .org/10.1007/978-3-319-59111-7_2.

Bahous, Sima. "Speech: Shaping a More Inclusive Digital Transformation with SDG 5 at the Core." UN Women, September 21, 2022. www.unwomen .org/en/news-stories/speech/2022/09/speech-shaping-a-more-inclusive-digi tal-transformation-with-sdg-5-at-the-core.

Bailey, Moya. *Misogynoir Transformed: Black Women's Digital Resistance.* New York: New York University Press, 2021.

Banco Mundial. "Costa Rica: Panorama general." Updated September 15, 2021. www.bancomundial.org/es/country/costarica/overview.

Banerjee, Pallavi, and Raewyn Connell. "Gender Theory as Southern Theory." In *Handbook of the Sociology of Gender*, edited by Barbara J. Risman, Carissa M. Froyum, and William J. Scarborough, 57–68. Handbooks of Sociology and Social Research. Cham: Springer International Publishing, 2018. https://doi.org/10.1007/978-3-319-76333-0_4.

Barnett, Megan. "How Corporate America Went Open-Source." *Fortune*, August 16, 2010. http://fortune.com/2010/08/16/how-corporate-america-went-open-source/.

Bateman, Milford, Maren Duvendack, and Nicholas Loubere. "Is Fin-tech the New Panacea for Poverty Alleviation and Local Development? Contesting Suri and Jack's M-Pesa Findings Published in *Science*." *Review of African Political Economy* 46, no. 161 (July 3, 2019): 480–95.

Beck, Erin. *How Development Projects Persist: Everyday Negotiations with Guatemalan NGOs.* Durham, NC: Duke University Press, 2017.

Bedford, Kate. *Developing Partnerships: Gender, Sexuality, and the Reformed World Bank.* Minneapolis: University of Minnesota Press, 2009.

Bello, Alessandro, Tonya Blowers, Susan Schneegans, and Tiffany Straza. "To Be Smart, the Digital Revolution Will Need to Be Inclusive: Excerpt from the *UNESCO Science Report*." Paris, France: UNESCO, 2021. https://unesdoc.unesco.org/ark:/48223/pf0000375429.

Beneria, Lourdes, Günseli Berik, and Maria Floro. "Gender and Development: A Historical Overview." In *Gender, Development and Globalization: Economics as If All People Mattered*, edited by Lourdes Beneria, Günseli Berik, and Maria Floro, 1–40. New York: Routledge, 2016.

Benjamin, Ruha. *Race after Technology: Abolitionist Tools for the New Jim Code.* Medford, MA: Polity, 2019.

Bergeron, Suzanne. "The Post-Washington Consensus and Economic Representations of Women in Development at the World Bank." *International Feminist Journal of Politics* 5, no. 3 (November 2003): 397–419.

Bergeron, Suzanne, and Stephen Healy. "Beyond the 'Business Case': A Community Economies Approach to Gender, Development and Social Economy." United Nations Research Institute for Social Development (UNRISD), 2013. Accessed May 23, 2017. www.unrisd.org/80256B3C00 5BCCF9/search/A920D10273890F62C1257B5F0059A7.

Bernal, Victoria, and Inderpal Grewal. "Introduction." In *Theorizing NGOs: States, Feminisms, and Neoliberalism*, edited by Victoria Bernal and Inderpal Grewal, 1–18. Durham, NC: Duke University Press, 2014.

Bernstein, Elizabeth, and Janet R. Jakobsen, eds. *Paradoxes of Neoliberalism: Sex, Gender and Possibilities for Justice.* New York: Routledge, 2021.

"Best Practice Forum on Gender and Access." Internet Governance Forum

(IGF), 2020. www.intgovforum.org/multilingual/index.php?q=filedepot_download/5004/2371.

Bhattacharya, Tithi. "Introduction: Mapping Social Reproduction Theory." In *Social Reproduction Theory: Remapping Class, Recentering Oppression*, 1–20. London, UK: Pluto Press, 2017.

Bobel, Chris. *The Managed Body: Developing Girls and Menstrual Health in the Global South*. New York: Palgrave Macmillan, 2019. https://doi.org/10.1007/978-3-319-89414-0.

Bonder, Gloria. *El enfoque de género en el ADN de la educación científico-tecnológica: Propuestas para la trasformación educativa en y para la Sociedad del Conocimiento*. 2014. https://dds.cepal.org/redesoc/publicacion?id=3665.

———. *From Access to Appropriation: Women and ICT Policies in Latin America and the Caribbean*. Prepared for Expert Group Meeting on Information and Communication Technologies and Their Impact on and Use as an Instrument for the Advancement and Empowerment of Women, UN Division for the Advancement of Women, Seoul, Korea, November 11–14, 2002. www.mujeresenred.net/zonaTIC/IMG/pdf/GBonder.pdf.

———. *The New Information Technologies and Women: Essential Reflections*. Santiago, Chile: Economic Commission for Latin America and the Caribbean, 2002. www.cepal.org/en/publications/5908-new-information-technologies-and-women-essential-reflections.

Boserup, Ester. *Woman's Role in Economic Development*. New York: St. Martin's Press, 1970.

Bouterse, Siko, and Anasuya Sengupta. *Decolonizing the Internet: Summary Report*. Whose Knowledge?, 2018. https://whoseknowledge.org/wp-content/uploads/2018/10/DTI-2018-Summary-Report.pdf.

Bowles, Nellie. "Thermostats, Locks and Lights: Digital Tools of Domestic Abuse." *New York Times*, June 23, 2018. www.nytimes.com/2018/06/23/technology/smart-home-devices-domestic-abuse.html.

Bradford Franklin, Sharon, and Greg Nojeim. "International Coalition Calls on Apple to Abandon Plan to Build Surveillance Capabilities into iPhones, iPads, and Other Products." *Center for Democracy and Technology* (blog). August 19, 2021. https://cdt.org/insights/international-coalition-calls-on-apple-to-abandon-plan-to-build-surveillance-capabilities-into-iphones-ipads-and-other-products/.

Breines, Wini. "Community and Organization: The New Left and Michels' 'Iron Law.'" *Social Problems* 27, no. 4 (1980): 419–29. https://doi.org/10.2307/800170.

Broadband Commission Working Group on Broadband and Gender. *Cyberviolence Against Women and Girls: A World-Wide Wake-Up Call*. v.2.0, updated October 2015. www.broadbandcommission.org/Documents/reports/bb-wg-gender-report2015.pdf.

———. *Doubling Digital Opportunities: Enhancing the Inclusion of Women and Girls in the Information Society*. Working Group Report. Geneva, Switzerland: ITU and UNDP, September 21, 2013. https://www.broad bandcommission.org/publication/doubling-digital-opportunities/.

Brock, André. *Distributed Blackness: African American Cybercultures*. New York: New York University Press, 2020.

brown, adrienne maree, ed. *Pleasure Activism: The Politics of Feeling Good*. Chico, CA: AK Press, 2019.

Brown, Wendy. *Undoing the Demos: Neoliberalism's Stealth Revolution*. New York: Zone Books, 2015.

Browne, Simone. *Dark Matters: On the Surveillance of Blackness*. Durham, NC: Duke University Press, 2015.

Burch, Sally. "ALAI: A Latin American Experience in Social Networking." In *Women@Internet: Creating New Cultures in Cyberspace*, 197–205. London: Zed Books, 1999.

Butler, Judith. "Judith Butler on Rethinking Vulnerability, Violence, Resistance." *Versobooks.com* (blog), 2020. www.versobooks.com/blogs/4583 -judith-butler-on-rethinking-vulnerability-violence-resistance.

Byrum, Greta, and Ruha Benjamin. "Disrupting the Gospel of Tech Solutionism to Build Tech Justice." *Stanford Social Innovation Review*, June 16, 2022. https://doi.org/10.48558/9SEV-4D26.

Cabnal, Lorena. *Feminismos diversos: El feminismo comunitario*. ACSUR Las Segovias, 2010. https://porunavidavivible.files.wordpress.com/2012/ 09/feminismos-comunitario-lorena-cabnal.pdf.

———. "TZK'AT, red de sanadoras ancestrales del feminismo comunitario desde Iximulew-Guatemala." *Ecología Política* (blog), 2018. www.ecolog iapolitica.info/?p=10247.

Calkin, Sydney. "Feminism, Interrupted? Gender and Development in the Era of 'Smart Economics.'" *Progress in Development Studies* 15, no. 4 (October 1, 2015): 295–307. https://doi.org/10.1177/1464993415592737.

Callison, William, and Zachary Manfredi, eds. "Introduction: Theorizing Mutant Neoliberalism." In *Mutant Neoliberalism: Market Rule and Political Rupture*, 1–37. New York: Fordham University Press, 2019.

———, eds. *Mutant Neoliberalism: Market Rule and Political Rupture*. New York: Fordham University Press, 2019.

Camacho, Kemly. *Análisis de la integración de la perspectiva de género en las agendas y políticas digitales de Latinoamérica y el Caribe*. Santiago, Chile: Comisión Económica para América Latina y el Caribe (CEPAL), April 2013. www.cepal.org/publicaciones/xml/0/49890/Analisisdelaintegracion .pdf.

———. "Mercantilización del territorio y reconfiguración de las violencias contra las mujeres: El caso de las lideresas en los movimientos ecologistas contra el monocultivo de la piña." *Sociología y Tecnociencia* 9, no. 1 (October 17, 2018): 86–106. https://doi.org/10.24197/st.1.2019.86-106.

Camps, Victoria. *Tiempo de cuidados: Otra forma de estar en el mundo.* Barcelona: Arpa Editores, 2021.

The Care Collective. *The Care Manifesto: The Politics of Interdependence.* New York: Verso, 2020.

Cavallero, Lucí, and Verónica Gago. *Una lectura feminista de la deuda.* Buenos Aires, Argentina: Tinta Limón, Fundación Rosa Luxemburgo, 2021. https://tintalimon.com.ar//libro/una-lectura-feminista-de-la-deuda/.

Cavallero, Lucí, Verónica Gago, and Celeste Perosino. "¿De qué se trata la inclusión financiera? Notas para una perspectiva crítica." *Realidad Económica* 51, no. 340 (2021): 9–30. https://ojs.iade.org.ar/index.php/re/article/view/153/117.

Centre for International Governance Innovation. *Non-Consensual Intimate Image Distribution: The Legal Landscape in Kenya, Chile, and South Africa.* Ontario, Canada: Centre for International Governance Innovation, June 14, 2021. www.cigionline.org/publications/non-consensual-intimate-image-distribution-the-legal-landscape-in-kenya-chile-and-south-africa/.

Centre for Internet and Society. "Revenge Porn Laws across the World." Centre for Internet and Society April 25, 2018. https://cis-india.org/internet-governance/blog/revenge-porn-laws-across-the-world.

Comisión Económica para América Latina y el Caribe (CEPAL)–Naciones Unidas. *El enfoque de brechas estructurales: Análisis del caso de Costa Rica.* Santiago, Chile: CEPAL, 2016. www.cepal.org/es/publicaciones/enfoque-brechas-estructurales-analisis-caso-costa-rica.

———. *Mujer y nuevas tecnologías.* Serie Mujer y Desarrollo. Santiago, Chile: CEPAL, 1990. www.cepal.org/es/publicaciones/5879-mujer-y-nuevas-tecnologias.

Chan, Anita Say. *Networking Peripheries: Technological Futures and the Myth of Digital Universalism.* Cambridge, MA: MIT Press, 2014.

Chant, Sylvia, and Caroline Sweetman. "Fixing Women or Fixing the World? 'Smart Economics,' Efficiency Approaches, and Gender Equality in Development." *Gender & Development* 20, no. 3 (November 1, 2012): 517–29. https://doi.org/10.1080/13552074.2012.731812.

Ciacci, Jes. "Imagining a Principle for a Feminist Internet Focusing on Environmental Justice." In *Global Information Society Watch 2020: Technology, the Environment and a Sustainable World: Responses from the Global South,* 38–41. Association for Progressive Communications (APC), 2021. www.giswatch.org/2020-technology-environment-and-sustainable-world-responses-global-south.

Cifor, M., P. Garcia, T.L. Cowan, J. Rault, T. Sutherland, A. Chan, J. Rode, A.L. Hoffman, N. Salehi, and L. Nakamura. *Feminist Data Manifest-No,* 2019. https://www.manifestno.com.

Citron, Danielle Keats. *Hate Crimes in Cyberspace.* Cambridge, MA: Harvard University Press, 2014.

———. "Sexual Privacy." *Yale Law Journal* 128, no. 7 (2019): 1792–2121. www.yalelawjournal.org/article/sexual-privacy.

Citron, Danielle Keats, and Mary Franks. "Criminalizing Revenge Porn." *Faculty Scholarship*, January 1, 2014. https://digitalcommons.law.umary land.edu/fac_pubs/1420.

Civil Society Declaration to the World Summit on the Information Society. "Shaping Information Societies for Human Needs." *Gazette* (Leiden, Netherlands) 66, no. 3–4 (June 1, 2004): 323–46. https://doi.org/10.1177/0016549204043615.

Cleaver, Harry M. "The Zapatista Effect: The Internet and the Rise of an Alternative Political Fabric." *Journal of International Affairs* 51, no. 2 (Spring 1998): 621.

Coleman, Gabriella. *Coding Freedom: The Ethics and Aesthetics of Hacking.* Princeton, NJ: Princeton University Press, 2012.

Collins, Patricia Hill. *Black Feminist Thought: Knowledge, Consciousness, and the Politics of Empowerment.* New York: Psychology Press, 2000.

Connell, Raewyn. "Decolonizing Sociology." *Contemporary Sociology* 47, no. 4 (July 1, 2018): 399–407. https://doi.org/10.1177/0094306118779811.

———. "Meeting at the Edge of Fear: Theory on a World Scale." *Feminist Theory* 16, no. 1 (April 1, 2015): 49–66. https://doi.org/10.1177/14647001 14562531.

———. *Southern Theory: Social Science and The Global Dynamics Of Knowledge.* Cambridge, MA: Polity, 2007.

Connell, Raewyn, and Nour Dados. "Where in the World Does Neoliberalism Come From?" *Theory and Society* 43, no. 2 (February 4, 2014): 117–38. https://doi.org/10.1007/s11186-014-9212-9.

Contreras, Randol. *The Stickup Kids: Race, Drugs, Violence, and the American Dream.* Berkeley, CA: University of California Press, 2012.

Cornwall, Andrea. "Buzzwords and Fuzzwords: Deconstructing Development Discourse." *Development in Practice* 17, no. 4/5 (August 1, 2007): 471–84. http://www.jstor.org/stable/25548244.

———. "Women's Empowerment: What Works?" *Journal of International Development* 28, no. 3 (April 1, 2016): 342–59. https://doi.org/10.1002/jid .3210.

Cornwall, Andrea, and Nana Akua Anyidoho. "Introduction: Women's Empowerment: Contentions and Contestations." *Development* 53, no. 2 (June 2010): 144–49. http://dx.doi.org.ezproxy.neu.edu/10.1057/dev.2010.34.

Cornwall, Andrea, Jasmine Gideon, and Kalpana Wilson. "Introduction: Reclaiming Feminism: Gender and Neoliberalism." *IDS Bulletin* 39, no. 6 (December 1, 2008): 1–9. https://doi.org/10.1111/j.1759-5436.2008.tb00 505.x.

Cornwall, Andrea, Elizabeth Harrison, and Ann Whitehead. "Gender Myths and Feminist Fables: The Struggle for Interpretive Power in Gender and

Development." *Development and Change* 38, no. 1 (January 1, 2007): 1–20. https://doi.org/10.1111/j.1467-7660.2007.00400.x.

Cornwall, Andrea, and Althea-Maria Rivas. "From 'Gender Equality' and 'Women's Empowerment' to Global Justice: Reclaiming a Transformative Agenda for Gender and Development." *Third World Quarterly* 36, no. 2 (February 2015): 396–415. https://doi.org/10.1080/01436597.2015.1013341.

Cortés, Nadia. "Generación incubadora." In *Tecnologías del cuidado.* Mexico, DF: Remediables; Centro de Cultura Digital, 2022.

Costanza-Chock, Sasha. "Design Justice, A.I., and Escape from the Matrix of Domination." *Journal of Design and Science.* July 16, 2018. https://doi.org /10.21428/96c8d426.

———. *Design Justice: Community-Led Practices to Build the Worlds We Need.* Cambridge, MA: MIT Press, 2020.

Couldry, Nick, and Ulises A. Mejías. *The Costs of Connection: How Data Is Colonizing Human Life and Appropriating It for Capitalism.* Stanford, CA: Stanford University Press, 2019.

Cox, Joy. "Equity in Health Technology: Where is Space for those Living in Larger Bodies?" *JusTech*, Social Science Research Council (blog). https:// just-tech.ssrc.org/articles/equity-in-health-technology-where-is-space-for -those-living-in-larger-bodies/.

Cummings, Sarah, Anastasia-Alithia Seferiadis, and Leah de Haan. "Getting Down to Business? Critical Discourse Analysis of Perspectives on the Private Sector in Sustainable Development." *Sustainable Development* 28, no. 4 (2020): 759–71. https://doi.org/10.1002/sd.2026.

Cupples, Julie, and Irving Larios. "A Functional Anarchy: Love, Patriotism, and Resistance to Free Trade in Costa Rica." *Latin American Perspectives* 37, no. 6 (2010): 93–108. www.jstor.org/stable/25750422.

Curiel, Ochy. "Descolonizando el feminismo: Una perspectiva desde América Latina y el Caribe." Presented at Primer Coloquio Latinoamericano sobre Praxis y Pensamiento Feminista realizado, Buenos Aires, 2009. http:// feministas.org/IMG/pdf/Ochy_Curiel.pdf.

Cyber Civil Rights Initiative. "48 States + DC + One Territory Now Have Revenge Porn Laws." *Cyber Civil Rights Initiative* (blog). Accessed May 19, 2021. www.cybercivilrights.org/revenge-porn-laws/.

Dados, Nour, and Raewyn Connell. "The Global South." *Contexts* 11, no. 1 (February 1, 2012): 12–13. https://doi.org/10.1177/1536504212436479.

Dalla Costa, Mariarosa, and Selma James. *The Power of Women and the Subversion of the Community.* Bristol: Falling Wall Press Ltd, 1975.

Daniels, Jessie. "Rethinking Cyberfeminism(s): Race, Gender, and Embodiment." *WSQ: Women's Studies Quarterly* 37, no. 1 (2009): 101–24. https: //doi.org/10.1353/wsq.0.0158.

Daniels, Jessie, Karen Gregory, and Tressie McMillan Cottom, eds. *Digital Sociologies.* Bristol, UK: Policy Press, 2017.

Davis, Angela Y. *Are Prisons Obsolete?* Open Media Book. New York: Seven Stories Press, 2003.

———. *Freedom Is a Constant Struggle: Ferguson, Palestine, and the Foundations of a Movement*. Chicago: Haymarket Books, 2016.

Davis, Angela Y., Gina Dent, Erica Meiners, and Beth Richie. *Abolition. Feminism. Now.* Chicago: Haymarket Books, 2021.

Dean, Jodi. "Feminist Solidarity, Reflective Solidarity." *Women & Politics* 18, no. 4 (January 26, 1998): 1–26. https://doi.org/10.1300/J014v18n04_01.

Demaria, Federico, and Ashish Kothari. "The Post-Development Dictionary Agenda: Paths to the Pluriverse." *Third World Quarterly* 38 (August 16, 2017): 1–12. https://doi.org/10.1080/01436597.2017.1350821.

Demirgüç-Kunt, Asli, Leora Klapper, Dorothe Singer, and Saniya Ansar. *The Global Findex Database 2021: Financial Inclusion, Digital Payments, and Resilience in the Age of COVID-19*. Washington, DC: World Bank, 2022. www.worldbank.org/en/publication/globalfindex/Report.

Demirgüç-Kunt, Asli, Leora Klapper, Dorothe Singer, Saniya Ansar, and Jake Hess. *The Global Findex Database 2017: Measuring Financial Inclusion and the Fintech Revolution*. Washington, DC: World Bank, 2018. https://openknowledge.worldbank.org/handle/10986/29510.

Desai, Manisha. *Gender and the Politics of Possibilities: Rethinking Globablization*. New York: Rowman & Littlefield Publishers, 2008.

"Digital Agenda for Latin America and the Caribbean (eLAC 2022)." UN Economic Commission for Latin America and the Caribbean, November 2020. https://conferenciaelac.cepal.org/7/sites/elac2020/files/20-00902_cmsi.7_digital_agenda_elac2022.pdf.

Doha NGO Group on Financing for Development. "Declaration from Doha Civil Society on Financing for Development." 2008. https://www.un.org/esa/ffd/wp-content/uploads/2014/09/Doha_Declaration_FFD.pdf.

Dolker, Tenzin. *Where Is the Money for Feminist Organizing?* Association for Women's Rights in Development (AWID). May 24, 2021. www.awid.org/news-and-analysis/new-brief-where-money-feminist-organizing.

Donner, Francesca, and Alisha Haridasani Gupta. "António Guterres Wants Gender Parity at the U.N. It May Take Time." *New York Times*. March 7, 2020. www.nytimes.com/2020/03/05/world/antonio-guterres-un.html.

Downing, John. *Radical Media: Rebellious Communication and Social Movements*. Thousand Oaks, CA: Sage, 2000.

Dunn, Suzie. *Technology-Facilitated Gender-Based Violence: An Overview*. Series: Supporting a Safer Internet. Centre for International Governance Innovation, December 7, 2020. www.cigionline.org/publications/technology-facilitated-gender-based-violence-overview/.

Eade, Deborah, and Andrea Cornwall, eds. *Deconstructing Development Discourse: Buzzwords and Fuzzwords*. Warwickshire, UK: Practical Action Publications & Oxfam GB, 2010.

Economic Commission for Latin America and the Caribbean (ECLAC). *Brasilia Consensus*. 11th session of the Regional Conference on Women in Latin America and the Caribbean. ECLAC, July 16, 2010. www.cepal.org /mujer/noticias/paginas/6/40236/ConsensoBrasilia_ING.pdf.

———. *Data, Algorithms and Policies: Redefining the Digital World*. LC/ CMSI.6/4. ECLAC, April 18, 2018. https://repositorio.cepal.org//handle/11 362/43515.

———. *Digital Technologies for a New Future*. LC/TS.2021/43. ECLAC, 2021. https://repositorio.cepal.org/handle/11362/46817.

———. "Mexico City Consensus." 9th session of the Regional Conference on Women in Latin America and the Caribbean. ECLAC, 2004. www.cepal .org/mujer/direccion/Consensus_Mx.pdf.

———. *Montevideo Strategy for Implementation of the Regional Gender Agenda within the Sustainable Development Framework by 2030*. ECLAC, 2016. www.cepal.org/en/publications/41013-montevideo-strategy -implementation-regional-gender-agenda-within-sustainable.

———. *Santo Domingo Consensus: 12th Session of the Regional Conference on Women in Latin America and the Caribbean*. ECLAC, 2013. www. cepal.org/12conferenciamujer/noticias/paginas/5/49995/PLE_CRM.12 -Santo_Domingo_Consensus.pdf.

———. *Women in the Digital Economy· Breaking through the Equality Threshold*. ECLAC, 2013. www.cepal.org/en/publications/women-digital -economy-breaking-through-equality-threshold.

———. "Women's Autonomy, Gender Equality and the Building of a Care Society are a Precondition, Path and Catalyst for Sustainable Development," press release. ECLAC, January 26, 2022. https://www.cepal.org/en /pressreleases/womens-autonomy-gender-equality-and-building-care -society-are-precondition-path-and.

———. *Women's Autonomy in Changing Economic Scenarios*. LC/CRM.14/3. ECLAC, December 30, 2019. https://repositorio.cepal.org//handle/11362/ 45037.

Eisenstein, Hester. "A Dangerous Liaison? Feminism and Corporate Globalization." *Science & Society* 69, no. 3 (July 1, 2005): 487–518. www.jstor .org/stable/40404269.

———. "Feminism Seduced: Globalisation and the Uses of Gender." *Australian Feminist Studies* 25, no. 66 (December 1, 2010): 413–31. https://doi .org/10.1080/08164649.2010.525210.

Elyachar, Julia. "Empowerment Money: The World Bank, Non-Governmental Organizations, and the Value of Culture in Egypt." *Public Culture* 14, no. 3 (September 1, 2002): 493–513. http://muse.jhu.edu.ezproxy.neu.edu/jour nals/public_culture/vo14/14.3elyachar.html.

———. *Markets of Dispossession: NGOs, Economic Development, and the State in Cairo*. Durham, NC: Duke University Press, 2005.

EQUALS Global Partnership. *10 Lessons Learnt: Closing the Gender Gap in*

Internet Access and Use Insights from the EQUALS Access Coalition. GSMA and EQUALS Global Partnership for Gender Equality in the Digital Age. www.gsma.com/mobilefordevelopment/resources/10-lessons-learnt-closing-the-gender-gap-in-internet-access-and-use/.

Eschle, Catherine, and Bice Maiguashca. "Reclaiming Feminist Futures: Co-opted and Progressive Politics in a Neo-Liberal Age." *Political Studies* 62, no. 3 (October 1, 2014): 634–51. https://doi.org/10.1111/1467-9248.12046.

Escobar, Arturo. *Designs for the Pluriverse: Radical Interdependence, Autonomy, and the Making of Worlds.* Durham, NC: Duke University Press Books, 2018.

———. *Encountering Development: The Making and Unmaking of the Third World.* Princeton, NJ: Princeton University Press, 1995.

Espinosa Gutiérrez, Aline. "Agresiones contra periodistas y defensoras de DH va en aumento en el espacio digital." *CIMAC Noticias* (blog), March 25, 2021. https://cimacnoticias.com.mx/2021/03/25/agresiones-contra-periodistas-y-defensoras-de-dh-va-en-aumento-en-el-espacio-digital.

Espinosa Miñoso, Yuderkys. *De por qué es necesario un feminismo descolonial.* Vilassar de Dalt, Barcelona: Icaria Editorial, 2022.

Eubanks, Virginia. *Automating Inequality: How High-Tech Tools Profile, Police, and Punish the Poor.* New York: St. Martin's Press, 2017.

Fajardo, Margarita. *The World That Latin America Created: The United Nations Economic Commission for Latin America in the Development Era.* Cambridge, MA: Harvard University Press, 2022.

Falcón, Sylvanna M. *Power Interrupted: Antiracist and Feminist Activism inside the United Nations.* Seattle: University of Washington Press, 2016.

———. "Transnational Feminism as a Paradigm for Decolonizing the Practice of Research." *Frontiers: A Journal of Women Studies* 37, no. 1 (March 2016): 174–94. https://doi.org/10.5250/fronjwomestud.37.1.0174.

Federici, Silvia. *Beyond the Periphery of the Skin: Rethinking, Remaking, and Reclaiming the Body in Contemporary Capitalism.* Oakland, CA: PM Press, 2020. www.pmpress.org/index.php?l=product_detail&p=1045.

———. *Caliban and the Witch: Women, the Body, and Primitive Accumulation.* New York, NY: Autonomedia, 2004.

———. "Feminism and the Politics of the Commons." *The Commoner,* 2011. http://uzbuna.org/en/journal/conversations-new-feminisam-and-art/feminism-and-politics-commons.

———. *Revolution at Point Zero: Housework, Reproduction, and Feminist Struggle.* 2nd ed. Oakland, CA: PM Press, 2020.

———. *Witches, Witch-Hunting, and Women.* Oakland, CA: PM Press, 2018.

Ferguson, James. "The Uses of Neoliberalism." *Antipode* 41 (January 1, 2010): 166–84. https://doi.org/10.1111/j.1467-8330.2009.00721.x.

Ferrari, Verónica, and Paula Martins. "Notes on the 50th Session of the

Human Rights Council." *Association for Progressive Communications* (APC) (blog), July 14, 2022. https://www.apc.org/en/news/notes-50th-session-human-rights-council.

Ferree, Myra Marx, and Aili Mari Tripp. *Global Feminism: Transnational Women's Activism, Organizing, and Human Rights.* New York: New York University Press, 2006.

Fisher, Bernice, and Joan C. Tronto. "Toward a Feminist Theory of Caring." In *Circles of Care: Work and Identity in Women's Lives*, 35–62. Albany: SUNY Press, 1990.

Foucault, Michel. *The Birth of Biopolitics: Lectures at the Collège de France, 1978–79*, edited by Michel Senellart. New York: Palgrave Macmillan, 2008.

———. *The History of Sexuality.* Vol. 1: *An Introduction.* Reissue ed. New York: Vintage, 1990.

"Francia Márquez: 'Vivir sabroso es vivir sin miedo.'" *El País América Colombia*, June 23, 2022. https://elpais.com/america-colombia/elecciones-presidenciales/2022-06-23/francia-marquez-vivir-sabroso-es-vivir-sin-miedo.html.

Franks, Mary Anne. "Democratic Surveillance." *Harvard Journal of Law & Technology.* 30 (January 1, 2017): 425. https://repository.law.miami.edu/fac_articles/473.

Fraser, Nancy. "Contradictions of Capital and Care." *New Left Review.* August 2016. https://newleftreview.org/issues/II100/articles/nancy-fraser-contradictions-of-capital-and-care.

———. *Fortunes of Feminism: From State-Managed Capitalism to Neoliberal Crisis.* New York: Verso, 2013.

Freeman, Carla. *Entrepreneurial Selves: Neoliberal Respectability and the Making of a Caribbean Middle Class.* Durham, NC: Duke University Press, 2014.

Friedman, Elisabeth J. *Interpreting the Internet: Feminist and Queer Counterpublics in Latin America.* Berkeley: University of California Press, 2016.

Gabor, Daniela. "The Wall Street Consensus." *Development and Change* 52, no. 3 (2021): 429–59. https://doi.org/10.1111/dech.12645.

Gabor, Daniela, and Sally Brooks. "The Digital Revolution in Financial Inclusion: International Development in the Fintech Era." *New Political Economy* 22, no. 4 (July 4, 2017): 423–36. https://doi.org/10.1080/13563467.2017.1259298.

Gago, Verónica. *Feminist International: How to Change Everything.* Translated by Liz Mason-Deese. New York: Verso, 2020.

———. "Is There a War 'on' the Body of Women? Finance, Territory, and Violence." *Viewpoint Magazine*, March 7, 2018. www.viewpointmag.com/2018/03/07/war-body-women-finance-territory-violence/.

Gajjala, Radhika. "Woman and Other Women: Implicit Binaries in Cyberfeminisms." *Communication and Critical/Cultural Studies* 11, no. 3 (July 3, 2014): 288–92. https://doi.org/10.1080/14791420.2014.926241.

Gajjala, Radhika, and Dinah Tetteh. "Relax, You've Got M-PESA: Leisure as Empowerment." *Information Technologies & International Development* 10, no. 3 (September 10, 2014): 31–46. https://itidjournal.org/index.php/itid/article/view/1282.html.

Gargallo, Francesca. *Feminismos desde Abya Yala*. Ciudad de México, México: Editorial Corte y Confección, 2014. https://francescagargallo.files.wordpress.com/2014/01/francesca-gargallo-feminismos-desde-abya-yala-ene20141.pdf.

Gates, Bill. "Digital Tech is Turning the Unbanked into the Banked." *GatesNotes: The Blog of Bill Gates*, June 29, 2022. https://www.gatesnotes.com/Development/Global-Findex-2022.

Gates, Melinda. "Melinda Gates: I'm Committing $1 Billion to Gender Equality." *Time*, October 5, 2019. https://time.com/5690596/melinda-gates-empowering-women/.

"Gender in the Information Society: Emerging Issues." Asia-Pacific Development Information Programme (APDIP); United Nations Development Program (UNDP), 2006. Accessed February 17, 2016. www.unapcict.org/ecohub/resources/gender-in-the-information-society-emerging-issues.

GenderIT. "Declaración: II Encuentro Internacional Ciberfeminista: Descolonizando internet." GenderIT.org, May 4, 2018. https://www.genderit.org/es/resources/declaraci%C3%B3n-ii-encuentro-internacional-ciberfeminista-descolonizar-internet.

Generation Equality Forum. "Action Coalitions Commitment Makers." 2021. https://forum.generationequality.org/sites/default/files/2021-09/GEF%20Commitment%20Makers.pdf.

———. "Action Coalitions Global Acceleration Plan Executive Summary." 2021. https://forum.generationequality.org/sites/default/files/2021-06/UNW%20-%20GAP%20Report%20-%20EN%20-%20Executive%20Summary.pdf.

———. "Action Coalitions Leadership Structures," 2021. Accessed July 1, 2021.

———. "Technology and Innovation for Gender Equality Action Coalition," 2021. Accessed July 1, 2021.

Gibson-Graham, J. K. "Post-Development Possibilities for Local and Regional Development." In *Handbook of Local and Regional Development*, edited by A. Pike, A. Rodriguez-Pose, and J. Tomaney, 226–36. London: Routledge, 2011. www.communityeconomies.org/site/assets/media/KatherineGibson/2009-Post-developmental-possibilities-for-local-and-regional-development.pdf.

Gilmore, Ruth Wilson. *Change Everything: Racial Capitalism and the Case*

for Abolition, edited by Naomi Murakawa. Chicago: Haymarket Books, 2022.

———. *Golden Gulag: Prisons, Surplus, Crisis, and Opposition in Globalizing California*. Berkeley: University of California Press, 2007.

Glasgow, Brad. "United Nations Apologizes for Fault-Ridden Cyberviolence Report." *Motherboard/Vice*, October 7, 2015. http://motherboard.vice.com/read/united-nations-apologizes-for-fault-ridden-cyberviolence-report.

Gobierno de México. Ley Olympia. http://ordenjuridico.gob.mx/violenciagenero/LEY%20OLIMPIA.pdf.

Goldberg, Emma. "Fake Nudes and Real Threats: How Online Abuse Holds Back Women in Politics." *New York Times*, June 4, 2021. www.nytimes.com/2021/06/03/us/disinformation-online-attacks-female-politicians.html.

Google Developers. Women Techmakers (website). Accessed October 4, 2022. https://developers.google.com/womentechmakers.

Gordon, Avery F. *Ghostly Matters*. 2nd ed. Minneapolis: University of Minnesota Press, 1997.

Graeber, David, and Andrej Grubačić. "Introduction." In *Mutual Aid: An Illuminated Factor of Evolution*. Oakland, CA: PM Press, 2021.

Gray, Mary L., and Siddharth Suri. *Ghost Work: How to Stop Silicon Valley from Building a New Global Underclass*. Boston: Mariner Books, 2019.

Green, W. Nathan, and Maryann Bylander. "The Exclusionary Power of Microfinance Over-Indebtedness and Land Dispossession in Cambodia." *Sociology of Development* 7, no. 2 (June 1, 2021): 202–29. https://doi.org/10.1525/sod.2021.7.2.202.

Greenberg, Andy. "Hacker Eva Galperin Has a Plan to Eradicate Stalkerware." *Wired*, April 3, 2019. www.wired.com/story/eva-galperin-stalkerware-kaspersky-antivirus/.

Greene, Daniel. *The Promise of Access: Technology, Inequality, and the Political Economy of Hope*. Cambridge, MA: MIT Press, 2021.

Grupo de Trabajo de Género eLAC. *ELAC 2015 Plan de Trabajo: Grupo de Trabajo de Género*. Comisión Económica para América Latina y el, Santiago, Chile, July 11, 2011. www.genderit.org/es/resources/elac2015-plan-de-trabajo-del-grupo-de-g%C3%A9nero.

GSMA and Oslo Metropolitan University for the EQUALS Leadership Coalition. *Perceptions of Power: Championing Female Leadership in Tech*. London and Oslo: EQUALS Global Partnership, 2020. https://o4bfff6c-3bf3-4ba6-bc89-b071fa61e8a9.usrfiles.com/ugd/o4bfff_c9c836a4097544f687532f85024d3c01.pdf.

Gurumurthy, Anita. *Gender and ICTs: Overview Report*. Institute of Development Studies, London, 2004. Accessed June 1, 2017. www.bridge.ids.ac.uk/ids-document/A52909?lang=en#lang-pane-en.

————. *A History of Feminist Engagement with Development and Digital Technologies*. Johannesburg: Association for Progressive Communications (APC), 2017. www.apc.org/en/pubs/history-feminist-engagement-development-and-digital-technologies.

Gurumurthy, Anita, and Nandini Chami. "Data: The New Four-Letter Word for Feminism." *GenderIT.Org* (blog), 2016. www.genderit.org/articles/data-new-four-letter-word-feminism.

————. "Development Justice in the Digital Paradigm: Agenda 2030 and Beyond." *Development* 62, no.1 (December 1, 2019): 19–28.

————. *A Feminist Action Framework on Development and Digital Technologies*. Association for Progressive Communications (APC), May 29, 2017. www.apc.org/en/pubs/feminist-action-framework-development-and-digital-technologies.

Guterres, António. "Tackling Inequality: A New Social Contract for a New Era, Nelson Mandela Annual Lecture 2020." United Nations, July 18, 2020. https://www.un.org/en/coronavirus/tackling-inequality-new-social-contract-new-era.

Gutiérrez Aguilar, Raquel. "Argumentos en discusión con las ideas que sostienen Lang y Segato en su provocación: Justicia Feminista ante el estado ausente: Un debate urgente." *Luchadoras* (blog), 2021. https://luchadoras.mx/argumentos-en-discusion-con-las-ideas-que-sostienen-lang-y-segato/.

————. "Because We Want Ourselves Alive, Together We Are Disrupting Everything: Notes for Thinking about the Paths of Social Transformation Today." *Viewpoint Magazine*. March 7, 2018. https://viewpointmag.com/2018/03/07/want-alive-together-disrupting-everything-notes-thinking-paths-social-transformation-today/.

————. "Women's Struggle against All Violence in Mexico: Gathering Fragments to Find Meaning." Translated by Liz Mason-Deese. *South Atlantic Quarterly* 117, no. 3 (July 1, 2018): 670–81. https://doi.org/10.1215/0038 2876-6942245.

Hafkin, Nancy, and Nancy Taggart. "Executive Summary." *Gender, Information Technology, and Developing Countries: An Analytic Study*. Washington, DC: United States Agency for International Development (USAID), 2001. http://pdf.usaid.gov/pdf_docs/Pnacm871.pdf.

Hao, Karen. "How Facebook and Google Fund Global Misinformation." *MIT Technology Review*, November 20, 2021. www.technologyreview.com/2021/11/20/1039076/facebook-google-disinformation-clickbait/.

Haraway, Donna J. *Staying with the Trouble: Making Kin in the Chthulucene*. Durham, NC: Duke University Press, 2016.

Haraway, Donna Jeanne. *Simians, Cyborgs, and Women: The Reinvention of Nature*. New York: Routledge, 1991.

Harcourt, Wendy. "Body Politics and Postdevelopment." In *Postdevelopment in Practice*. Routledge, 2019.

————. "Gender and Development: Looking Back, Looking Forward." *Devel-*

opment 61, no. 1 (December 1, 2018): 9–13. https://doi.org/10.1057/s41301-018-0185-2.

———. "What a Gender Lens Brings to Development Studies." In *Building Development Studies for the New Millennium*, edited by Isa Baud, Elisabetta Basile, Tiina Kontinen, and Susanne von Itter, 361–80. EADI Global Development Series. Cham, Switzerland: Springer International Publishing, 2019. https://doi.org/10.1007/978-3-030-04052-9_16.

Harding, Sandra. "Introduction." In *The Postcolonial Science and Technology Studies Reader*, edited by Sandra Harding, 1–31. Durham, NC: Duke University Press, 2011.

———. "Latin American Decolonial Social Studies of Scientific Knowledge: Alliances and Tensions." *Science, Technology, & Human Values* 41, no. 6 (November 1, 2016): 1063–87. https://doi.org/10.1177/0162243916656465.

Hardt, Michael, and Antonio Negri. *Commonwealth*. Cambridge, MA: Harvard University Press, 2011.

Harvey, David. *A Brief History of Neoliberalism*. New York: Oxford University Press, 2005.

Heath, Alex. "Leaked Files Show Facebook Is in Crisis Mode over Losing Young People." *The Verge*, October 25, 2021. www.theverge.com/22743744/facebook-teen-usage-decline-frances-haugen-leaks.

Heeks, Richard. "Digital Inequality beyond the Digital Divide: Conceptualizing Adverse Digital Incorporation in the Global South." *Information Technology for Development*. July 7, 2022. http://www.tandfonline.com/doi/abs/10.1080/02681102.2022.2068492.

———. "From Digital Divide to Digital Justice in the Global South: Conceptualising Adverse Digital Incorporation." *ArXiv:2108.09783 [Cs]*. August 22, 2021. http://arxiv.org/abs/2108.09783.

———. "From the Digital Divide to Digital Justice in the Global South." In *12th ACM Conference on Web Science Companion*, 10–11. Southampton United Kingdom: ACM, 2020. https://doi.org/10.1145/3394332.3402821.

Heikkilä, Melissa. "António Guterres' Role Questioned in UN Harassment Case." *POLITICO*, May 19, 2021. www.politico.eu/article/antonio-guterres-harassment-united-nations-fabrizio-hochschild-drummond/.

Held, Virginia. *The Ethics of Care: Personal, Political, and Global*. New York: Oxford University Press, 2007.

Hendl, Tereza, and Bianca Jansky. "Tales of Self-Empowerment through Digital Health Technologies: A Closer Look at 'Femtech.'" *Review of Social Economy* 80, no. 1 (2022): 29–57.

Hernandez, Joe. "Reversing a Planned Ban, OnlyFans Will Allow Pornography on Its Site After All." *NPR*, August 25, 2021. www.npr.org/2021/08/25/1030949680/onlyfans-explicit-content-pornography-sex-workers-reverses-ban.

Hernández Bauzá, Valentina. *2010–2020: Sucesos regulatorios en materias de privacidad e internet en Latinoamérica*. Santiago, Chile: Derechos Digitales, December 2020. www.derechosdigitales.org/wp-content/uploads/tendencias-privacidad-latam.pdf.

Hesse-Biber, Sharlene Nagy, and Michelle L. Yaiser. *Feminist Perspectives on Social Research*. New York: Oxford University Press, 2004.

Hierro, Graciela. *La ética del placer*. Mexico, DF: Universidad Nacional Autónoma de México, 2001. https://cieg.unam.mx/detalles-libro.php?l=MTEx.

Hoang, Kimberly Kay. *Dealing in Desire: Asian Ascendancy, Western Decline, and the Hidden Currencies of Global Sex Work*. Oakland: University of California Press, 2015.

Hobart, Hiʻilei Julia Kawehipuaakahaopulani, and Tamara Kneese. "Radical Care: Survival Strategies for Uncertain Times." *Social Text* 38, no. 1 (142) (March 1, 2020): 1–16. https://doi.org/10.1215/01642472-7971067.

hooks, bell. "Marginality as a Site of Resistance." In *Out There: Marginalization and Contemporary Cultures*, edited by Russell Ferguson, Martha Gever, T. Minh-Ha Trinh, and Cornel West, 341–43. Cambridge, MA: MIT Press, 1990.

Hull, Gloria T., Patricia Bell Scott, and Barbara Smith. *But Some of Us Are Brave: All the Women Are White, All the Blacks Are Men: Black Women's Studies*. New York: Feminist Press at CUNY, 1993.

Huyer, Sophia, and Marilyn Carr. "Information and Communication Technologies: A Priority for Women." *Gender, Technology and Development* 6, no. 1 (March 1, 2002): 85–100. https://doi.org/10.1177/097185240200600105.

Huyer, Sophia, and Swasti Mitter. "ICTs, Globalisation and Poverty Reduction: Gender Dimensions of the Knowledge Society." Gender Advisory Board of the UN Commission on Science and Technology for Development. 2003. http://unpan1.un.org/intradoc/groups/public/documents/unpan/unpano37351.pdf.

hvale vale. "Introduction." In *EroTICs South Asia Exploratory Research: Sex, Rights, and the Internet*. APC Women's Networking Support Programme. 2017.

INCITE! "Critical Resistance Statement: Statement on Gender Violence and the Prison Industrial Complex," 2001. www.incite-national.org/page/incite-critical-resistance-statement.

INCITE! Women of Color Against Violence. *The Revolution Will Not Be Funded: Beyond the Non-Profit Industrial Complex*. Durham, NC: Duke University Press, 2017.

Iniciativa Mesoamericana de Mujeres Defensoras de Derechos Humanos. "El Salvador: Organizaciones preocupadas por incremento de violencia digital contra defensoras." June 19, 2020. http://im-defensoras.org/2020/06/el-salvador-organizaciones-preocupadas-por-incremento-de-violencia-digital-contra-defensoras/.

Instituto Nacional de Fomento Cooperativo. *Cooperativismo autogestion-*

ario: Un modelo para emprendedores. San José, Costa Rica: Instituto Nacional de Fomento Cooperativo, 2004. www.infocoop.go.cr/biblioteca/fasciculos/cooperativismo_autogestionario_modelo_emprendedores.pdf.

International Telecommunications Union (ITU). *Measuring Digital Development: Facts and Figures 2020.* New York: ITU, 2021.

———. *Measuring Digital Development: Facts and Figures 2021.* Geneva, Switzerland: ITU, 2021.

International Telecommunication Union (ITU) and UN Women. *Action Plan to Close the Digital Gender Gap.* 2015. www.itu.int/en/action/gender-equality/Documents/ActionPlan.pdf.

"ITU World Information Society Award Ceremony: Statement by Laureate Professor Muhammad Yunus (as Delivered) Managing Director of Grameen Bank, Bangladesh." International Telecommunications Union, 2006. www.itu.int/wisd/2006/award/statements/yunus.html.

Irani, Lilly. *Chasing Innovation: Making Entrepreneurial Citizens in Modern India.* Princeton, NJ: Princeton University Press, 2019.

Ismail, Feyzi, and Sangeeta Kamat. "NGOs, Social Movements and the Neoliberal State: Incorporation, Reinvention, Critique." *Critical Sociology* 44, no. 4–5 (July 1, 2018): 569–77. https://doi.org/10.1177/0896920517749804.

Jackson, Sarah J., Moya Bailey, and Brooke Foucault Welles. *#HashtagActivism: Networks of Race and Gender Justice.* Cambridge, MA: MIT Press, 2020.

Jaggar, Alison M. "Love and Knowledge: Emotion in Feminist Epistemology." In *Gender/Body/Knowledge: Feminist Reconstructions of Being and Knowing,* 145–71. New Brunswick, NJ: Rutgers University Press, 1989.

James, Selma. *Our Time Is Now: Sex, Race, Class, and Caring for People and Planet.* Oakland, CA: PM Press, 2021.

Jane, Emma A. *Misogyny Online: A Short (and Brutish) History.* Los Angeles, CA: Sage, 2017. https://doi.org/10.4135/9781473916029.

Jarrett, Kylie. "Digital Labor." In *The International Encyclopedia of Gender, Media, and Communication,* 1–5. New York: John Wiley & Sons, 2020. https://doi.org/10.1002/9781119429128.iegmc008.

Jeong, Sarah. 'I'm Disappointed': Zoe Quinn Speaks Out on UN Cyberviolence Report. *Motherboard/Vice,* October 1, 2015. http://motherboard.vice.com/read/im-disappointed-zoe-quinn speaks-out-on-un-cyberviolence-report.

Jolly, Susie, Andrea Cornwall, and Kate Hawkins, eds. *Women, Sexuality, and the Political Power of Pleasure.* London: Zed Books, 2013.

Jones, Angela. *Camming: Money, Power, and Pleasure in the Sex Work Industry.* New York: New York University Press, 2020.

Jong, Sara de, and Susanne Kimm. "The Co-Optation of Feminisms: A Research Agenda." *International Feminist Journal of Politics* 19, no. 2 (April 3, 2017): 185–200. https://doi.org/10.1080/14616742.2017.1299582.

Juris, Jeffrey S. *Networking Futures: The Movements against Corporate Globalization.* Durham, NC: Duke University Press, 2008.

Kaba, Mariame. *We Do This 'Til We Free Us: Abolitionist Organizing and Transforming Justice.* Chicago, IL: Haymarket Books, 2021.

Kabeer, Naila. "Gender Equality and Women's Empowerment: A Critical Analysis of the Third Millennium Development Goal 1." *Gender & Development* 13, no. 1 (March 1, 2005): 13–24. https://doi.org/10.1080/135520 70512331332273.

———. "Gender, Poverty, and Inequality: A Brief History of Feminist Contributions in the Field of International Development." *Gender & Development* 23, no. 2 (May 4, 2015): 189–205. https://doi.org/10.1080/13552074 .2015.1062300.

Kapuściński, Ryszard. *Los cinco sentidos del periodista.* México, DF: Fondo de Cultura Económica, 2003.

Karim, Lamia. *Microfinance and Its Discontents: Women in Debt in Bangladesh.* Minneapolis: University of Minnesota Press, 2011.

Kee, Jac SM. *Cultivating Violence through Technology? Exploring the Connections between Information Communication Technologies (ICT) and Violence Against Women (VAW).* Johannesburg, South Africa: Association for Progressive Communications, December 11, 2007. www.apc.org/ en/pubs/issue/gender/all/cultivating-violence-through-technology.

Kemble, Emma, Lucy Pérez, Valentina Sartori, Gila Tolub, and Alice Zheng. "The Dawn of the FemTech Revolution." McKinsey & Company, 2022. https://www.mckinsey.com/industries/healthcare-systems-and-services/ our-insights/the-dawn-of-the-femtech-revolution.

Khoja-Moolji, Shenila. "Becoming an 'Intimate Publics': Exploring the Affective Intensities of Hashtag Feminism." *Feminist Media Studies* 15, no. 2 (March 4, 2015): 347–50. https://doi.org/10.1080/14680777.2015.1008 747.

KPMG Global. *Pulse of Fintech H2'21.* KPMG, 2022. https://assets.kpmg/ content/dam/kpmg/xx/pdf/2022/02/pulse-of-fintech-h2-21.pdf.

Lal, Shivani. "How One Can Imagine Embodiment in Our 'Disembodied' Online Lives?" *GenderIT.Org* (blog), March 14, 2020. www.genderit.org /feminist-talk/how-one-can-imagine-embodiment-our-disembodied-on line-lives.

Lancet. "Violence against Women: Tackling the Other Pandemic." *Lancet Public Health* 7, no. 1 (January 1, 2022): e1. https://doi.org/10.1016/S2468 -2667(21)00282-6.

Lang, Miriam, and Rita Segato. "Justicia Feminista ante el estado ausente: Un debate urgente. Reflexiones sobre estrategias frente a la violencia patriarcal." *Luchadoras* (blog), July 7, 2021. https://luchadoras.mx/justicia-femi nista-ante-el-estado-ausente-un-debate-urgente-reflexiones-sobre-estrate gias-frente-a-la-violencia-patriarcal/.

Latour, Bruno. "Where Are the Missing Masses? The Sociology of a Few

Mundane Artifacts." In *Shaping Technology/Building Society: Studies in Socio-Technical Change*, edited by Wiebe E. Bijker and John Law, 225–58. Cambridge, MA: MIT Press, 1992.

Law, Victoria. *"Prisons Make Us Safer": And 20 Other Myths about Mass Incarceration*. Boston: Beacon Press, 2021.

Lee, Micky. "UNESCO's Conceptualization of Women and Telecommunications 1970–2000." *Gazette* (Leiden, Netherlands) 66, no. 6 (December 1, 2004): 533–52. https://doi.org/10.1177/0016549204047575.

Lenhart, Amanda, Michele Ybarra, Kathryn Zickuhr, and Myeshia Price-Feeney. "Online Harassment, Digital Abuse, and Cyberstalking in America." *Data & Society*, January 18, 2016. https://datasociety.net/blog/2017/01/18/online-harassment-digital-abuse/.

Levey, Tania G. *Sexual Harassment Online: Shaming and Silencing Women in the Digital Age*. Boulder, CO: Lynne Rienner Publishers, 2018.

Levine, Marne. "Helping to Close the Gender Data Gap." *Facebook* (blog), March 10, 2020. https://about.fb.com/news/2020/03/closing-the-gender-data-gap/.

Leye, Veva. "UNESCO, ICT Corporations and the Passion of ICT for Development: Modernization Resurrected." *Media, Culture & Society* 29, no. 6 (November 1, 2007): 972–93. https://doi.org/10.1177/0163443707081711.

Liboiron, Max. *Pollution Is Colonialism*. Durham, NC: Duke University Press, 2021.

Liinason, Mia. "'Drawing the Line' and Other Small-Scale Resistances: Exploring Agency and Ambiguity in Transnational Feminist and Queer NGOs." *International Feminist Journal of Politics* 23, no. 1 (January 1, 2021): 102–24. https://doi.org/10.1080/14616742.2020.1775489.

López, Eugenia. "Lorena Cabnal: Sanar y defender el territorio-cuerpo-tierra." *Avispa Midia* (blog), June 26, 2018. https://pruebas2.avispa.org/lorena-cabnal-sanar-y-defender-el-territorio-cuerpo-tierra/.

Lorde, Audre. *Sister Outsider: Essays and Speeches*. Berkeley, CA: Crossing Press, 1984.

———. "Uses of the Erotic: The Erotic as Power." In *Sister Outsider: Essays and Speeches*, 53–59. Berkeley, CA: Crossing Press, 1984.

Luchadoras. *La violencia en línea contra las mujeres en México*. Luchadoras, December 18, 2017. http://luchadoras.mx/informe-onu/.

———. *Violencia política a través de las tecnologías*. Luchadoras, October 24, 2018. https://luchadoras.mx/informe-violencia-politica/.

Luchadoras et al. "Sociedad civil insta a la Cámara de Diputados a atender violencia digital de forma integral." April 16, 2021. https://articulo19.org/sociedad-civil-insta-a-la-camara-de-diputados-atender-violencia-digital-de-forma-integral.

Lugones, María. "Heterosexualism and the Colonial/Modern Gender System." *Hypatia* 22, no. 1 (February 1, 2007): 186–219. https://doi.org/10.1111/j.1527-2001.2007.tb01156.x.

———. "Toward a Decolonial Feminism." *Hypatia* 25, no. 4 (October 1, 2010): 742–59. https://doi.org/10.1111/j.1527-2001.2010.01137.x.

Lukacs, Martin, and Rajiv Sicora. "Will Bill Gates and His Billionaire Friends Save the Planet?" *The Guardian*, December 1, 2015. www.theguardian. com/environment/true-north/2015/dec/01/will-bill-gates-and-his -billionaire-friends-save-the-planet.

Maddocks, Sophie. "Feminism, Activism and Non-consensual Pornography: Analyzing Efforts to End 'Revenge Porn' in the United States." *Feminist Media Studies*. April 11, 2021, 1–16. https://doi.org/10.1080/14680777.20 21.1913434.

———. "From Non-Consensual Pornography to Image-Based Sexual Abuse: Charting the Course of a Problem with Many Names." *Australian Feminist Studies* 33, no. 97 (July 3, 2018): 345–61. https://doi.org/10.1080/ 08164649.2018.1542592.

———. "'Revenge Porn': 5 Important Reasons Why We Should Not Call It by That Name." *GenderIT.Org* (blog), 2019.

Malala, Joy. *Law and Regulation of Mobile Payment Systems: Issues Arising "Post" financial Inclusion in Kenya.* New York: Routledge, 2019.

Maldonado, Rery. "Sonia Montaño tras su alejamiento de Cepal: 'Uno de los errores estratégicos cometido por el movimiento de mujeres fue alejarse del pensamiento crítico feminista.'" *América Economía*, 2015. www. americaeconomia.com/politica-sociedad/sociedad/sonia-montano-tras-su -alejamiento-de-cepal-uno-de-los-errores-estrategico.

Mantilla, Karla. "Gendertrolling: Misogyny Adapts to New Media." *Feminist Studies* 39, no. 2 (2013): 563–70. www.jstor.org/stable/23719068.

Marcus, George E. "Ethnography in/of the World System: The Emergence of Multi-Sited Ethnography." *Annual Review of Anthropology* 24 (January 1, 1995): 95–117. https://doi.org/10.2307/2155931.

Martin, Randy. *Financialization of Daily Life.* Philadelphia: Temple University Press, 2002.

Martins, Paula, and Veronica Ferrari. "Human Rights Online at the Human Rights Council 47th Session." *Association for Progressive Communications* (blog), June 21, 2021. www.apc.org/en/news/human-rights-online -human-rights-council-47th-session.

Marwick, Alice E. "Morally Motivated Networked Harassment as Normative Reinforcement." *Social Media + Society* 7, no. 2 (April 1, 2021): 2056 3051211021376. https://doi.org/10.1177/20563051211021378.

Marwick, Alice E., and Robyn Caplan. "Drinking Male Tears: Language, the Manosphere, and Networked Harassment." *Feminist Media Studies* 18, no. 4 (July 4, 2018): 543–59. https://doi.org/10.1080/14680777.2018.1450 568.

Marwick, Alice E., and Ross W. Miller. "Online Harassment, Defamation, and Hateful Speech: A Primer of the Legal Landscape." *SSRN Scholarly Paper.* June 10, 2014. Rochester, NY: Social Science Research Network.

Masiero, Silvia. "Biometric Infrastructures and the Indian Public Distribution System." *South Asia Multidisciplinary Academic Journal*, no. 23 (September 15, 2020). https://doi.org/10.4000/samaj.6459.

———. "Should We Still Be Doing ICT4D Research?" *Electronic Journal of Information Systems in Developing Countries* n/a, no. n/a (2022): e12215. https://doi.org/10.1002/isd2.12215.

Masiero, Silvia, and Soumyo Das. "Datafying Anti-Poverty Programmes: Implications for Data Justice." *Information, Communication & Society* 22, no. 7 (June 7, 2019): 916–33. https://doi.org/10.1080/1369118X.2019.1575448.

Masiero, Silvia, and S. Shakthi. "Grappling with Aadhaar: Biometrics, Social Identity and the Indian State." *South Asia Multidisciplinary Academic Journal*, no. 23 (September 15, 2020). https://doi.org/10.4000/samaj.6279.

McGlynn, Clare, and Erika Rackley. "Research Briefing: Image-Based Sexual Abuse: More Than Just 'Revenge Porn.'" Birmingham, UK: University of Birmingham, 2016.

McKinsey Global Institute. "AI, Automation, and the Future of Work: Ten Things to Solve For: Briefing Note Prepared for the Tech4good Summit, Organized by the French Presidency." McKinsey Global Institute, 2018. Accessed August 24, 2021. www.mckinsey.com/featured-insights/future-of-work/ai-automation-and-the-future-of-work-ten-things-to-solve-for.

———. "The Future of Women at Work: Transitions in the Age of Automation." Executive Summary. McKinsey Global Institute (MGI), 2019.

McMillan Cottom, Tressie. "Where Platform Capitalism and Racial Capitalism Meet: The Sociology of Race and Racism in the Digital Society." *Sociology of Race and Ethnicity* 6, no. 4 (October 1, 2020): 441–49. https://doi.org/10.1177/2332649220949473.

Medina, Eden, Ivan da Costa Marques, and Christian Holmes. "Introduction: Beyond Imported Magic." In *Beyond Imported Magic: Essays on Science, Technology, and Society in Latin America*, edited by Eden Medina, Ivan da Costa Marques, and Christian Holmes, 1–23. Cambridge, MA: MIT Press, 2014.

Mendel, Jonathan, and Kiril Sharapov. "Human Trafficking and Online Networks: Policy, Analysis, and Ignorance." *Antipode* 48, no. 3 (2016): 665–84. https://doi.org/10.1111/anti.12213.

Menjívar, Cecilia. *Enduring Violence: Ladina Women's Lives in Guatemala*. Berkeley: University of California Press, 2011.

Mesa-Lago, Carmelo. *Market, Socialist, and Mixed Economies: Comparative Policy and Performance: Chile, Cuba, and Costa Rica*. Baltimore, MD: Johns Hopkins University Press, 2000.

Mies, Maria, and Vandana Shiva. *Ecofeminism*. 2nd ed. London: Zed Books, 2014.

Mignolo, Walter D. *Local Histories/Global Designs: Coloniality, Subaltern Knowledges, and Border Thinking*. Rev. ed. Princeton, NJ: Princeton University Press, 2012.

Milan, Stefania, and Emiliano Treré. "Big Data from the South(s): Beyond Data Universalism." *Television & New Media* 20, no. 4 (May 1, 2019): 319–35. https://doi.org/10.1177/1527476419837739.

Miller, Julia, Angelika Arutyunova, and Cindy Clark. *New Actors, New Money, New Conversations: A Mapping of Recent Initiatives for Women and Girls*. Association for Women's Rights in Development (AWID), 2013. www.awid.org/publications/new-actors-new-money-new-conversations.

Ministerio de Ciencia, Tecnología y Telecomunicaciones (MICITT) de Costa Rica. "Estrategia de transformación digital del bicentenario." October 17, 2018. https://presidencia.go.cr/comunicados/2018/10/gobierno-presento-estrategia-de-transformacion-digital-del-bicentenario/.

———. *National Telecommunications Development Plan (PNDT) 2015–2021: Costa Rica: A Connected Society*. 2015. https://www.micitt.go.cr/wp-content/uploads/2022/07/PNDT_2015-2021.-English-Version-Web.pdf.

———. *Plan Nacional de Desarrollo de las Telecomunicaciones 2022-2027: Costa Rica: Hacia la disrupción digital inclusive*. 2022. https://www.micitt.go.cr/wp-content/uploads/2022/12/PNDT-2022-2027-V12-12-22.pdf.

———. *Política Nacional para la Igualdad entre Mujeres y Hombres en la Formación, el Empleo y el Disfrute de los Productos de la Ciencia, la Tecnología, las Telecomunicaciones y la Innovación 2018–2027*. 2017. https://www.micitt.go.cr/wp-content/uploads/2022/04/pdf.

———. "Se oficializa la creación de la promotora costarricense de innovación e investigación." 2021. https://micit.go.cr/noticias/se-oficializa-la-creacion-la-promotora-costarricense-innovacion-e-investigacion.

Ministerio de Economía, Industria y Comercio de Costa Rica (MEIC). *Política nacional de empresariedad 2019–2030*. San José, Costa Rica: Gobierno de Costa Rica, Administración Alvarado Quesada 2018–2022, 2020. http://reventazon.meic.go.cr/informacion/pyme/MEIC_PNE_2030.pdf.

Mishra, Paro, and Yogita Suresh. "Datafied Body Projects in India: Femtech and the Rise of Reproductive Surveillance in the Digital Era." *Asian Journal of Women's Studies* 27, no. 4 (October 2, 2021): 597–606. https://doi.org/10.1080/12259276.2021.2002010.

Mitter, Swasti. "ICTs, Globalisation and Poverty Reduction: Gender Dimensions of the Knowledge Society." Gender Advisory Board of the UN Commission on Science and Technology for Development. 2003. http://unpan1.un.org/intradoc/groups/public/documents/unpan/unpan037351.pdf.

Moeller, Kathryn. *The Gender Effect: Capitalism, Feminism, and the Corporate Politics of Development*. Berkeley, CA: University of California Press, 2018.

Mohanty, Chandra Talpade. *Feminism without Borders: Decolonizing Theory, Practicing Solidarity*. Durham, NC: Duke University Press, 2003.

———. "Under Western Eyes: Feminist Scholarship and Colonial Discourses."

Feminist Review, no. 30 (October 1, 1988): 61–88. https://doi.org/10.2307/1395054.

Molinier, Helene. *Leveraging Digital Finance for Gender Equality and Women's Empowerment.* New York: UN Women, September 2019. www.unwomen.org/digital-library/publications/2019/09/discussion-paper-leveraging-digital-finance-for-gender-equality-and-womens-empowerment.

Moolman, Jan. "Recognition of Online GBV in International Law: The Highs and Lows" (editorial). *GenderIT.Org* (blog), June 17, 2018. www.genderit.org/editorial/editorial-recognition-online-gbv-international-law-highs-and-lows.

Moraga, Cherríe. "La Güera." In *This Bridge Called My Back: Writings by Radical Women of Color*, 4th ed., edited by Cherríe Moraga and Gloria Anzaldúa, 22–29. Albany: SUNY Press, 2015.

Moraga, Cherríe, and Gloria Anzaldúa, eds. *This Bridge Called My Back: Writings by Radical Women of Color.* 4th ed. Albany: SUNY Press, 2015.

Morgan, Joan. "Why We Get Off: Moving Towards a Black Feminist Politics of Pleasure." *Black Scholar* 45, no. 4 (October 2, 2015): 36–46. https://doi.org/10.1080/00064246.2015.1080915.

Morris, Charlotte, Paul Boyce, Andrea Cornwall, Hannah Frith, Laura Harvey, and Yingying Huang, eds. *Researching Sex and Sexualities.* London: Zed Books, 2018.

Moussié, Rachel. *Challenging Corporate Power: Struggles for Women's Rights, Economic and Gender Justice.* Toronto and Mexico City: Association for Women's Rights in Development (AWID) and the Solidarity Center, September 2, 2016. www.awid.org/publications/challenging-corporate-power-struggles-womens-rights-economic-and-gender-justice.

Mozur, Paul. "A Genocide Incited on Facebook, With Posts From Myanmar's Military." *New York Times.* October 15, 2018. www.nytimes.com/2018/10/15/technology/myanmar-facebook-genocide.html.

Murphy, Michelle. *The Economization of Life.* Durham, NC: Duke University Press, 2017.

———. "Unsettling Care: Troubling Transnational Itineraries of Care in Feminist Health Practices." *Social Studies of Science* 45, no. 5 (2015): 717–37. www.jstor.org/stable/43829053.

Musto, Jennifer Lynne, and danah boyd. "The Trafficking Technology Nexus." *Social Politics: International Studies in Gender, State & Society* 0, no. 0 (August 26, 2014): 1–23. https://doi.org/10.1093/sp/jxu018.

Nagar, Richa. "Footloose Researchers, 'Traveling' Theories, and the Politics of Transnational Feminist Praxis." *Gender, Place & Culture* 9, no. 2 (June 1, 2002): 179–86. https://doi.org/10.1080/09663960220139699.

———. *Muddying the Waters: Coauthoring Feminisms across Scholarship and Activism.* Urbana: University of Illinois Press, 2014.

Nagar, Richa, and Susan Geiger. "Reflexivity, Positionality, and Languages of Collaboration in Feminist Fieldwork." In *Muddying the Waters: Coau-*

thoring Feminisms across Scholarship and Activism, 81–94. Urbana: University of Illinois Press, 2014.

Naples, Nancy A. *Feminism and Method: Ethnography, Discourse Analysis, and Activist Research*. New York: Routledge, 2003.

Nash, Jennifer C. "Black Sexualities." *Feminist Theory* 19, no. 1 (April 1, 2018): 3–5. https://doi.org/10.1177/1464700117742865.

Nast, Kendra, and Afsaneh Rigot. "Apple and Google Still Have an LGBTQ Problem." *Wired UK*, August 8, 2021. www.wired.co.uk/article/apple -google-lgbtq-apps.

Nelson, Maggie. *On Freedom: Four Songs of Care and Constraint*. Minneapolis, MN: Graywolf Press, 2021.

Nichols, Michelle. "U.N. Chief Puts Technology Envoy on Leave over Harassment Inquiry." Reuters, January 28, 2021. www.reuters.com/world/americas /un-chief-puts-technology-envoy-leave-over-harassment-inquiry-2021-01-28/.

Noble, Safiya Umoja. *Algorithms of Oppression: How Search Engines Reinforce Racism*. New York: New York University Press, 2018.

———. "A Future for Intersectional Black Feminist Technology Studies." *S&F Online*, no. 13.3–14.1 (2016). http://sfonline.barnard.edu/traversing-tech nologies/safiya-umoja-noble-a-future-for-intersectional-black-feminist -technology-studies/.

Noronha, Frederick, and Karen Higgs. "The Internet Is a 'Radically Different' Place Because of APC." *APC News* (blog), 2010. www.apc.org/en/node/ 10678/.

Office of ECOSOC Support and Coordination, UN-DESA. *Background Note: Funding Situation of the UN Development System*. New York: United Nations, September 26, 2016. http://archive.ipu.org/conf-e/135/un -funding.pdf.

ONU Mujeres. "Plataforma virtual conectará a más de 3,8 millones de mujeres en América Latina y el Caribe en torno a la tecnología y el emprendimiento." ONU Mujeres América Latina y el Caribe, 2022. https://lac.un women.org/es/stories/noticia/2022/01/todasconectadas-plataforma-virtual -conectara-a-millones-de-mujeres-en-america-latina-y-el-caribe.

Orloff, Ann Shola, Raka Ray, and Evren Savci. "Introduction: Perverse Politics? Feminism, Anti-Imperialism, Multiplicity." In *Political Power and Social Theory: Perverse Politics? Feminism, Anti-Imperialism, Multiplicity*, 1–17. Bradford, West Yorkshire, UK: Emerald Group Publishing Limited, 2016.

Orloff, Ann Shola, and Talia Shiff. "Feminism/s in Power: Rethinking Gender Equality after the Second Wave." In *Political Power and Social Theory: Perverse Politics? : Feminism, Anti-Imperialism, Multiplicity*, 109–34. Bradford, West Yorkshire, UK: Emerald Group Publishing Limited, 2016.

Padte, Richa Kaul. *Cyber Sexy: Rethinking Pornograohy*. London: India Penguin, 2018.

Paredes, Julieta. "El feminismocomunitario: La creación de un pensamiento propio." *Corpus: Archivos virtuales de la alteridad americana* 7, no. 1 (June 26, 2017). https://doi.org/10.4000/corpusarchivos.1835.

Paredes, Julieta, and Comunidad Mujeres Creando Comunidad. *Hilando fino: Desde el feminismo comunitario*. La Paz, Bolivia: El Rebozo, Zapateándole, Lente Flotante, En cortito que's palargo y AliFem AC, 2010. https://sjlatinoamerica.files.wordpress.com/2013/06/paredes-julieta-hilan do-fino-desde-el-feminismo-comunitario.pdf.

Paredes, Julieta, and Adriana Guzmán. *El tejido de la rebeldía: ¿Qué es el feminismo comunitario?: Bases para la despatriarcalización*. La Paz, Bolivia: Mujeres Creando Comunidad, 2014.

Pateman, Carole. *The Sexual Contract*. Stanford, CA: Stanford University Press, 1988.

Paul, Kari, and Dan Milmo. "Facebook Putting Profit before Public Good, Says Whistleblower Frances Haugen." *The Guardian*. October 4, 2021. www.theguardian.com/technology/2021/oct/03/former-facebook-em ployee-frances-haugen-identifies-herself-as-whistleblower.

Pedwell, Carolyn. "Affective (Self-) Transformations: Empathy, Neoliberalism and International Development." *Feminist Theory* 13, no. 2 (August 1, 2012): 163–79. https://doi.org/10.1177/1464700112442644.

Peña, Paz. "Recommendations on Technology-Related Violence Against Women (VAW) for the UN." *Medium* (blog), March 1, 2018. https://medi um.com/@pazpena/recommendations-on-technology-related-violence -against-women-vaw-for-the-un-5e27b544e6b2.

———. *Reporte de la situación de América Latina sobre la violencia de género ejercida por medios electrónicos*. Asociación por los Derechos Civiles, Coding Rights, Derechos Digitales, Hiperderecho, Fundación Karisma, InternetLab, IPANDETEC, Red en Defensa de los Derechos Digitales (R3D), TEDIC. 2017. https://hiperderecho.org/wp-content/up loads/2018/03/Reporte_Violencia_Genero_Linea_Latinoamerica.pdf.

Peña, Paz, and Joana Varon. *Consent to Our Data Bodies: Lessons from Feminist Theories to Enforce Data Protection*. Coding Rights, March 8, 2019. https://www.apc.org/en/pubs/consent-our-data-bodies-lessons-fem inist-theories-enforce-data-protection.

Pereira, Charmaine. *Changing Narratives of Sexuality: Contestations, Compliance and Womens Empowerment*. London: Zed Books, 2014.

Pérez Orozco, Amaia. *The Feminist Subversion of the Economy: Contributions for a Dignified Life Against Capital*. Translated by Liz Mason-Deese. New York: Common Notions, 2022.

Pew Research Center, and Emily Vogels. *The State of Online Harassment*. Pew Research Center, January 13, 2021. www.pewresearch.org/internet/ 2021/01/13/the-state-of-online-harassment/.

Phillips, Lynne, and Sally Cole. "Feminist Flows, Feminist Fault Lines: Women's Machineries and Women's Movements in Latin America." *Signs* 35, no. 1 (September 1, 2009): 185–211. https://doi.org/10.1086/599327.

Phillips, Nelson, and Cynthia Hardy. *Discourse Analysis: Investigating Processes of Social Construction.* Thousand Oaks, CA: Sage, 2002.

Posetti, Julie, Nermine Aboulez, Kalina Bontcheva, Jackie Harrison, and Silvio Waisbord. "ICFJ-UNESCO Study: Online Violence, Fueled by Disinformation and Political Attacks, Deeply Harms Women Journalists." International Center for Journalists (ICFJ), 2021. www.icfj.org/news/icfj-unesco-study-online-violence-fueled-disinformation-and-political-attacks-deeply-harms.

Primo, Natasha. *Gender Issues in the Information Society.* Paris, France: UNESCO, 2003.

Privacy International. *No Body's Business But Mine: How Menstruation Apps Are Sharing Your Data.* September 9, 2019. https://privacyinternational.org/long-read/3196/no-bodysbusiness-mine-how-menstruations-apps-are-sharing-your-data.

Promotora de Comercio Exterior (PROCOMER) con la colaboración de la Cámara de Tecnologías de la Información y Comunicación (CAMTIC). "Mapeo de tecnologías digitales 2019." In *Caracterización del sector de Tecnologías de Información y Comunicación (TICs) en Costa Rica.* San José, Costa Rica: PROCOMER and CAMTIC, 2019. www.camtic.org/wp-content/uploads/2019/09/Caracterizaci%C3%B3n-del-sector-de-tecnolog%C3%ADas-de-informaci%C3%B3n-y-comunicaci%C3%B3n-TICs-en-Costa-Rica-2019.pdf.

Prügl, Elisabeth. "Neoliberalising Feminism." *New Political Economy* 20, no. 4 (July 4, 2015): 614–31. https://doi.org/10.1080/13563467.2014.951614.

Puig de la Bellacasa, María. *Matters of Care: Speculative Ethics in More than Human Worlds.* Minneapolis: University of Minnesota Press, 2017.

———. "'Nothing Comes Without Its World': Thinking with Care:" *Sociological Review* 60, no. 2 (May 1, 2012). https://journals-sagepub-com.ezp.fandm.edu/doi/10.1111/j.1467-954X.2012.02070.x.

Pyati, Ajit. "WSIS: Whose Vision of an Information Society?" *First Monday*, May 2, 2005. https://firstmonday.org/ojs/index.php/fm/article/download/1241/1161.

Quijano, Aníbal. "Coloniality and Modernity/Rationality." *Cultural Studies* 21, no. 2–3 (March 1, 2007): 168–78. https://doi.org/10.1080/09502380601164353.

Radhakrishnan, Smitha. "Empowerment, Declined: Paradoxes of Microfinance and Gendered Subjectivity in Urban India." *Signs: Journal of Women in Culture and Society* 44, no. 1 (2018): 83. www.academia.edu/37247560/Empowerment_Declined_Paradoxes_of_Microfinance_and_Gendered_Subjectivity_in_Urban_India.

———. "'Low Profile' or Entrepreneurial? Gender, Class, and Cultural Adaptation in the Global Microfinance Industry." *World Development* 74 (October 2015): 264–74. https://doi.org/10.1016/j.worlddev.2015.05.017.

———. *Making Women Pay: Microfinance in Urban India.* Durham, NC: Duke University Press, 2022.

Rankin, Joy Lisi. "For 50 Years, Tech Companies Have Tried to Increase Diversity by Fixing People Instead of the System." *Slate Magazine.* March 31, 2021. https://slate.com/technology/2021/03/google-acm-digital-skills-training-diversity-history.html.

Rankin, Katharine N. "Governing Development: Neoliberalism, Microcredit, and Rational Economic Woman." *Economy and Society* 30, no. 1 (January 1, 2001): 18–37. https://doi.org/10.1080/03085140020019070.

———. "Social Capital, Microfinance, and the Politics of Development." *Feminist Economics* 8, no. 1 (January 1, 2002): 1–24. https://doi.org/10.1080/13545700210125167.

Rathgeber, Eva M. "WID, WAD, GAD: Trends in Research and Practice." *Journal of Developing Areas* 24, no. 4 (1990): 489–502. www.jstor.org/stable/4191904.

Ravindranath, Paul. "Introducing the Inaugural Class of the Google for Startups Accelerator, India Women Founders." Google. October 3, 2022. https://blog.google/intl/en-in/introducing-the-inaugural-class-of-the-google-for-startups-accelerator-india-women-founders/.

Razavi, Shahra, and Carol Miller. "From WID to GAD: Conceptual Shifts in the Women and Development Discourse." United Nations Research Institute for Social Development (UNRISD). 1995. Accessed June 21, 2021. www.unrisd.org/80256B3C005BCCF9/(httpPublications)/D9C3FCA/8D3DB32E80256B67005B6AB5.

Reinharz, Shulamit. *Feminist Methods in Social Research.* Oxford: Oxford University Press, 1992.

Ressa, Maria. "Propaganda War: Weaponizing the Internet." *Rappler* (blog). 2016. November 21, 2021. www.rappler.com/nation/propaganda-war-weaponizing-internet.

Reyes, Ángela. "¿Qué significa realmente el 'vivir sabroso' de Francia Márquez? Historia de una filosofía del Pacífico que ahora resuena en Colombia." *CNN* (blog). June 22, 2022. https://cnnespanol.cnn.com/2022/06/22/vivir-sabroso-francia-marquez-colombia-que-es-orix/.

Riaño Alcalá, Pilar. *Women in Grassroots Communication: Furthering Social Change.* Thousand Oaks, CA: Sage Publications, 1994.

Ricaurte, Paola. "Mapping." In *Technoaffections: For Politics of Shared Responsibility.* Mexico, DF: Sursiendo, 2022.

Richie, Beth E. "Reimagining the Movement to End Gender Violence: Anti-Racism, Prison Abolition, Women of Color Feminisms, and Other Radical Visions of Justice Converge Reimagining the Movement to End Gender Violence Keynote Transcript." *University of Miami Race and Social Justice Law Review* 5, no. 2 (2015): 257–74. https://heinonline.org/HOL/P?h=hein.journals/umrsj5&i=275.

223

Rivera Cusicanqui, Silvia. "Ch'ixinakax Utxiwa: A Reflection on the Practices and Discourses of Decolonization." *South Atlantic Quarterly* 111, no. 1 (January 1, 2012): 95–109. https://doi.org/10.1215/00382876-1472612.

Roberts, Adrienne. "The Political Economy of 'Transnational Business Feminism': Problematizing the Corporate-Led Gender Equality Agenda." *International Feminist Journal of Politics* 17, no. 2 (April 3, 2015): 209–31. https://doi.org/10.1080/14616742.2013.849968.

Roberts, Sarah T. *Behind the Screen: Content Moderation in the Shadows of Social Media.* New Haven, CT: Yale University Press, 2019.

Robertson, Adi. "A Federal 'Revenge Porn' Ban Could Transform Online Harassment Laws." *The Verge*, April 15, 2021. www.theverge.com/2021/4/15/22340260/vawa-shield-act-revenge-porn-first-amendment-questions.

Rodríguez, Clemencia. *Fissures in the Mediascape: An International Study of Citizens' Media.* Cresskill, NJ: Hampton Press, 2001.

Rodríguez Moreno, Celenis. "Mujer y desarrollo: Un discurso colonial." *El Cotidiano* 184 (March-April 2014): 31–37. https://www.redalyc.org/articulo.oa?id=32530724002

Rolnik, Suely. *Esferas de la insurrección: Apuntes para descolonizar el inconsciente.* Translated by Cecilia Palmeiro, Marcía Cabrera, and Damian Kraus. Buenos Aires, Argentina: Tinta Limón, 2019.

Rosas, Celia. "The Future Is Femtech: Privacy and Data Security Issues Surrounding Femtech Applications." *Hastings Business Law Journal* 15, no. 2 (2019): 319–41.

Rose, Nikolas. *Powers of Freedom: Reframing Political Thought.* Cambridge, UK: Cambridge University Press, 2010.

Roy, Ananya. *Poverty Capital: Microfinance and the Making of Development.* New York: Routledge, 2010.

——. "Subjects of Risk: Technologies of Gender in the Making of Millennial Modernity." *Public Culture* 24, no. 1 66 (January 1, 2012): 131–55. https://doi.org/10.1215/08992363-1498001.

Roy, Arundhati. "The NGO-Ization of Resistance." *Pambazuka News*, September 23, 2014. https://revolutionaryfrontlines.wordpress.com/2014/09/25/ngoisation-of-resistance-arundhati-roy/.

Roy, Srila. "Enacting/Disrupting the Will to Empower: Feminist Governance of 'Child Marriage' in Eastern India." *Signs: Journal of Women in Culture and Society* 42, no. 4 (June 2017): 867–91. https://doi.org/10.1086/690954.

——. "The Indian Women's Movement: Within and Beyond NGOization." *Journal of South Asian Development* 10, no. 1 (April 1, 2015): 96–117. https://doi.org/10.1177/0973174114567368.

——. "The Positive Side of Co-optation? Intersectionality: A Conversation between Inderpal Grewal and Srila Roy." *International Feminist Journal of Politics* 19, no. 2 (April 3, 2017): 254–62. https://doi.org/10.1080/1461 6742.2017.1291225.

Rubio, Irene García, and Rita Laura Segato. "'Todas las revoluciones han sido hechas por barbudos': Entrevista con Rita Segato." *Minerva: Revista del Círculo de Bellas Artes*, no. 28 (2017): 41–44. https://dialnet.unirioja.es/servlet/articulo?codigo=6043056.

Ruddick, Sara. "Care as Labor and Relationship." In *Norms and Values: Essays on the Work of Virginia Held*, edited by Joram Graf Haber and Mark S. Halfon, 3–25. Lanham, MD: Rowman & Littlefield, 1998.

———. "Maternal Thinking." *Feminist Studies* 6, no. 2 (1980): 342–67. https://doi.org/10.2307/3177749.

Sachs, Wolfgang, ed. *The Development Dictionary*. 2nd ed. New York: Zed Books, 2010. First published 1992 by Zed Books.

Sahay, Ratna, Ulric Eriksson von Allmen, Amina Lahrèche-Révil, Purva Khera, Sumiko Ogawa, Majid Bazarbash, and Kimberly Beaton. *The Promise of Fintech: Financial Inclusion in the Post COVID-19 Era*. Department Paper Series, no. 20, 09. Washington, DC: International Monetary Fund, 2020.

Saldroite. "Queer Lust and Internet Orgasms." *GenderIT.Org* (blog). 2021. June 10, 2021. https://genderit.org/articles/queer-lust-and-internet-orgasms.

Santiago, Karen. "Lorena Cabnal: Sanación, feminismo y defensa comunitaria." *Luchadoras* (blog), May 14, 2018. https://luchadoras.mx/lorena-cabnal-sanacion/.

Saunders, Kriemild. *Feminist Post-Development Thought: Rethinking Modernity, Post-Colonialism & Representation*. London: Zed, 2004.

Schiebinger, Londa. *Harnessing Technology and Innovation to Achieve Gender Equality and Empower all Women and Girls*. Background Paper in Support of the Sixty-Seventh Session of the Commission on the Status of Women (CSW67). UN Women, 2022. https://www.unwomen.org/sites/default/files/2022-12/BP.2_Londa%20Schiebinger.pdf.

Schoenebeck, Sarita, Oliver L. Haimson, and Lisa Nakamura. "Drawing from Justice Theories to Support Targets of Online Harassment." *New Media & Society* 23, no. 5 (May 1, 2021): 1278–300. https://doi.org/10.1177/1461444820913122.

Schumacher, E. F. *Small Is Beautiful; Economics as If People Mattered*. New York: Harper & Row, 1973.

Scott, James C. *Seeing Like a State: How Certain Schemes to Improve the Human Condition Have Failed*. New Haven, CT: Yale University Press, 1999.

Segato, Rita Laura. *La escritura en el cuerpo de las mujeres asesinadas en Ciudad Juárez*. Buenos Aires, Argentina: Tinta Limón, 2013. http://journals.openedition.org/amerika/7531.

———. *La guerra contra las mujeres*. Madrid: Traficantes de Sueños, 2016.

Segato, Rita Laura, and Pedro Monque. "Gender and Coloniality: From Low-Intensity Communal Patriarchy to High-Intensity Colonial-Modern Patri-

archy." *Hypatia* 36, no. 4 (ed 2021): 781–99. https://doi.org/10.1017/hyp
.2021.58.

———. "Género y colonialidad: En busca de claves de lectura y de un vocabu-
lario estratégico descolonial." In *Feminismos y poscolonialidad: Descolonizando el feminismo desde y en América Latina*, edited by Karina
Bidaseca and Vanesa Vazquez Laba, 17–48. Buenos Aires: Ediciones
Godot, 2011.

Seitz, Karolin, and Jens Martens. "Philanthrolateralism: Private Funding and
Corporate Influence in the United Nations." *Global Policy* 8, no. S5 (2017):
46–50. https://doi.org/10.1111/1758-5899.12448.

Sen, Gita, Caren Grown, and Development Alternatives with Women for a
New Era (Project). *Development, Crises, and Alternative Visions: Third
World Women's Perspectives.* New York: Monthly Review Press, 1987.

Shaw, Adrienne. "The Internet Is Full of Jerks, Because the World Is Full of
Jerks: What Feminist Theory Teaches Us About the Internet." *Communication and Critical/Cultural Studies* 11, no. 3 (July 3, 2014): 273–77. https:
//doi.org/10.1080/14791420.2014.926245.

Shaw, Amanda, and Kalpana Wilson. "The Bill and Melinda Gates Foundation and the Necro-Populationism of 'Climate-Smart' Agriculture."
Gender, Place & Culture 27, no. 3 (March 3, 2020): 370–93. https://doi.
org/10.1080/0966369X.2019.1609426.

Shiva, Vandana. *Staying Alive: Women, Ecology and Development.* London:
Zed Books, 1988.

Shokooh Valle, Firuzeh. "Moving beyond Co-optation: Gender, Development, and Intimacy." *Sociology of Development* 4, no. 4 (December 1,
2018): 325–45.

Simpson, Betasamosake Leanne. *As We Have Always Done: Indigenous Freedom Through Radical Resistance.* Minneapolis: University of Minnesota
Press, 2017.

Singal, Jesse. "The U.N.'s Cyberharassment Report Is Really Bad." *New York
Magazine.* September 28, 2015. https://www.thecut.com/2015/09/uns-cy
berharassment-report-is-really-bad.html

Smith, Linda Tuhiwai. *Decolonizing Methodologies: Research and Indigenous Peoples.* 2nd ed. London: Zed Books, 2012.

Sobieraj, Sarah. *Credible Threat: Attacks against Women Online and the
Future of Democracy.* New York: Oxford University Press, 2020.

Souza, Ladyane, and Joana Varon. *Violencia política de género en internet:
Policy Paper América Latina y El Caribe.* AlSur, 2021. www.alsur.lat/
reporte/violencia-politica-genero-en-internet.

Spade, Dean. *Mutual Aid: Building Solidarity during This Crisis.* New York:
Verso, 2020.

Special Rapporteur on the Promotion and Protection of the Right to Freedom
of Opinion and Expression, Irene Khan. *Gender Justice and Freedom of*

Expression—Report of Special Rapporteur on the Promotion and Protection of the Right to Freedom of Opinion and Expression. A/76/258. UN Human Rights Council, July 30, 2021. https://www.ohchr.org/en/documents/thematic-reports/a76258-gender-justice-and-freedom-expression-report-special-rapporteur.

Special Rapporteur on the Promotion and Protection of the Right to Freedom of Opinion and Expression, Frank La Rue. *Promotion and Protection of All Human Rights, Civil, Political, Economic, Social and Cultural Rights, Including the Right to Development.* A/HRC/17/27. UN Human Rights Council, May 16, 2011. https://www2.ohchrs.org/english/bodies/hrcouncil/docs/17session/a.hrc.17.27_en.pdf.

Special Rapporteur on Violence against Women, Dubravka Šimonović. *Report of the Special Rapporteur on Violence against Women, Its Causes and Consequences on Online Violence against Women and Girls from a Human Rights Perspective.* A/HRC/38/47. UN Human Rights Council, June 18, 2018. http://digitallibrary.un.org/record/1641160.

Spivak, Gayatri. *The Spivak Reader: Selected Works of Gayati Chakravorty Spivak.* New York: Routledge, 2013.

Srnicek, Nick. *Platform Capitalism.* Malden, MA: Polity, 2017.

Stacey, Judith. "Can There Be a Feminist Ethnography?" *Women's Studies International Forum* 11, no. 1 (January 1, 1988): 21–27. https://doi.org/10.1016/0277-5395(88)90004-0.

Stake, Robert E. *Multiple Case Study Analysis.* New York: Guilford Press, 2006.

Steele, Catherine Knight. *Digital Black Feminism.* New York: New York University Press, 2021.

Stoler, Ann Laura. *Carnal Knowledge and Imperial Power: Race and the Intimate in Colonial Rule.* Berkeley: University of California Press, 2002.

Suarez Estrada, Marcela. "Feminist Struggles against Criminalization of Digital Violence: Lessons for Internet Governance from the Global South." *Policy & Internet* 14, no. 2 (2022): 410–23. https://doi.org/10.1002/poi3.277.

Sunkel, Osvaldo. "National Development Policy and External Dependence in Latin America." *Journal of Development Studies* 6, no. 1 (October 1, 1969): 23–48. https://doi.org/10.1080/00220386908421311.

Suri, Tavneet, and William Jack. "The Long-run Poverty and Gender Impacts of Mobile Money." *Science* 354, no. 6317 (December 9, 2016): 1288–92. https://www.science.org/doi/10.1126/science.aah5309.

Swarr, Amanda Lock, and Richa Nagar. *Critical Transnational Feminist Praxis.* Albany: SUNY Press, 2012.

TallBear, Kim. "Standing with and Speaking as Faith: A Feminist-Indigenous Approach to Inquiry." *Journal of Research Practice* 10, no. 2 (July 1, 2014): 1–7. http://jrp.icaap.org/index.php/jrp/article/view/405.

———. "Why Interspecies Thinking Needs Indigenous Standpoints." *Society*

for Cultural Anthropology, Fieldsights, November 18, 2011. https://
culanth.org/fieldsights/why-interspecies-thinking-needs-indigenous
-standpoints.

Task Force on Digital Financing of the Sustainable Development Goals. *People's Money: Harnessing Digitalization to Finance a Sustainable Future.*
New York: United Nations, 2020. https://unsdg.un.org/resources/peoples
-money-harnessing-digitalization-finance-sustainable-future.

Taub, Amanda, and Max Fisher. "Facebook Fueled Anti-Refugee Attacks in
Germany, New Research Suggests." *New York Times.* October 10, 2018.
www.nytimes.com/2018/08/21/world/europe/facebook-refugee-attacks
-germany.html.

Taylor, Linnet, and Dennis Broeders. "In the Name of Development: Power,
Profit and the Datafication of the Global South." *Geoforum* 64 (August 1,
2015): 229–37. https://doi.org/10.1016/j.geoforum.2015.07.002.

Telleria, Juan. "Power Relations? What Power Relations? The De-politicising
Conceptualisation of Development of the UNDP." *Third World Quarterly*
38, no. 9 (September 2, 2017): 2143–58. https://doi.org/10.1080/01436597
.2017.1298437.

Thayer, Millie. *Making Transnational Feminism: Rural Women, NGO Activists, and Northern Donors in Brazil.* London: Routledge, 2010.

Todd, Zoe. "An Indigenous Feminist's Take on the Ontological Turn: 'Ontology' Is Just Another Word for Colonialism." *Journal of Historical Sociology* 29, no. 1 (2016): 4–22. https://doi.org/10.1111/johs.12124.

Toledo, Amalia. "Misoginia en internet: bombardeo a campo abierto contra
las periodistas." Fundación Karisma, February 24, 2016. https://karisma.
org.co/misoginia-en-internet-bombardeo-a-campo-abierto-contra-las
-periodistas/.

Tuck, Eve, and K. Wayne Yang. "Decolonization Is Not a Metaphor." *Decolonization: Indigeneity, Education & Society* 1, no. 1 (September 8,
2012): 1–40. https://jps.library.utoronto.ca/index.php/des/article/view/
18630.

United Nations. "Inequality in a Rapidly Changing World." In *World Social
Report 2020*, ch. 2. New York: UN Department of Economic and Social
Affairs, February 2020. www.un.org/development/desa/dspd/wp-content/
uploads/sites/22/2020/02/World-Social-Report-2020-Chapter-2.pdf.

———. *Our Common Agenda–Report of the Secretary-General.* United Nations, 2021. https://www.un.org/en/content/common-agenda-report/assets
/pdf/Common_Agenda_Report_English.pdf.

———. *Report of the Secretary-General: Roadmap for Digital Cooperation.*
United Nations, June 2020. https://www.un.org/en/content/digital
-cooperation-roadmap/assets/pdf/Roadmap_for_Digital_Cooperation_
EN.pdf.

———. *Sustainable Development Goals Report 2021.* New York: United Nations, 2021. https://unstats.un.org/sdgs/report/2021/.

United Nations and World Conference on Women. *Beijing Declaration and Platform of Action.* Adopted September 15, 1995. https://www.un.org/womenwatch/daw/beijing/pdf/BDPfA%20E.pdf.

United Nations Children's Fund (UNICEF) and ITU. *Towards an Equal Future: Reimagining Girls' Education through STEM.* New York: UNICEF, 2020. https://www.unicef.org/media/84046/file/Reimagining -girls-education-through-stem-2020.pdf.

United Nations Conference on Trade and Development (UNCTAD). *Applying a Gender Lens to Science, Technology, and Innovation.* Geneva: UNCTAD, 2011. https://unctad.org/webflyer/applying-gender-lens-science -technology-and-innovation#.

———. *Technology and Innovation Report: Catching Technological Waves Innovation with Equity.* Geneva: UNCTAD, 2021. https://unctad.org/webflyer/technology-and-innovation-report-2021.

United Nations Development Programme (UNDP). *Gender Equality Strategy 2022–2025.* New York: UNDP, 2022. www.undp.org/publications/gender -equality-strategy-2022-2025.

United Nations Division for the Advancement of Women (UNDAW). *Information and Communication Technologies and Their Impact on and Use as an Instrument for the Advancement and Empowerment of Women: Report of the Expert Group Meeting Seoul, Republic of Korea, 11–14 November 2002.* UNDAW, International Telecommunication Union, and UN ICT Task Force Secretariat, December 23, 2002. https://www.un.org/womenwatch/daw/egm/ict2002/reports/EGMFinalReport.pdf.

United Nations Division for the Advancement of Women (UNDAW) and United Nations Division of Economic and Social Affairs (UNDESA). *Gender Equality and Empowerment of Women through ICT.* Women2000 and Beyond, September 2005. https://www.un.org/womenwatch/daw/public/w2000-09.05-ict-e.pdf.

———. *Women2000: Women and the Information Revolution.* October 1996. www.un.org/womenwatch/daw/public/Women2000%20-%20Women%20and%20the%20Information%20Revolution.pdf.

United Nations Division for the Advancement of Women (UNDAW) and United Nations Educational, Scientific and Cultural Organization (UNESCO). *Gender, Science Technology Expert Group Report.* Paris: UNDAW, UNESCO. 2010. www.itu.int/en/ITU-D/Digital-Inclusion/Wo men-and-Girls/Documents/ReportsModules/Final-Report-EGM-ST% 20Gender%20science%20technology%20expert%20group%20report .pdf.

United Nations Educational, Scientific and Cultural Organization (UNESCO). "Artificial Intelligence and Gender Equality: Key Findings of UNESCO's Global Dialogue." Paris, France: UNESCO, August 31, 2020. https://en. unesco.org/AI-and-GE-2020.

———. "UNESCO Science Report: The Race against Time for Smarter Devel-

opment." Paris: UNESCO, 2021. www.unesco.org/reports/science/2021/
en.

———. "Women, Science, and Technology: Towards a New Development?"
Paris: UNESCO, 1999. https://unesdoc.unesco.org/ark:/48223/pf0000011
8131.

United Nations Educational, Scientific and Cultural Organization (UNESCO),
UN Women, ITU, Microsoft. *Girls in STEM and ICT Careers: The Path
Toward Gender Equality.* Paris: UNESCO, UN Women, ITU, and Microsoft, 2014. https://www.empowerwomen.org/en/resources/documents/
2014/1/girls-in-stem-and-ict-careers-the-path-toward-gender-equality?
lang=en.

United Nations General Assembly (UNGA). "A/RES/70/1 Transforming Our
World: The 2030 Agenda for Sustainable Development," 2015.

———. *The 2030 Agenda for Sustainable Development.* New York: UNGA,
2015. www.un.org/pga/wp-content/uploads/sites/3/2015/08/120815_out
come-document-of-Summit-for-adoption-of-the-post-2015-development
-agenda.pdf.

United Nations Inter-agency Task Force on Financing for Development. *Financing for Sustainable Development Report 2022.* New York: United
Nations, 2022. https://developmentfinance.un.org/fsdr2022.

United Nations Secretary-General. *UN Secretary-General's Strategy on New
Technologies.* New York: United Nations, 2018. www.un.org/en/newtech
nologies/.

United Nations Secretary-General's High-level Panel on Digital Cooperation.
The Age of Digital Interdependence. New York: United Nations, 2019.
https://www.un.org/en/pdfs/DigitalCooperation-report-for%20web.pdf.

United Nations University and EQUALS. *Taking Stock: Data and Evidence
on Gender Equality in Digital Access, Skills, and Leadership.* New York:
United Nations University Institute on Computing and Society, International Telecommunications Union, EQUALS Research Group, March 15,
2019. https://i.unu.edu/media/cs.unu.edu/attachment/4040/EQUALS-Re
search-Report-2019.pdf.

United Nations Women. "Beijing Declaration and Platform for Action; Beijing
+5 Political Declaration and Outcome." UN Women, 2014, 1995. www.
unwomen.org/~/media/headquarters/attachments/sections/csw/pfa_e_
final_web

———. *COVID-19 and Ending Violence Against Women and Girls.* UN
Women, 2020. https://www.unwomen.org/sites/default/files/Headquarters
/Attachments/Sections/Library/Publications/2020/Issue-brief-COVID-19
-and-ending-violence-against-women-and-girls-en.pdf.

———. *Innovation for Gender Equality.* New York: UN Women, 2019. www
.unwomen.org/digital-library/publications/2019/03/innovation-for-gender
-equality.

———. *Measuring the Shadow Pandemic: Violence Against Women during*

COVID-*19*. New York: UN Women, Women Count, 2021. https://data. unwomen.org/publications/vaw-rga.

———. "Online and ICT-Facilitated Violence against Women and Girls during COVID-19." April 2020. www.unwomen.org/en/digital-library/publica tions/2020/04/brief-online-and-ict-facilitated-violence-against-women -and-girls-during-covid-19.

———. *SDG Monitoring Report: Turning Promises into Action: Gender Equality in the 2030 Agenda for Sustainable Development*. New York: UN Women, 2018. www.unwomen.org/en/digital-library/sdg-report.

United Nations Women and United Nations Development Programme (UNDP). *Government Responses to COVID-19: Lessons on Gender Equality for a World in Turmoil*. New York: UN Women and UNDP, June 2022. www.unwomen.org/en/digital-library/publications/2022/06/govern ment-responses-to-covid-19-lessons-on-gender-equality-for-a-world-in-tur moil.

Vaca-Trigo, Iliana. *Oportunidades y desafíos para la autonomía de las mujeres en el futuro escenario del trabajo*. Santiago, Chile: Comisión Económica para América Latina y el Caribe (CEPAL). January 18, 2019. www.cepal.org/es/publicaciones/44408-oportunidades-desafios-la-autono mia-mujeres-futuro-escenario-trabajo.

Vaca-Trigo, Iliana, and María Elena Valenzuela. *Digitalización de las mujeres en América Latina y el Caribe: Acción urgente para una recuperación trans formadora y con igualdad*. Documentos de Proyectos (LC/TS.2022/79). Santiago, Chile: Comisión Económica para América Latina, 2022.

Valencia, Sayak. *Gore Capitalism*. Cambridge, MA: MIT Press, 2018.

van Dijck, Jose. *The Culture of Connectivity: A Critical History of Social Media*. New York: Oxford University Press, 2013.

Van Waeyenberge, Elisa. "The Post-Washington Consensus." In *The Essential Guide to Critical Development Studies*. New York: Routledge, 2017.

———. *The Private Turn in Development Finance*. Working Paper 140. Fi nancialisation, Economy, Society & Sustainable Development Project, April 1, 2016. https://ideas.repec.org/p/fes/wpaper/wpaper140.html.

Varga, Dávid. "Fintech, the New Era of Financial Services." *Vezetéstudomány— Budapest Management Review* 48, no. 11 (November 2017): 22–32. https: //doi.org/10.14267/VEZTUD.2017.11.03.

Vargas, Virginia. "International Feminisms: The World Social Forum." In *Feminist Agendas and Democracy in Latin America*, edited by Jane S. Ja quette, 145–64. Durham, NC: Duke University Press Books, 2009.

Vaughan-Nichols, Steven J. "The Corporation Has Gone Open Source." *IT world*. August 6, 2010. www.itworld.com/article/2754345/business/the -corporation-has-gone-open-source.html.

Vera Ramírez, Natalia. "El abrazo fintech del Grupo Santander." *América- Economía*, November 12, 2021. www.americaeconomia.com/negocios -industrias/cl-abrazo-fintech-del-grupo-santander.

Vo, Samantha. "Concern for Community: A Case Study of Cooperatives in Costa Rica." *Journal of Community Practice* 24, no. 1 (January 2, 2016): 56–76. https://doi.org/10.1080/10705422.2015.1127304.

von Schnitzler, Antina. "Citizenship Prepaid: Water, Calculability, and Techno-Politics in South Africa." *Journal of Southern African Studies* 34, no. 4 (December 2008): 899–917. https://doi.org/10.1080/0305707080245 6821.

Wajcman, Judy. *Feminism Confronts Technology.* University Park: Pennsylvania State University Press, 1991.

Wall Street Journal. "The Facebook Files" (webpage). October 1, 2021. www .wsj.com/articles/the-facebook-files-11631713039.

Walsh, Catherine E. "Decoloniality In/As Praxis." In *On Decoloniality: Concepts, Analytics, Praxis,* 15–102. Durham, NC: Duke University Press, 2018.

Walsham, Geoff. "ICT4D Research: Reflections on History and Future Agenda." *Information Technology for Development* 23, no. 1 (January 2, 2017): 18–41. https://doi.org/10.1080/02681102.2016.1246406.

Weber, Heloise. "Politics of 'Leaving No One Behind': Contesting the 2030 Sustainable Development Goals Agenda." *Globalizations* 14, no. 3 (April 16, 2017): 399–414. https://doi.org/10.1080/14747731.2016.1275404.

Weinstein, Matthew, David Blades, and Shannon C. Gleason. "Questioning Power: Deframing the STEM Discourse." *Canadian Journal of Science, Mathematics and Technology Education* 16, no. 2 (April 2, 2016): 201–12. https://doi.org/10.1080/14926156.2016.1166294.

West, Mark, Rebecca Kraut, and Han Ei Chew. *I'd Blush If I Could: Closing Gender Divides in Digital Skills through Education.* New York: UNESCO for the EQUALS Skills Coalition, 2019.

White, Allen. "Arturo Escobar: Farewell to Development." Great Transition Initiative. March 20, 2018. https://greattransition.org/publication/farewell -to-development.

Wieringa, Saskia, and Horacio Sívori, eds. *The Sexual History of the Global South: Sexual Politics in Africa, Asia, and Latin America.* London: Zed Books, 2013.

Williams, Logan D. A., and Georgia H. Artzberger. "Developing Women as ICT Users: A Miniature Scoping Review of Gender and ICTs for Development." *Gender, Technology and Development* 23, no. 3 (September 2, 2019): 234–56. https://doi.org/10.1080/09718524.2019.1679330.

Wilson, Kalpana. "Towards a Radical Re-Appropriation: Gender, Development and Neoliberal Feminism." *Development and Change* 46, no. 4 (June 1, 2015): 803–32. https://doi.org/10.1111/dech.12176.

Winner, Langdon. "Do Artifacts Have Politics?" *Daedalus* 109, no. 1 (1980): 121–36. www.jstor.org/stable/20024652.

Women Will (website). Accessed October 4, 2022. https://womenwill.google/.

World Bank. *World Development Report 2016: Digital Dividends.* Washington, DC: World Bank, 2016. https://www.worldbank.org/en/publication/wdr2016.

World Health Organization (WHO). "Violence against Women." Fact sheet. March 9, 2021. www.who.int/news-room/fact-sheets/detail/violence-against-women.

World Summit on the Information Society. Tunis Commitment. November 18, 2005. www.itu.int/net/wsis/docs2/tunis/off/7.pdf.

World Wide Web Foundation. "Facebook, Google, TikTok and Twitter Make Unprecedented Commitments to Tackle the Abuse of Women on Their Platforms." *World Wide Web Foundation* (blog), July 1, 2021. https://webfoundation.org/2021/07/generation-equality-commitments/.

———. "The Online Crisis Facing Women and Girls Threatens Global Progress on Gender Equality." *World Wide Web Foundation* (blog), March 12, 2020. https://webfoundation.org/2020/03/the-online-crisis-facing-women-and-girls-threatens-global-progress-on-gender-equality/.

———. *Women's Rights Online: Translating Access into Empowerment.* World Wide Web Foundation, October 20, 2015. http://webfoundation.org/wp-content/uploads/2015/10/WomensRightsOnlineWF_Oct2015.pdf.

Zakaria, Rafia. *Against White Feminism: Notes on Disruption.* New York: W. W. Norton & Company, 2021.

Zerai, Assata. *African Women, ICT and Neoliberal Politics: The Challenge of Gendered Digital Divides to People-Centered Governance.* New York: Routledge, 2019.

Ziai, Aram, ed. *Exploring Post-Development: Theory and Practice, Problems and Perspectives.* New York: Routledge, 2013.

Zilli, Bruno, and Horacio Sívori. "Introduction." In *EROTICS Global Survey 2017: Sexuality, Rights, and Internet Regulations.* Association for Progressive Communications, 2017. www.apc.org/en/pubs/erotics-global-survey-2017-sexuality-rights-and-internet-regulations.

Zuboff, Shoshana. *The Age of Surveillance Capitalism: The Fight for a Human Future at the New Frontier of Power.* New York: Public Affairs, 2019.

INDEX

Page numbers in italics denote figures, and endnotes are indicated by "n" followed by the endnote number.

235

Argentina, 23, 39, 104, 120

Arora, Payal, 13, 41, 132

Association for Progressive Communications, Women's Rights Programme (APC WRP): on anticapitalist approaches, 106; author's methodology, 21–22, 23–24, 27, 159–62, *161*, 166–67; centering of body and pleasure, 1–2, 103; challenging victimization tropes, 107–9; embodiment principle, 112–18, *118*; EROTICS project, *109*, 109–11; Feminist Principles of the Internet (FPIs), 111–12, 144; funding model, 144–47; history of, 103–5; mandate, 10–11, 170n24; on online gender-based violence, 53, 118–21, 122–25, 126–27, 129, 130–32, 152; open letter to Apple, 102

Association for Women's Rights in Development (AWID), 137–38

Australia, 125

Bahous, Sima, 62

Banerjee, Pallavi, 28

Bárcena, Alicia, 60

Bateman, Milford, 40

Beijing Platform for Action (1995), 31, 34, 44, 48–49, 50–51, 56, 129

Benjamin, Ruha, 76–77

Bergeron, Susan, 35

Bernal, Victoria, 18, 135

Bill and Melinda Gates Foundation, 37, 38, 55, 139, 141

Black and Brown communities: artificial and harmful inclusion, 45–46, 76–77; Black pleasure and joy, 9; in community-based media, 56; health disparities during COVID-19, 40; bell hooks on marginality, 26; impacts of criminalization, 125–26, 133;

online gender-based violence toward, 123; prominence in care economy, 35; sexualities, stigmatization of, 115; Sulá Batsú hackathons and, 78–80

body: body politics, 108; body-territory connection, 68–69, 114; embodiment and resistance, 112–18, *118*, 132; reappropriation of, 103

Bonder, Gloria, 58–59

Boserup, Ester, 12

Bosnia and Herzegovina, 104

Brazil, 110

Bribri people, 63–64, 79–80, 92

Brooks, Sally, 39

brown, adrienne maree, 105

Brown, Wendy, 20

Browne, Simone, *Dark Matters,* 67

Butler, Judith, 116

Cabécar people: centering relationality, 67; Sulá Batsú hackathons and, 79–80; on technology of feeling, 63–64, 92, 102, 152. *See also* Sulá Batsú cooperative

Cabnal, Lorena, 9, 28, 69, 114

Cáceres, Berta, 9

Camacho, Kemly: author's work with, 27, 165–66; on conflict and adversity, 94, 96, 97, 98; on corporate agendas in STEM fields, 77; on decentering technology, 66, 67, 81; on digital sovereignty, 67–68; on entrepreneurship, 81, 87–88, 89–90, 93; on private funding, 141–43; on Sulá Batsú hackathons, 79–80; on technology of feeling, 63, 64; on TIC-as project, 70

Camelia (APC WRP activist), 116, 121

Canada, 23, 93, 104, 125

Canadian International Development Research Center (IDRC), 65

236

capitalism: anticapitalist approaches, 106–7, 111–12; corporatization, 49, 54–56, 77, 137–43, 145–48; defense of life vs., 116–17; feminist entrepreneurship and, 90–91; gender-based violence and, 119–21; inclusion practices furthering, 76–78, 86–87, 117; paradox of technology and, 20–21, 129; politics of connections vs. politics of things, 7–8; predatory inclusion, 33, 121–22, 149–50. *See also* neoliberalism

capitalist-colonial order: body politics and, 108; body-territory connection and, 114; "capital-life conflict," 33; "colonial" used herein, 175n109; digital violence and, 102; gender-based violence and, 119–21; paradox of technology and, 20–21, 129; pleasure, in disrupting paradigms of, 8–9, 115; term usage herein, 24, 25

care: in activism mandates, 10–11, 128, 152; commodification of, 15–16, 31, 33–35, 60, 89–90; conceptualizations of, 4–5; in development discourse, 3, 34–35; erasure of, 11; pleasure as fundamental to, 101–3; relationships of connection and, 91–94, 99–100; in restoration of justice, 127–28; solidarity and pleasure as politics of, 6–9. *See also* development discourse; pleasure; solidarity

Cavallero, Luci, 39, 42
Changeling (APC WRP activist), 116
Chant, Sylvia, 49
Chew, Han Ei, *I'd Blush If I Could,* 34, 37, 44
Chile, 56, 60
China, 140
Chowdhury, Rumman, 132

Clara (Sulá Batsú member), 97
College of Information and Computation Professionals of Costa Rica, 80
Collins, Patricia Hill, 127
colonialism. *See* capitalist-colonial order
Commission on the Status of Women (CSW), 22, 50, 128–29, 131
Committee on Payments and Market Infrastructure (CPMI), 37
commons, concept of, 89
Connell, Raewyn, 25, 28
cooperative activism. *See* Sulá Batsú cooperative
Cornwall, Andrea, 8–9, 16, 27
corporatization: of development, 137–43, 145–48; of gender equality, 49, 54–56; inclusion practices furthering, 76–78, 86–87, 117; in STEM fields, 77. *See also* capitalism; neoliberalism
Costanza-Shock, Sasha, 102
Costa Rica, inclusion initiatives in, 82–87. *See also* Sulá Batsú cooperative
Costa Rican Promoter of Innovation and Investigation (CONICIT), 84, 85
Costa Rica United States Foundation for Cooperation (CRUSA), 85
COVID-19 pandemic: digital banking technology and, 39; economization of care, 31, 32; geopolitical climate, 24; online violence increase, 123; requiring feminist recovery, 60; urgency of inclusion and, 19, 33, 38, 61, 85
criminalization of online violence, 125–28
Curiel, Ochy, 122
Cyberviolence Against Women and Girls (UN report), 129

239

EROTICS project, *109*, 109–11; feminist activism and, 48; feminist principles of, 111–12, 144, 186n32; within neoliberal agenda, 51; as space of embodiment, 113. *See also* digital technology; online gender-based violence

Internet Governance Forum (IGF), 51–54

Irani, Lilly, 42

Israel, 125

Jack, William, 40

Japan, 125, 140

Jones, Angela, 106

Juan (Sulá Batsú member), 64, 94, 95

Julia (APC WRP activist), 107, 108, 124–25, 130–31, 144, 145–47

Juris, Jeffrey, 89

Kaba, Mariame, 156

Kapuściński, Ryszard, 157

Keila (APC WRP activist), 126–27, 144–45

Kempadoo, Kamala, 25

Kenya, 40

Khan, Irene, 53

Kneese, Tamara, 5

knowledge: commodification of, 46; Indigenous, 80–81

Koç Holding, 55

Kraut, Rebecca, *I'd Blush If I Could*, 34, 37, 44

Lal, Shivani, 113, 114

language, in decolonial methodology, 167

Latin America, development discourse in, 56–60. *See also* global South

Laura (APC WRP activist), 131–32

La voz de las chicas del Centro de América project, 71, 72, 142

Lebanon, 104, 110

Lee, Micky, 49

legibility and inclusion, 12

LGBTQ+ community: health disparities during COVID-19, 40; sexualities, stigmatization of, 115; sexual rights activists, *109*, 109–11; shifts in development funding and, 138. *See also* online gender-based violence

Lila (Sulá Batsú member), 65, 75, 91, 93

Limón, Costa Rica, 79–80

"live deliciously" *(vivir sabroso)*, 9

Lorde, Audre, 9

Loubere, Nicholas, 40

Lugones, María, 114

Maiguashca, Bice, 88, 136, 147

Malaysia, 104

Marcela (Sulá Batsú member), 88–89, 91, 93, 97

Marcus, George, 158

marginalized, term usage herein, 26

Marina (Sulá Batsú member), 65, 94

Márquez, Francia, 9

Martin, Randy, 17

Marwan, Ezrena, *118*

Marx, Karl, 20

Mastercard Inc., 60

Max (APC WRP activist), 106, 111, 119–20, 122, 127

McMillan Cottom, Tressie, 27, 33

Meta Platforms Inc., 45, 145–46, 179n61, 183n8

#MeToo movement, 128, 190n92

Mexico, 23

microfinancing, 15, 50

Microsoft Corporation, 55, 60, 83

Min (APC WRP activist), 108, 118, 131

Ministerio de Ciencia, Innovación, Tecnología y Telecomunicaciones (MICITT), 83–84, 86

Ministerio de Economía, Industria y Comercio (MEIC), 82, 83
Mohanty, Chandra Talpade, 7, 108
Mora, Alejandra, 86–87
Moussié, Rachel, 138–39
M-Pesa (money transfer service), 40
"multiplier effect" and digital technology, 35–37
Murphy, Michelle, 5
Mutual Aid (Graeber and Grubačić), 11

Nagar, Richa, 167
National Institute of Women (INAMU), 84, 85, 86
Navarro Castillo, Mauren, 86
Nelson, Maggie, 7, 106
neoliberalism: activist critiques of, 57, 58, 59; commodification of care, 33–34, 61; co-optation of feminisms, 135–37; corporatization of development, 137–39; corporatization of gender equality, 54–56; depoliticization of digital technology, 50–51; feminist entrepreneurship and, 90–91; inclusion practices furthering, 76–78, 86–87, 117; STEM fields and, 86–87; term usage herein, 24–25; *Vitalpolitik* (politics of life) and, 15–16; women as ideal entrepreneurs, 41–43. *See also* capitalism; Third World Technological Woman
NGOs (non-governmental organizations), 135–37
Noble, Safiya Umoja, 45, 102

Okama Süei application, 80
online gender-based violence: characterizing, 122–25, 187n63; criminalization, 125–28; in development discourse, 53–54; global South perspective, 118–22;

in UN discourse, 128–32; violence against women and, 144, 145
OnlyFans, 102
open source software, 89, 104, 184n37
oppressed, term usage herein, 26
Orloff, Ann Shola, 134, 136

Pabru (Sulá Batsú member), 65, 95, 96–97
Paredes, Julieta, 69
PayPal Holdings Inc., 55
Pedwell, Carolyn, 16–17
Peña, Paz, 128
Pérez Orozco, Amaia, 33
Perosino, Celeste, 39
Pétalo (journalist), 117
Philippines, 125
pineapple cultivation, 68, 143
pleasure: defined, 7; APC WRP history and, 103–5; in APC WRP mandate, 10, 103, 170n24; critical perspectives including, 58; as dimension of care, 101–3; disrupting colonial paradigms, 8–9; embodiment, 112–18, *118*; EROTICS project, *109*, 109–11; Feminist Principles of the Internet (FPIs), 111–12, 144; as feminist technopolitical tactic, 1–2, 6–9, 105–7, 132, 150–56; victimization narratives and, 107–9. *See also* online gender-based violence; solidarity
"politics of connections," 7–8, 34, 66, 100, 105, 116, 150–51
politics of life *(Vitalpolitik)*, 5, 15–16, 34
post-development, 14, 90
Prebisch, Raúl, 56
privacy, 39, 53
process vs. outcome, 1, 88–89, 92–93, 150

CPSIA information can be obtained
at www.ICGtesting.com
Printed in the USA
JSHW080049270723
45479JS00004B/6